Sentenced to Serve

The operation and impact of community service by offenders

GILL McIVOR
Social Work Research Centre
University of Stirling

Ashgate

Published by
Ashgate Publishing Limited
Gower House
Croft Road
Aldershot
Hants GU11 3HR
England

Ashgate Publishing Company
131 Main Street
Burlington, VT 05401-5600 USA

Ashgate website: http://www.ashgate.com

A CIP catalogue record for this book is available from the British Library and the US Library of Congress.

ISBN 1 85628 329 1

Reprinted 2002

Printed and bound in Great Britain by Biddles Limited, Guildford and King's Lynn.

Contents

Series Editor's Preface   viii

Acknowledgements   xi

Introduction   xii

Chapter 1: Community service in Scotland   1

Introduction   1
The development of community service in England and Wales   3
The development of community service in Scotland   8

Chapter 2: The research programme   19

Introduction   19
An evaluative study of community service by offenders in Scotland   19
The comparative costs of community service and custody   26
Sentencers' perceptions of community service by offenders   28
Community service orders: assessing the benefit to the community   30
Reconviction among offenders sentenced to community service   32

Chapter 3: Offenders, offences, orders and outcomes   35

Introduction   35
Who gets community service?   35
Who is unsuitable for community service?   38
The community service order   41
The outcomes of orders   47
Factors associated with non-compliance and breach   52
Summary   55

Chapter 4: Identifying effective practice   57

Introduction   57
Assessing offenders' suitability   57
Matching offenders to work placements   61
Time to complete   65
Enforcement   68
Work placements and outcomes   72
The nature and impact of social work support   74
Summary   79

Chapter 5: A worthwhile experience?   82

Introduction   82
Offenders' attitudes towards community service   84
Offenders' attitudes and placement characteristics   89
What did offenders gain from community service?   93
Continuing on a voluntary basis   98
Is community service punitive?   100
Summary   102

Chapter 6: A worthwhile service?   104

Introduction   104
Individual beneficiaries   106
The agency perspective   114
Summary   127

Chapter 7: Community service and custody   129

Introduction   129
The sentencing of unsuccessful referrals   133

The outcomes of breaches and other revocations 134
Risk of custody and custodial sentencing 137
Sentencers' views 138
Tariff escalation 142
Informed consent 144
The comparative costs of community service and custody 146
Enhancing consistency of practice 147
Summary 148

Chapter 8: Offenders' experiences and subsequent reconviction 150

Introduction 150
Predicted likelihood of re-offending 153
The rate of reconviction 154
Reconviction while completing community service 156
The nature and frequency of reconviction before and after
community service 157
Factors associated with reconviction 162
How well are offenders able to predict whether they will
re-offend? 170
Some methodological issues 171
Summary 172

Chapter 9: Progress and prospects 174

Community service: what has been achieved? 174
The future of community service revisited 184

Bibliography 189

Index 198

Series Editor's Preface

Evaluative Studies in Social Work brings together research which has explored the impact of social work services in a variety of contexts and from several perspectives. The vision of social work in this series is a broad one. It encompasses services in residential, fieldwork and community settings undertaken by workers with backgrounds in health and welfare. The volumes will therefore include studies of social work with families and children, with elderly people, people with mental and other health problems and with offenders.

This approach to social work is consistent with contemporary legislation in many countries, including Britain, in which social work has a key role in the assessment of need and in the delivery of personal social services, in health care and in criminal justice. It also continues a long tradition which perceives an integral relationship between social work, social research and social policy. Those who provide social work services are acquainted with the complexities of human need and with the achievements and shortcomings of major instruments of social policy. This knowledge was exploited by, amongst others, Booth, Rowntree and the Webbs in their studies of poverty. Politicians and sociologists have also recognised that, together with the people they try to help, social workers can provide a commentary on the human meaning of public policies and the social issues that grow from private troubles.

This knowledge and experience of the recipients and practitioners of social work is not, of course, immediately accessible to the wider community. A major purpose of research is to gather, organise and interpret this information and, in the studies in this series, to evaluate the impact of social work. Here there are many legitimate interests to consider. First and foremost are direct service users and those who care for them. These are the people who should be the main beneficiaries of social work services. Also to be considered are the personnel of other services for whom liaison and collaboration with social work is essential to their own successful functioning. The needs and views of these different groups may well conflict and it is the researcher's task to identify those tensions and describe social work's response to them.

The problems which confront social work are often extremely complex. They may need to be tackled in a variety of ways; for example, through practical assistance, advocacy, counselling and supervision. Outcomes may be similarly varied and studies of the effectiveness of social work must demonstrate the different kinds of impact it can have. These may entail changes in users' circumstances, behaviour or well being. On these changes, and on the kind of help they have received, users' perspectives must be of great significance. Also of central interest to those who provide or manage services is an understanding of their form and content and the relationship between the problems identified and the statutory responsibilities of social workers and the help given. Social work researchers must therefore take care to study what is actually delivered through social work and how, as well as its outcomes, aspirations and objectives. For good and ill social work has an impact on large and increasing number of citizens. A major aim of *Evaluative Studies in Social Work* is to increase well informed understanding of social work, based on knowledge about its real rather than imagined activities and outcomes.

The identification of effectiveness, in its various forms, can also not be the end of the story. The costs of the associated services must be studied, set in the context of their effectiveness, to allow the most efficient use of resources.

These demands present major challenges to researchers who have to use, adapt and develop a wide range of research methods and designs. Ingenuity and persistence are both required if evaluative research in social work is to be pursued in contexts often regarded as beyond the scope of such enquiry. *Evaluative Studies in Social Work* intends to make widely available not only the research findings about the impact of social work but also to demonstrate and discuss possible approaches and methods in this important and developing field of enquiry.

The first volumes in this series describe studies undertaken in the Social Work Research Centre at the University of Stirling. The Centre is funded by the Economic and Social Research Council and the Scottish Office to evaluate the effectiveness of social work services. Later volumes may include work carried out elsewhere.

Sentenced to Serve is probably the most comprehensive evaluation of community service for offenders so far conducted. It integrates studies of the effectiveness of different approaches to organisation and practice. It also explores the views of sentencers, of offenders who have been 'sentenced to serve', and of those who have received their services. The comparative costs of community service and custody are reported; and the reconviction of a sample of offenders three years after their sentence is examined. The volume is therefore an excellent example of evaluative research in the light it throws on all important aspects of community service and on the interaction of social work and criminal justice.

Juliet Cheetham

Acknowledgements

A great many people, too numerous to mention individually, have contributed in various ways to the programme of research reported in this book. I am indebted to colleagues in the Social Work Research Centre who have given generously of their ideas, encouragement and time, to Pam Lavery and June Watson for their limitless patience and excellent secretarial support and to Ann Barham who compiled the index. The help and advice provided by colleagues in the Scottish Office, the Scottish Criminal Records Office and the research sections of the social work departments have also been much appreciated.

The community service staff throughout Scotland who participated in the research did so with extraordinary commitment and enthusiasm. Special thanks are due to them and to the offenders, agencies and beneficiaries who gave so much of their time to convey their experiences and views.

The research reported in this book was conducted on the core-funding provided to the Social Work Research Centre by the Economic and Social Research Council and the Social Work Services Group of the Scottish Office. Preparation of parts of the book was facilitated by a further research grant from the Carnegie Trust for the Universities of Scotland.

Gill McIvor
June 1992

Introduction

In 1986, the Social Work Research Centre at Stirling University embarked upon a programme of research which sought to evaluate the impact of the community service order and ascertain the extent to which a range of policy objectives associated with this innovative sentencing option had been achieved.

The introduction of community service in England and Wales in the early 1970s resulted in a flurry of research activity over the next ten or so years. But much of that research was descriptive in nature or had a narrow geographical or substantive focus. In Scotland, more especially, there had been no analysis of community service since the early evaluative studies of the first five experimental schemes.

There was no reason to assume, however, that the findings from these initial studies would still be applicable several years later, when practice had evolved and schemes had settled down. Other important questions remained unanswered or had been only partially addressed. What types of offenders were being sentenced to community service? Who were considered by schemes to be unsuitable for community service and why? What types of work were offenders carrying out? Who was most likely to complete a community service order and who was most likely to fail? Which methods of assessment and matching were most effective? How effective was the provision of help to offenders who had problems while completing their community service work? How might schemes maximise offenders' compliance with their orders? What did offenders think of community service, what did they get out of community service and what types of placements were considered most rewarding and worthwhile? How much did the community benefit from community service work? How was community service regarded and used by the courts? How costly were different methods of operation and how did the costs of community service orders compare with the costs of the prison sentences they were intended to replace? How many people were reconvicted after being sentenced to community service, how often and for what types of offences? Finally, did offenders' experiences of community service have any influence upon subsequent reconviction?

These were among the questions that five separate, but inter-related, studies aimed to address. This book focuses in particular upon the findings of three of these studies: the evaluation of practice across community service schemes (McIvor, 1989); the survey of individual and agency beneficiaries (McIvor, 1990a); and the exploration of reconviction following community service (McIvor, 1992a). Additional reference is made, where appropriate, to the cost effectiveness study and to the study of sentencers' views, both of which are fully reported elsewhere (Knapp et al., 1989, 1992; Carnie, 1990). Although the research was conducted entirely in Scotland, the operation of community service in this country is sufficiently similar to that in the rest of Britain to make most of the findings and conclusions equally applicable to England and Wales.

The first two chapters chart the development of community service in Scotland and describe the programme of research on which the book is based. The results from the different studies are interwoven in the following six chapters. Chapter 3 describes the characteristics of offenders sentenced to community service orders in twelve community service schemes, the orders they received and their outcomes, and identifies the factors associated with increased risk of failure to comply. Offenders who were ordered to perform community service are compared with others who were referred for a community service assessment but who subsequently received an alternative disposal, and the criteria employed by schemes in assessing suitability are discussed.

In Chapter 4 the variations in practice across the twelve schemes are described and the relative effectiveness of different operational arrangements is assessed. The emphasis is upon the major components of community service practice, including the assessment of offenders' suitability, the matching of offenders to work placements and the supervision and enforcement of orders.

The community service work experiences and views of the offenders are reported in Chapter 5, while Chapter 6 documents the experiences and attitudes of individual members of the public and of voluntary and statutory agencies who had work performed on their behalf by offenders on community service orders. The views of sentencers are considered in Chapter 7, which also assesses the extent to which community service orders had replaced sentences of imprisonment as opposed to other non-custodial penalties.

Chapter 8 examines the level and frequency of reconviction following community service. The factors associated with an increased risk or frequency of reconviction are identified and the relationship between offenders' experiences of community service and reconviction is explored. This chapter concludes by examining the relationship between predicted re-offending and reconviction.

The main findings and conclusions are summarised in Chapter 9. This concluding chapter discusses the likely impact of recent policy developments and speculates upon the future of community service in the context of wider organisational and legislative changes in the criminal justice systems in Scotland and in England and Wales.

1 Community service in Scotland

Introduction

Community service orders, which require convicted offenders to perform unpaid work for the benefit of the community, have now been available as a sentencing option in Britain for almost twenty years. Although numerous examples of criminal sanctioning with an emphasis on the performance of work with a socially useful purpose can be identified historically (see, for example, Hoggarth, 1991; Young, 1979; van Kalmthout and Tak, 1988) the first modern community service programme was developed in Alameda County, California in 1966 when certain traffic offenders were required by the municipal court to perform unpaid work for the community. Since then, the use of community service has spread throughout the United States, being most often implemented as only one component of a package of measures (which might include house arrest, counselling, financial compensation to victims or drug testing) imposed upon the probationer.

The development of community service in the United States received a particular impetus when, in 1976, the Law Enforcement Assistance Administration made available funding for the development of community service programmes for adult offenders. Two years later the Office of Juvenile Justice and Delinquency Prevention provided resources to enable the development of community service programmes for juvenile offenders in eighty-five counties and states. Although many programmes ceased when

1

the initial funding ran out (see, for example, McDonald, 1986) others obtained alternative sources of finance, including local and state support.

In contrast with the British experience, community service orders in the United States tend, as Morris and Tonry (1990, p. 154) have indicated:

> ...to flourish among white-collar offenders, in juvenile courts, and for minor offenses; they have less frequently been applied in this country to the poor and to those convicted of repeated though less serious offenses against property - and rarely to those convicted of crimes of violence.

Morris and Tonry concluded from their overview that community service could be applied to a wider range of offenders than was typically the case and proposed that this sentencing option could be further developed in the United States in three distinct ways. First, as a substitute for other nominal punishments for minor offences; second, for more serious offences as a stand alone alternative to short periods of incarceration or to monetary penalties for those without the means to pay; and third, as part of a package of non-custodial measures and conditions imposed on serious offenders with the intention of increasing public safety while addressing offenders' underlying motivations and needs.

Community service is also available in differing formats in several other non-European countries including Australia (e.g. Australian Institute of Criminology, 1983; Rook, 1978), Canada (e.g. Menzies, 1986; Menzies and Vass, 1989; Polonoski, 1981; Vass and Menzies, 1990) and New Zealand (e.g. Leibrich et al., 1984a; Leibrich, 1985). Its use in various parts of Europe has been most recently documented by Albrecht and Schädler (1986), by van Kalmthout and Tak (1988) and by Bishop (1988). Community service has been most often been introduced, as in Britain, as a direct alternative to short periods of incarceration. In some countries (such as Luxembourg and Norway) community service may be substituted for prison as a condition of pardon while in others (such as Germany, Italy and Switzerland) community service orders may be imposed instead of imprisonment for fine default.

As Tak (1986) noted, however, a few countries have, for various reasons, resisted the addition of community service to their repertoire of criminal sanctions. Spain, for instance, lacks a formalised probation service which might administer a community service programme and other practical problems (such as increasing unemployment) might, it was anticipated, have undermined the credibility of such a sentence were it introduced. Sweden, on the other hand, rejected community service on the basis of its apparently limited ability to reduce the use of imprisonment and its incompatibility with a social structure which regards work as a privilege.

Community service has perhaps been most enthusiastically embraced in Britain where it has proved to be a popular measure with the courts. Community service orders were first introduced on a legislated basis in England and Wales. The formal incorporation of community service into the criminal justice system was watched with interest by other countries and the British experience served as a model for schemes that were subsequently developed elsewhere.

Since detailed descriptions of the development of community service in England and Wales are available (Pease, 1980a, 1985; Vass, 1984; Wright, 1984; Young, 1979) a brief overview will, for present purposes, suffice.

The development of community service in England and Wales

By the late 1960s and early 1970s it had become widely recognised that custodial sentences were generally ineffective as a deterrent against further offending (Home Office, 1965) and the rehabilitative efficacy of institutional treatment was increasingly being called into question (Bailey, 1966; Lipton et al., 1975; Martinson, 1974; Robison and Smith, 1971). Imprisonment had, moreover, been recognised as having detrimental effects upon individual offenders and their families and concern was being expressed at this time both about the levels of overcrowding in penal establishments, particularly in England and Wales, and about the increasing costs of incarcerating offenders (Home Office, 1969).

Against this background, the Advisory Council on the Penal System, chaired by Baroness Wootton, was set the task of devising alternatives to custodial sentences and expanding the range of non-custodial disposals for offenders who would not, in any case, attract a custodial sentence. In its 1970 report, the Wootton Committee considered, among other measures, the possibility of introducing community service orders which would require selected adult offenders to perform unpaid work of benefit to the community.

Community service, which was described by the chair of the Advisory Council on the Penal System as the 'most imaginative and hopeful' of the Committee's recommendations (Advisory Council on the Penal System, 1970, p. v), gained legislative expression, albeit in an amended form, in the 1972 Criminal Justice Act. At the beginning of 1973, the community service order was introduced on an experimental basis in six pilot areas and in the following year community service was extended to other parts of the country.

The probation services in England and Wales assumed responsibility for

3

the administration of the new orders which required convicted offenders aged 17 years or older to perform between 40 and 240 hours of unpaid work for the community, to be completed within one year of the order being made (the Criminal Justice Act 1982 subsequently extended the availability of community service orders to 16-year-olds in England and Wales, but set a maximum limit of 120 hours on the number of hours of unpaid work that offenders of this age could be ordered to perform). Community service orders were available as a sentencing option for offenders who had been convicted of offences that were punishable by imprisonment, with the court retaining the option of re-sentencing the offender for the original offence if, for any reason, the requisite number of hours were not completed. Offenders were required to consent to an order being imposed and before sentencing an offender to community service the court had to be satisfied that the offender was suitable for an order and that arrangements could be made for the offender to undertake unpaid work.

In advocating the introduction of community service, the Wootton Committee had recommended that 'as with any new penal experiment, provision for the study of the working of the community service project should be incorporated into the scheme from the outset' (Advisory Council on the Penal System, 1970, para. 63). The Home Office Research Unit (Pease et al., 1975) undertook an evaluation of the community service experiment which sought to describe: the background to the scheme and its rationale; the criteria used by probation officers in assessing offenders' suitability for an order, the characteristics of offenders ordered to perform community service and the operation of the scheme; and the attitudes and views expressed about community service by probation managers and staff, by the courts, by offenders and by the media.

Despite variations in practice across schemes and in the use of community service by the courts, the Home Office researchers were led to conclude that:

> The community service experience shows that the scheme is viable; orders are being made and completed, sometimes evidently to the benefit of the offenders concerned. However, the effect on the offenders as a whole is not known; the penal theory underlining the scheme is thought by some to be uncertain; it has not made much of an impact on the prison population because of the manner of its use by the courts; in practice a few supervisors may be able to subvert some orders of the court unless good contact at the work-site is maintained by the probation and after-care service; and neither the type of offender for whom it is suitable, nor the most desirable work

placements for different individuals on community service are as yet known. The writers feel much more optimistic about the scheme than this list implies, but have tried throughout not to state the case for community service any more strongly than the evidence currently available justifies.

(Pease et al., 1975, p. 70)

The confusion of purpose alluded to by Pease et al. could be traced to the Wootton Committee's proposal that the community service order could appeal to different varieties of penal philosophy and could fulfil, though not necessarily simultaneously, a number of sentencing aims. Community service could punish offenders by requiring that they sacrifice some of their leisure time; it could enable offenders to make amends to the community for their wrongdoing; and it might, in some instances, promote a changed outlook on the part of the offender. There was, in addition, ambiguity about whether community service should be regarded as a sentence in its own right or as a tariff measure intended for use only where a custodial sentence would otherwise be imposed. Its wider use had been advocated by the Wootton Committee and the legislation enabled a community service order to be imposed even if an immediate sentence of imprisonment was unlikely. However, a different view was conveyed by the Home Secretary who implied that community service should be reserved for offenders who would otherwise receive short custodial sentences. Probation staff in the experimental schemes were divided in their opinions. Some regarded the new order as a sentence in its own right and others as an alternative to imprisonment (Pease et al., 1975). Further analysis of data from these schemes suggested that community service orders had been imposed by the courts in lieu of prison sentences in only 45-50 per cent of cases (Pease et al., 1977).

Despite this lack of clarity, and apparently with little or no regard to the outcomes of the evaluation (Pease, 1983), the government announced in 1974 that the scheme would be extended to other parts of England and Wales. The diversity of practice which evolved over the following years has been clearly documented. The lack of agreement among sentencers and among probation staff concerning the appropriate use of community service remained unresolved (see, for example, Vass, 1984). The use of community service orders varied from area to area (Young, 1979) as did the types of work that offenders on community service were required to perform, with schemes differing widely in their relative use of agency, group and 'fallback' placements (Fletcher, 1983; B. McWilliams 1980; Read, 1980). Schemes likewise differed in the manner in which absences from placements were categorised (as acceptable or not) and in the way

5

in which the requirements of orders were enforced (B. McWilliams, 1980; Young, 1979). Vass (1984) documented the 'creative' recording of hours worked and the reluctance of community service staff to return offenders to court who were in breach of their requirements while Young (1979) concluded from his review of practice that:

> It was evident that there were no consistent principles, either within or between areas, for determining the appropriate point for initiation of breach proceedings. The perceived need to pay due regard to individualised factors, and to give the offender as much opportunity as possible to respond to the order by becoming involved in voluntary work, militated against the formulation of such principles. Thus organisers could to some extent manipulate their 'success' rate, in the eyes of the court, by tolerating more unacceptable absenteeism and avoiding the need for breach proceedings in some cases.
>
> (Young, 1979, p. 66)

The use of community service orders grew during the 1970s and early 1980s before levelling off at around 7-8 per cent of offenders convicted of indictable offences in any year (Home Office, 1990a). The introduction by the Home Office of national standards for community service schemes in 1989 was intended to eliminate much of the existing diversity in practice and, more especially, to promote the community service order as a tough and demanding sentencing option. The Home Office circular which accompanied the national standards (Home Office, 1989) identified the purposes of community service as punishment, reparation and benefit to the community. Although the national standards were clearly aimed at enhancing the credibility of community service with the public and with the courts, and encouraging the increased use of community service as an alternative to custody (Home Office, 1988a, 1990b), the circular acknowledged, on the basis of Appeal Court guidance, that a short community service order 'may properly be ordered for an offence which would not justify a custodial sentence' (Home Office, 1989, p. 3).

The Community Service Orders Rules 1989, which came into force on 1 April of that year to co-incide with the implementation of the national standards, introduced the requirement that most offenders sentenced to orders of 60 or more hours should complete their community service orders in team placements, engaged in manual work. Manual tasks which improve the appearance and amenities of a neighbourhood might, according to the national standards, include clearing litter, removing graffiti and clearing overgrown cemeteries (Home Office, 1988b). The national standards also introduced requirements for the recording of hours worked and specified the procedures to be adopted in the event of an offender's failure to comply with his or her community service order.

The national standards, and particularly the first draft, which was seen as containing a number of unreasonable and unworkable proposals, were widely criticised (e.g. McWilliams, 1989) and disappointment was expressed (e.g. by Allen, 1988) that the government had published standards when a Home Office funded evaluation of community service practice in several probation areas, being conducted by researchers at the University of Birmingham, had just begun.

In the Green Paper 'Punishment, Custody and the Community' (Home Office, 1988a) the government suggested that community service might be combined with other community-based sentences in a new supervision and restriction order and sought views on whether amendments should be made to the maximum or minimum number of hours of work that an offender sentenced to community service could be ordered to perform. The subsequent White Paper (Home Office, 1990b) indicated that the maximum of 240 hours and minimum of 40 hours should remain unchanged, but proposed the introduction of combined probation and community service orders and the opportunity for courts to impose community service orders concurrently with curfew orders enforced, if necessary, by electronic monitoring.

The government's proposals gained legislative expression in the Criminal Justice Act 1991 which comes into effect in October 1992. The Act makes provision for the maximum number of hours that can be imposed upon a 16 year-old to be increased from 120 to 240 and introduces a requirement that courts obtain and consider a pre-sentence report before passing a sentence of community service. Most significantly, however, the new Act will enable community service orders to be combined with other community sentences and makes available to the courts for the first time the power to make a 'combination order' of probation and community service, in which the probation component must be for not less than 12 months (and may include additional requirements) and the community service component must fall within the range of 40 to 100 hours. Commenting on the new arrangements for community penalties, which are viewed by the government as sentences in their own right rather than as alternatives to custody, Wasik and Taylor (1991, p. 4) concluded that:

> It may, perhaps be doubted whether this 'cafeteria' style of sentencing can achieve very much, except further to confuse sentencing principles. It seems to owe more to the rather old-fashioned belief that a precise form of sentence can be selected to achieve a specific rehabilitative effect, than to the coherent grading of community orders. It seems to

run contrary to the government's own stated preference for penalty scaling and tends to undermine recent official moves to standardise the operational and breach arrangements for community orders.

The practical ramifications of the 1991 Criminal Justice Act, so far as it relates to the community service order, will be considered in the final chapter of this book.

The development of community service in Scotland

Community service orders were introduced in Scotland in October 1977 with the development of the first experimental schemes in Grampian and Tayside regions. Within a few months, a total of five experimental schemes were operational in four local authorities, with initial funding provided by the Scottish Office for a period of two years.

Following the report of the Kilbrandon Committee in 1964, the government issued a white paper entitled 'Social Work and the Community' (Scottish Office, 1966) in which it proposed a total restructuring of the personal social services in Scotland, through the creation of comprehensive social work departments. When the proposals were implemented in 1969, the newly created generic departments assumed responsibility for the tasks previously undertaken by the probation service. Since then (and more recently in the case of prison social work) social work services to offenders and their families have been provided by the local authority social work departments who were, therefore, the obvious candidates for administering the new community service orders.

In the absence of specific enabling legislation, the first community service orders in Scotland were imposed as a requirement of probation. In February 1979, with the implementation of the Community Service by Offenders (Scotland) Act 1978, Scottish courts obtained the facility to make 'stand alone' orders of between 40 and 240 hours, while retaining the option of alternatively imposing a community service order as a requirement of probation. The two types of community service orders have become widely referred to as Section 1 and Section 7 orders respectively, based on the relevant enabling sections of the 1978 Act.

In most respects, the Scottish legislation was comparable to the earlier legislation that had been introduced in England and Wales, with community service orders being available for offenders who had been convicted of offences that were punishable by imprisonment. Legislation north and south of the border differed, however, in two notable respects. First, because community service had originally been introduced as a

8

requirement of probation, this option was retained when the specific community service legislation came into effect. In reality, however, many schemes did not, until recently, offer courts the facility of imposing Section 7 (combined) community service orders.

The minimum age at which a community service order could be imposed also differed in Scotland and in England and Wales, reflecting the differently organised criminal justice systems in these countries. Thus while community service was available from the outset for 16 year-olds in Scotland (and the full range of hours could be imposed), this option was only later extended to 16 year-olds in England and Wales.

Just as the Wootton Committee (Advisory Council on the Penal System, 1970) had identified several distinct but complementary objectives for community service, so too did the Scottish Office regard this new penal measure as having the ability to fulfil a number of aims. As Duguid (1982) noted in his evaluation of the five experimental schemes, the main features of community service were:

1. Community service involves punishment. Regular attendance at placements deprives the offender of free use of his leisure time.
2. Community service also has a rehabilitative element. The offender must spend time helping others, and this it is hoped will help to restore his sense of personal dignity and to improve his standing in the community.
3. It also contains an indirect element of reparation. The unpaid work which the offender does benefits either the community in general or specific, usually disadvantaged, sections of that community.
4. In contrast to imprisonment, community service allows the offender to retain his job and continue to support his family. For the unemployed offender, it helps to maintain or develop the work habit and assists in overcoming social isolation.
5. It saves public resources by relieving pressure on the prison system and, arguably, by providing a cheaper alternative to incarceration.

(Duguid, 1982, p. 1)

The Scottish Office evaluation of the experimental schemes was largely descriptive in nature but revealed that the new sentencing option was operating broadly as planned. A similar conclusion was reached by O'Boyle and Parsloe (1980) in their study of the Grampian community service scheme.

Following the apparent viability and success of community service, its availability was gradually extended to other parts of the country. Partial funding was provided by the Scottish Office (80 per cent for the first five years and 70 per cent for the subsequent five years) and operational guidance was introduced (Social Work Services Group, 1980). By 1986, community service was available in 50 Sheriff Court Districts. With the gradual development of community service schemes over the years, there was a steady annual increase in the numbers of orders imposed. In 1986, 3,453 community service orders were made in Scotland, representing 1.6 per cent of all offenders against whom a charge was proved in that year (Social Work Services Group, 1988).

Despite the issuing of operational guidance by central government, wide variations in practice emerged. Social work departments were required to adopt a form of operation and management appropriate to their organisational structure and to local geographical and sentencing contexts. In some instances, several different models of practice could be found within a single regional department. Staffing arrangements likewise varied widely across the country.

Community service practitioners and managers began to express concerns about the impact of such operational diversity, which was further highlighted by a survey of policy and practice conducted in 1985 by the policy sub-group of the Scottish Community Service Group, which represented schemes throughout Scotland. Most schemes viewed the community service order as being simultaneously a punitive, reparative and rehabilitative sanction. There was a broad consensus that community service should be retained as an alternative to custody and many schemes believed that a high proportion of orders fell into this category. Some worrying discrepancies were, however, revealed in the final report which was published in August 1986, particularly in relation to enforcement and breach:

> Eighty-seven per cent of schemes described their breach procedure as being generally flexible in terms of what they viewed as acceptable or unacceptable conduct for the initiation of breach. It is of some concern, however, that the majority of schemes examined indicate that their assessment of acceptable reasons for absence appears to depend entirely upon subjective professional assessments, rather than by the utilisation or reference to an overall checklist as used by certain schemes...In terms of initiating breach proceedings, it is evident that whilst generally speaking, uniformity is found in the principle of using verbal and written warnings, wide discrepancies can be found in the number of absences allowed.
>
> (Scottish Community Service Group, 1986, p. 13)

Variations in practice were also identified, among other areas, in relation to the role of community service staff at the pre-sentence stage and in the types of information provided to offenders before being sentenced.

The introduction of nationwide standards of practice was argued to be necessary to minimise inequities which might otherwise arise when offenders were sentenced to community service in different parts of the country. The sub-group report contained 35 policy and practice recommendations which were subsequently debated at the Scottish Community Service Group annual conference later that year. The recommendations covered areas such as: insurance; assessment procedures; the provision of information to offenders prior to sentence; travel time and expenses; the location of units in relation to social work offices and the courts; staffing levels and designation; and workload management.

In order that the credibility of community service as a high tariff sentencing option could be maintained, the report recommended against the further extension of community service orders to the District Courts and for primarily practical reasons recommended against the introduction of community service as an alternative to imprisonment for fine default. The policy sub-group further recommended that schemes should provide individual (agency) placements for suitable offenders, that the work undertaken by offenders should be constructive and that 'the positive benefits of community service to the offender and the community should also be recognised as of equal importance and schemes should be encouraged towards good practice in this respect' (Scottish Community Service Group, 1986, p. 17).

With regard to enforcement, the report recommended the implementation of a nationwide checklist of important and unavoidable reasons for absence which would include only attendance at funerals, illness, job interviews, lawyers' appointments, court appearances and child birth. A standardised system of enforcement was proposed which would require the initiation of breach proceedings after the transmission of one verbal and three written warnings by personal or recorded delivery. Finally, on a more general level, a recommendation was made that all schemes in Scotland should arrange for the provision of unpaid work as a requirement of probation.

The continued funding of community service was also a topical issue at that time, with several schemes approaching the end of their first ten years of financial support from the Scottish Office. Thereafter, local authorities were expected to assume full responsibility for the costs of their community service schemes. However, as a result of its incremental development, community service was still not available to all Sheriff Courts and under the existing arrangements the development of additional schemes was dependent upon local authority social work departments making available a portion of the operational costs. Existing schemes were similarly constrained by the availability of resources and several had found it necessary to undergo temporary periods of closure in the face of excessive demands for community service orders by the courts.

A review of the existing funding arrangements was acknowledged by the government to be necessary if new schemes were to be developed in areas where community service had been hitherto unavailable to the courts and if schemes were to be adequately resourced to meet sentencers' demands for orders. Scheme closures and, in some cases, lax enforcement practices were viewed as having the potential to undermine seriously the credibility of the community service order with the Scottish courts.

It was against this background that Michael Forsyth, the Minister with responsibility for social work at the Scottish Office, announced in December 1987 the government's intention of providing 100 per cent funding for community service schemes with effect from 1 April 1989. Commenting on the proposals, Mr Forsyth said:

> The Government places a high value on community service, but we do not think it has yet realised its full potential. Considerable progress has been achieved in the eight years since community service schemes were introduced. Nevertheless, I am anxious to remove any obstacles to their further development and accordingly we propose to change the basis on which community service is funded...The Government consider it important that the courts should have available to them a tough realistic alternative to imprisonment, which they can use in cases where the offence merits custody, but the court considers that a non-custodial sentence would be more appropriate.
>
> (Scottish Office, 1987)

Following the announcement, the Scottish Office convened a consultative group, which included representatives from the Scottish Office, the Association of Directors of Social Work, the Convention of Scottish Local Authorities (COSLA), the Crown Office, the Sheriffs' Association, the District Courts Administration and the police. The consultative group was set the task of developing national standards and objectives for the operation of Scottish community service schemes to be introduced with the advent of full central funding from April 1989. The change to 100 per cent funding was not intended to involve a centralisation of the management of community service schemes: community service would continue to operate in the context of the local authority social work departments and staff would continue to be accountable within the existing local authority management structures. Standardisation of policy and practice was, however, seen as both desirable and necessary for a number of reasons. National standards would serve to redress the inequities that were known to exist; they would facilitate the monitoring of schemes (which, in turn, would inform subsequent decisions regarding resource allocation); and they would, it was argued, further enhance the credibility of community service, encouraging its increased use by the courts as a direct alternative to imprisonment.

Limiting the use of imprisonment for less serious offenders was a central policy objective of the government in the late 1980s, highlighted thus in the Kenneth Younger Memorial Lecture delivered in November 1988 to the Howard League (Scotland) by Malcolm Rifkind, then Secretary of State for Scotland:

> There will always be those who commit serious or violent crimes and who pose a threat to society which requires them to be confined for significant periods. Nevertheless, there are many good reasons for wishing to ensure that, as a society, we use prisons as sparingly as possible...If offenders can remain in the community, under suitable conditions, they should be able to maintain their family ties, opportunities for work or training and they may be better placed to make some reparation for their offence.
>
> (Rifkind, 1989, p. 85)

In the mid to late 1980s Scotland had witnessed a series of serious disturbances in several prisons which had resulted in roof-top protests and the taking of staff as hostages. The 1980s had also been characterised by high levels of imprisonment in both British and European terms. In 1988, for example, the average daily sentenced population in Scottish prisons was 4,385, or 108 per 100,000 of the total adult (16 years and over) population. At the same time, there was some evidence that community service had, since its introduction, been used less and less as a direct alternative to imprisonment or detention. The proportion of offenders sentenced to community service who were, on the basis of their prior sentencing history, judged to be at a higher risk of imprisonment had gradually decreased, while the proportion deemed to be at a lower risk of custody had risen steadily (Social Work Services Group, 1988).

A primary objective of the national standards was, therefore, to reduce the unnecessary use of custody by the Scottish courts. According to paragraph 1.2.2, one of the main operational objectives would be:

To seek to ensure that community service is used for those offenders whose offences genuinely warrant a custodial sentence, except where the court considers that other factors, such as the protection of the public, require a period of detention or imprisonment.

(Social Work Services Group 1989, para. 1.2.2)

The national standards were, in addition, aimed at encouraging the increased participation of local communities in responding to crime and in facilitating the re-integration of offenders, and at promoting community service as a sentence which is credible and fair in the eyes of courts, local communities and offenders alike. Schemes were required to provide work opportunities and facilities for offenders with particular needs, to provide good quality supervision and to offer offenders access to advice and help with personal, social or family problems which might otherwise interfere with the work ordered by the court. Community service placements should be characterised by:

...work which is clearly of value to the community, the agency and the offender...work which is within the capacity of the offender and capable of enhancing his/her social responsibility and self-respect...work which enables the offender to make reparation to the community for his/her offending behaviour...(and) clear, realistic and challenging standards of behaviour and work.

(Social Work Services Group, 1989, para. 1.2.8)

A substantial increase in expenditure on community service, to increase the number of places available to the courts, would be justified if the new guidelines had the intended impact of increasing the numbers of offenders sentenced to community service instead of custody. It quickly became apparent, however, that the national standards would, in themselves, have a limited impact upon sentencing practice. This was confirmed by interviews with sentencers, which were conducted shortly after the national standards were introduced (Carnie, 1990).

A range of methods, such as increasing the maximum number of hours that could be ordered, were considered by the Scottish Office as a means of encouraging the courts to use community service more often as an alternative to imprisonment. However, the timely introduction in 1990 of a law reform bill afforded the government an opportunity to amend the existing community service legislation in such a way as to restrict the use of community service orders to those offenders who would otherwise receive a sentence of imprisonment or detention. While some provisions in the bill (such as the proposed introduction of a unit fine system) were lost in its rapid passage through parliament, the community service amendment survived and came into effect on 1 April 1991 following the publication of the Law Reform (Miscellaneous Provisions) (Scotland) Act 1990 in November of that year. Other provisions in the Act have indirect implications for the operation of community service in Scotland.

The Law Reform Act introduced a new option - the supervised attendance order - for use by the courts in dealing with those who default on payment of their fines. The fine is by far the most commonly used disposal in Scotland, accounting for approximately 80 per cent of all sentences. Although the majority of those thus sentenced pay their fines, a small percentage (7.1 per cent in 1988) fail to do so and are imprisoned as a result. Because of the extensive use of monetary penalties, however, this group is numerically large. A total of 9,714 offenders were received into penal establishments in Scotland for defaulting on their fine repayments in 1988. In that year, fine defaulters accounted for 47.4 per cent of all sentenced adult receptions and 6.1 per cent of the average daily sentenced adult population in Scottish prisons. Twenty-six per cent of all fine defaulters imprisoned in 1988 for non-payment were under 21 years of age (Scottish Home and Health Department, 1990).

It had been shown that many people default on their fine repayments not because they are unwilling to pay, but because they have insufficient income to meet the instalments required (Nicholson, 1990). The introduction of fines enforcement officers to Scottish courts was found to have had a limited impact upon the numbers of defaulters received into prison, partly as a result of 'certain offenders with very poor financial means making rational decisions to serve time rather than pay their fines irrespective of any advice and assistance which the fines officer could offer' (Nicholson and Millar, 1989, p. viii).

In 1987, a working party convened by the Association of Directors of Social Work (ADSW) recommended in favour of the introduction of a unit fine system, which would gear the level of monetary penalties more realistically to offenders' ability to pay (see, for example, Hillsman, 1990) and suggested that further attention should be directed towards the introduction of an attendance centre order, or some similar measure, to expand the range of non-custodial options and decrease the courts' reliance on monetary penalties for offenders without the necessary financial means.

The ADSW working group also recommended that courts should have the option, in cases of default, of imposing other non-custodial sanctions such as probation or community service. Although legislative provision has existed in England and Wales to enable community service to be considered as an option for fine defaulters, West (1978) has argued

15

persuasively against extending the use of community service in this way. West highlighted, in particular, the resource implications for schemes and the practical and administrative difficulties that would be created through offenders having the opportunity to 'buy themselves out' of their community service work.

Alive to these issues, the Scottish Office rejected the extension of community service to fine defaulters and introduced instead the supervised attendance order. Initially conceived of as an addition to the existing range of non-custodial sanctions at first sentence and in cases of default, the supervised attendance order was subsequently introduced solely as an option for fine defaulters who would otherwise be imprisoned as a consequence of their non-payment.

Under the new order, offenders who are in default of their fine payments, and who face imprisonment as a result, may be given 10-60 hours of attendance at specified activities supervised by the local authority social work department:

> The aim will be to provide constructive activity which is likely to include sessions on life skills as well as unpaid work, carried out wherever possible on a group basis. Supervised attendance orders will not be geared to tackling individual offending behaviour, but will, in effect, constitute a fine on the offender's free time.
>
> (Social Work Services Group, 1991a)

At the time of writing, the first experimental schemes were being established by three regional social work departments.

The Law Reform Act also contained the legislative changes necessary for the introduction of full central government funding of all other statutory social work services to the criminal justice system. From April 1991, probation, court services and through-care became subject to 100 per cent Scottish Office funding and, following a process of consultation similar to that which had previously occurred with community service, national standards for these other statutory social work services were introduced (Social Work Services Group, 1991b). The new arrangements were aimed at improving the quality and targeting of community-based social work disposals to further decrease the reliance of Scottish courts upon the use of detention and imprisonment. The creation of a specialist social work service to offenders and their families was viewed as necessary to increase the confidence of the courts in probation supervision. The probation order had to a large extent fallen from grace since the creation of generic social work departments in 1969.

The comparatively low use of probation in Scotland appears at least in part to have been influenced by the low level of probation recommendations in social enquiry reports (Curran and Chambers, 1982; Williams et al., 1991). Although Roberts and Roberts (1982) questioned whether resource availability alone could account for the varying use of probation and community service across probation areas in England and Wales, it was acknowledged in some areas to be a determining factor. With other client groups competing for limited social work resources, and with increased emphasis upon statutory child protection work, generic social workers in Scotland had little incentive to recommend the making of probation orders and add to their already overburdened caseloads which encompassed the entire spectrum of service provision and need.

The courts gradually became increasingly disillusioned with the quality of supervision afforded to offenders who were made subject to probation and became increasingly reluctant to make use of this option. This process was summarised succinctly by one sheriff as follows:

> For a while, certainly, probation was the sick man of the criminal justice system. The abandoning of supervision by specialist probation officers in favour of generic social workers was followed though not necessarily caused by a collapse of judicial confidence in this particular disposal. Orders it seemed were not being allocated in such a way as to allow the offender to go directly from the hands of the court to those of the social work department; supervision was neither strict nor frequent enough; and finally no particular effort was being required of many offenders although unfairly perhaps someone who re-offended during a period of probation was likely to be treated by the court as an even more lamentable case in that he was deemed to have spurned social work assistance which all too often had not been made properly available in the first place. There were exceptions naturally but by and large there seemed to be little which effectively distinguished probation from a simple deferred sentence.
>
> (Lothian, 1991)

The provision of full central funding for probation, court services and through-care was accompanied by a re-organisation within social work departments of their services to offenders. Under the previous funding arrangements, resources that were allocated by central government for work with offenders were frequently swallowed up by other forms of service provision. The new financial arrangements were introduced to ensure that financial allocation for statutory social work services in the criminal justice system was being put to its intended purpose. The separate budgets for offender services (including community service) could be most effectively administered through the creation of specialist workers or teams. In some areas, specialist offender workers have begun to incorporate the administration and supervision of community service orders into their wider caseloads.

The national standards which were simultaneously introduced were intended to promote minimum standards of practice across the country and to increase the credibility of social work disposals with the courts. Some amendments were made to the earlier community service guidelines to bring procedures (such as enforcement) into line with those which had been introduced for the supervision of probation orders but the overall operational objectives for community service schemes remained largely unchanged. On an organisational level, however, community service should now become more closely integrated with other social work services to offenders and their families in Scotland.

2 The research programme

Introduction

The programme of research described in this book was conducted over a five year period from 1986-91. It evolved in an incremental fashion, with later studies being prompted by questions raised by the earlier research. The present chapter describes the series of studies in the order in which they were completed, outlining the aims and rationale of each study and the research methods employed.

An evaluative study of community service by offenders in Scotland

In 1986, shortly after its inception, the Social Work Research Centre (SWRC) was encouraged to undertake an evaluative study of Scottish community service schemes as part of its core-funded research activities. The request was initiated by a large local authority social work department with several community service schemes which differed from each other operationally in a number of potentially interesting respects.

The policy context

The reasons underlying the diversification of community service practice across Scotland have been outlined in the previous chapter. So too have the concerns being expressed by managers and practitioners by the mid 1980s about the possible negative consequences of existing operational inconsistencies both for clients and for the credibility of the scheme as a whole. The legislative framework had allowed for considerable flexibility in the manner in which schemes were organised and operated. In spite of the early introduction of centralised guidance (Social Work Services Group, 1980) differences could be found both between, and in some instances within, local authorities with respect both to staffing structures and to various aspects of operation and practice.

Initially, it was intended that the SWRC evaluation would concentrate upon a number of community service schemes within a single social work department. With the growing interest among practitioners in standardising, as far was practicable, the operation of schemes throughout the country, the focus of the study was expanded to include a total of twelve schemes in four local authorities. In addition to increasing the scale of the endeavour, the expansion of the study enabled a greater range of practice variation to be embraced by the research and, in so doing, provided an opportunity for more informed comment on the relative effectiveness of different approaches to practice.

In spite of community service having been available as a sentencing option in Scotland for almost ten years, and for even longer in England and Wales, much of the previous research which had been conducted into the operation of this measure in Britain had been largely descriptive in nature and had failed to elucidate whether or not different approaches to the operation of community service schemes were differentially effective. This, however, was the type of information required by practitioners and managers in Scotland who were attempting to align their practice in such a way that the most effective components would be retained.

The initial steps towards the development of a coherent national framework for community service practice were taken by the Scottish Community Service Group whose policy sub-group report and subsequent annual conference in 1986 explored the mechanisms by which standardisation might be achieved and the forms that it might take (Scottish Community Service Group, 1986). The issue of standardisation was further highlighted and formalised the following year with the announcement in December 1987 of the government's intention to review the operation of community service in Scotland and to introduce full central funding of schemes and national standards from 1 April 1989.

When the Scottish Office announced their future intentions for the operation and organisation of community service in Scotland the SWRC evaluation had been in progress for several months. The expected timescales of the research and the planned policy developments meant, however, that the findings could be made available to the consultation group in sufficient time to inform the contents of the national standards that were being produced. From its comparatively modest origins and aims, the research therefore assumed increased significance in helping to shape the future development of community service in Scotland.

Objectives and focus of enquiry

In broad terms, the research aimed to identify effective community service practice. To draw upon Pease's (1983) distinction, the study could be more appropriately described as 'improvement research' (which is aimed at optimising practice) than as 'evaluative research' (aimed at assessing the viability of a service and its effectiveness in relation to other measures). That is not, however, to deny the evaluative focus of the enterprise, since the identification of optimal practice was, in itself, critically dependent upon an assessment of the relative effectiveness of the varied operational arrangements that existed across schemes.

Within this overall framework the research sought to identify the characteristics of offenders sentenced to community service; to compare the participating schemes along a number of relevant dimensions of practice; to assess the relative effectiveness of different models of practice in achieving various outcomes; to document offenders' experiences on community service and their attitudes towards different types of work; and to estimate the extent to which community service was being used by the courts as an alternative to detention or imprisonment. Each of these objectives is discussed, in turn, more fully below.

Identifying the characteristics of offenders on orders. A primary objective of the research was to obtain a detailed picture of the types of offenders being sentenced to community service in Scotland. A description of the background characteristics of offenders made subject to community service orders in the experimental schemes had been provided by Duguid (1982). With the subsequent evolution and expansion of community service and its extension to other parts of the country it was by no means certain that this earlier profile would still be applicable. The annually published statistical data which were routinely collected from individual regions by central government painted a very broad picture of the manner in which community service was being used.

A range of information was therefore gathered for each offender in the research sample. This included various demographic variables (e.g. age, gender, employment status, marital status); sentencing variables (e.g. type of sentencing court, remand status prior to sentence; nature of offence/s for which the order was made; length of community service order; type of order (Section 1 or Section 7); previous criminal history (nature and number of previous convictions and disposals); history of social work involvement (recency and types of supervision as an adult and/or child); and social circumstances (e.g. accommodation status and history, employment history, family relationships and history of substance abuse or mental health problems).

Little, beyond the anecdotal level, was known about the characteristics of offenders in Scottish schemes who failed to comply with the requirements of their community service orders. As well as describing the characteristics of offenders on orders the research therefore aimed to identify the factors associated with an increased risk of breach.

Assessing the relative effectiveness of practice. The main focus of the study was upon the different procedures adopted by the schemes and their relative effectiveness in achieving certain specified outcomes. The primary outcome measure adopted was the rate of successful completion, based upon all orders completed or breached (that is, excluding orders revoked in the interests of justice). A comparison of success rates across schemes took into account the differential representation of high risk offenders across schemes.

Similar success rates across schemes may, nevertheless, mask underlying differences in the extent to which offenders fail to comply with the requirements of their orders. Previous studies (e.g. B. McWilliams, 1980) had identified absence from placement as the most common reason for offenders on community service orders being returned to court for failure to comply. The levels of acceptable and unacceptable absences sustained by offenders were therefore adopted as an intermediate outcome measure. The reason for each absence was documented (including whether or not prior permission for the absence had been given by community service staff) as was they manner in which the absence had been classified (acceptable or unacceptable) and the follow-up action, if any, that had been taken.

The aspects of practice examined in the research included the procedures for assessing offenders' suitability for a community service order; the methods adopted to match offenders to an appropriate work placement; the enforcement practices employed in response to failure to comply with the requirements; and the response of schemes to family, social or personal problems encountered by offenders while completing their community service orders.

Prior discussions with each of the schemes had revealed differences between them with respect to each of these areas of practice. The research therefore sought to establish whether there was a relationship between the variations in practice and the outcomes of community service orders.

Offenders' experiences and attitudes. It is possible that offenders' perceptions of the quality of their community service experience may have an influence upon their compliance with the requirements of their community service orders. That is, offenders who regard their work placements as constructive and worthwhile may be more motivated to attend for work as instructed and may, therefore, have fewer absences from placement and a lower likelihood of breach.

A widely held assumption was that agency placements were generally viewed by offenders as more rewarding than placements in community service teams and that work of a personalised nature was more highly valued than practical work. Some, on the other hand, (e.g. Ralphs, 1980; West, 1976) have argued that the quality of placements may more important than the broad characteristics of the work or the setting in which it is carried out. The research therefore examined the attitudes of offenders towards different types of work placements and aimed to identify those features of placements that enhanced the perceived quality of community service for offenders ordered to perform unpaid work.

The offenders' experiences and views were solicited through interviews and questionnaires. In addition to documenting the offenders' experiences of, and attitudes towards, unpaid work the questionnaires sought information about the types of family, social or personal problems experienced by the offenders; the offenders' understanding of the enforcement policies operational in the schemes; their views as to how community service might be improved; the incidence of offending (convictions and charges) while on community service; and their self-predicted likelihood of further offending. The offenders were also asked to indicate which sentence they believed that their community service order had replaced.

The use of community service by the courts. Perhaps the greatest debate surrounding community service concerns whether this option should serve solely as an alternative to a custodial sentence or whether the community service order should be regarded as a sentence in its own right which might justifiably be imposed in place of other non-custodial penalties such as fines. The evaluation of the experimental schemes conducted by Duguid (1982) indicated that in the first year in which community service was available to Scottish courts, sheriffs would have imposed a non-custodial sanction in just under thirty per cent of cases had community service not been available. More recent estimates (e.g. Social Work Services Group, 1988) suggested that the diversionary impact of community service had gradually declined over time.

A final objective of the research was, therefore, to examine the manner in which community service was being used by Scottish courts. More specifically, to what extent were community service orders being imposed in lieu of sentences of imprisonment or detention and to what extent as alternatives to other non-custodial measures?

Research methods and sample

As previously noted, a total of twelve community service schemes in four local authority social work departments participated in the research. The schemes were selected on the basis that they differed from each other organisationally or procedurally while being broadly representative of the range of practice throughout the country. Very small schemes (such as those operated by island authorities) were excluded on the grounds that they would not yield sufficient numbers of cases within the fieldwork period. Otherwise, schemes located in both rural and urban areas were represented in the study.

In view of the varying staffing structures in different parts of the country, the definition of what constituted a community service scheme varied accordingly. In most instances the unit of analysis was a complete scheme comprising an organiser with managerial responsibilities and one or more officers or assistants. In one of the larger schemes the caseload of one of four qualified community service officers formed the focus of the research while in another scheme the caseloads of two qualified officers were included. Such an approach was considered appropriate in schemes consisting of several qualified members of staff to prevent the emergence of a composite picture of practice that failed to reflect variations in practice among individual staff members.

The community service sample. The research focused upon all offenders in the participating schemes whose community service orders were terminated (successfully or otherwise) between 1 September 1987 and 31 May 1988. In the case of breach for failure to comply, offenders were excluded from the sample if breach proceedings had been instituted but the final outcome of the application for revocation was still unknown by the end of the recruitment period.

The total sample consisted of 406 offenders across the twelve schemes. Background information about each of these offenders and information relating to their experiences on community service (types of work placements, absences etc.) was extracted from their social enquiry reports and community service case files. All offenders in the sample were invited at the point of completing their orders, or as soon as possible thereafter, to complete a questionnaire. The questionnaires were distributed by community service staff and returned directly to the SWRC in the pre-paid envelopes provided.

Completed questionnaires were received from 136 offenders, representing a response rate of approximately a third. In addition, interviews were conducted with a sub-sample of 28 questionnaire respondents. The interviews, which were conducted in the offenders' homes, afforded a more detailed exploration of the topics included in the questionnaire and addressed additional areas of interest that could not otherwise have been covered.

A composite picture of practice within the schemes was obtained through aggregating the data extracted from individual case files. Details of scheme policy and practice were also derived through interviews with each of the organisers, officers and assistants in the twelve schemes and from staff questionnaires. Each of the schemes was visited by the researcher on an approximately monthly basis to extract information from the case files of those offenders who had completed their orders during the previous four weeks. These regular visits also offered an opportunity for informal discussion and facilitated the process of familiarisation with the policies and procedures that operated in the schemes.

Unsuccessful referrals. To gain some insight into the selection criteria adopted by schemes and the sentencing practices of the courts a study was also made of offenders who had been referred to the schemes for a community service assessment but who had, for various reasons, subsequently received an alternative sentence. Background information was obtained for each of the unsuccessful referrals to the twelve schemes between 1 April and 30 September 1987, a period during which many, though not all, of the community service sample had received their orders.

Less comprehensive background information was generally available for the unsuccessful referrals. Where available, information relating to the personal characteristics of offenders and their social and criminal histories was extracted from case files. A note was made of whether or not offenders had been assessed as suitable for a community service order, whether or not they had consented to an order being made and whether or not appropriate work could have been made available for them to perform. Where relevant the reasons for an offender being assessed as unsuitable were recorded and, when available, details of the alternative sentences received by sample were obtained.

The comparative costs of community service and custody

An analysis of the comparative costs of community service orders and the most likely alternative custodial sentences was conducted by Martin Knapp and Eileen Robertson of the Personal Social Services Research Unit (PSSRU) at the University of Kent. An additional research grant was provided by the Social Work Services Group of the Scottish Office to enable such a costing to be included in the evaluation of the twelve community service schemes.

Rationale and objectives

When the Wootton Committee (Advisory Council on the Penal System, 1970) first recommended the introduction of community service orders, one attraction of the proposed new sentencing option was its comparative cheapness. Particularly when prison overcrowding is high and large capital sums are required to expand prison capacity, policy makers look to non-custodial options as offering a cheaper, and perhaps even more effective, alternative to custody. Although some evidence of the costs of different sanctions existed (e.g. Shaw, 1980) the relative cheapness of various alternatives to custody had rarely been tested. Previous costings of community service and its alternatives (especially imprisonment) had failed to take into account the full range of direct and indirect costs both to society and to offenders and their families. Often the costs of various alternatives had been compared without due regard to the differences between offenders sentenced to different disposals and there had been no attempt to link the costs of community service or imprisonment with data concerning its effectiveness.

In broad terms the objectives of the costing study were three-fold. First, to compare the costs of community service orders across schemes and to seek to explain variations in costs with reference to variations in practice. Second, by linking data on costs with data on outcomes to examine whether different operational arrangements were differentially cost effective. Third, by comparing, on a comprehensive basis, the costs of community service orders and likely alternative custodial sentences that would have been imposed, to reach well informed conclusions about the relative cost effectiveness of these two penal options.

As originally conceived, the PSSRU research would have sought, additionally, to comment on the appropriateness of existing funding arrangements by identifying separately the direct and indirect costs of community service to local authority social work departments and to central government. More specifically, to what extent were the Scottish

Office justified in requiring that local authorities should, over time, meet an increasing proportion of the costs of schemes, when the savings which might result from the diversion of offenders from sentences of imprisonment would accrue not to the social work departments but to central government? In the event, this aspect of the costing was pre-empted by the Scottish Office's decision to assume, from April 1989, full financial responsibility for the operation of community service schemes.

The costing methodology

Full details of the costing methodology employed in the study have been reported elsewhere (Knapp et al, 1989, 1992; McIvor, 1989) and for this reason it will be outlined only briefly here.

The direct costs of community service orders. The costs of community service orders in the twelve schemes were derived from accounts for the year ended 31 March 1988. The community service expenditures obtained from regional headquarters were reduced to a consistent basis and grouped under ten headings: salary, national insurance and superannuation; travel and subsistence; property costs excluding rent and rates; insurance; office supplies and equipment; advertising; telephone and postage; other miscellaneous costs including community service equipment; and overheads calculated as eight per cent of the total of the other nine items.

To compute the average direct cost of a community service order in each of the schemes, the total costs of the following four activities were calculated: pre-sentence referrals and assessment; the matching of offenders to work placements; the ongoing supervision of placements; and the processing of breaches through the courts. The average costs of each of these activities were based upon corresponding workload measures: the number of pre-sentence assessments conducted by community service staff; the number of new orders started within the study year; the number of community service hours supervised by the scheme over the year; and the number of breach proceedings initiated. The total average direct cost of an order was obtained by summing the average costs of these four activities in each scheme. By initially disaggregating the costs of the component activities in this way it was possible to compare the relative costs and effectiveness of different operational arrangements across schemes.

The direct costs of imprisonment. The direct costs of alternative prison sentences were derived from the Scottish Home and Health Department prisons expenditure figures for 1986-7 and inflated by 6 per cent to 1987-88 prices to put them on an equal footing with the community service costs. The prison costs were slightly recalculated to exclude items not included in the available community service accounts (such as medical services and capital expenditure on buildings).

Having thus obtained the average weekly prison cost for young offenders and adults in Scotland, the costs were then adjusted to reflect the fact that the typical offender on a community service order will differ from the typical prison inmate: the anticipated costs of custody for the former will be lower than the average costs of imprisonment. Relevant local information was used to identify the predicted average prison costs for each scheme which were then converted to a cost per sentence based on the mean length of sentence received by the unsuccessful referrals who were imprisoned in each scheme and an assumption concerning the remission obtained.

The total costs of community service and custody. In order that comparisons could be made between the costs of community service orders and the likely alternative custodial sentence, the direct costs of each of these options had to be supplemented with indirect costs.

The direct costs of a prison sentence were adjusted to take into account the hidden costs to social work departments (estimated at 4 per cent of direct prison costs) and the savings to households of weekly living costs when an offender is in custody (based upon the Family Expenditure Survey).

There were equivalent indirect costs of community service, estimated for successfully completed orders at 3 per cent of the direct cost of an average length order. For breached orders there were estimated to be substantial additional costs of uncontested and contested cases coming before the courts (including solicitor and police costs). Added to this were the costs of prison sentences imposed when breached orders were revoked. Taken together, the estimates suggested an additional indirect and knock-on cost of, on average, around £2,500 per breached order. The total cost of an average length community service order was then calculated on the basis that just under 12 per cent of orders would result in breach.

Sentencers' perceptions of community service by offenders

The policy context

The introduction of full central government funding and national standards for the operation of Scottish community service schemes (Social Work

Services Group, 1989) was aimed at encouraging the courts to make increasing use of community service orders as alternatives to sentences of detention and imprisonment.

The popularity of community service among sentencers had been evidenced by the level of demand for orders by the courts. Indeed in some areas the demand for community service places was so great that schemes had found it necessary on a periodic basis to close to new referrals until existing caseloads had been reduced. There was growing evidence, however, both from Scotland (McIvor, 1989, 1990b; Social Work Services Group, 1988) and from England and Wales (Pease et al., 1977; Willis, 1977) that community service orders were frequently being imposed, and in as many as a small majority of cases, in lieu of other non-custodial sentences. In Scotland, moreover, it appeared that since its introduction, the use of community service as an alternative to custody had lessened over time. By simply increasing the resources made available to existing schemes there was no guarantee that a significant impact upon the level of custodial sentencing would result. There was, on the contrary, a clear danger that the additional places would be used to an even greater extent than before for offenders who would not otherwise have been dealt with by means of a custodial sentence.

The survey of sentencers' attitudes towards, and use of, the community service order was intended in part to assess the extent to which one of the primary objectives of the new arrangements for community service in Scotland would be achieved.

Objectives and methods

The study of Scottish sentencers' perceptions of community service was conducted by Jim Carnie and funded by the Criminology and Law Group of the Scottish Home and Health Department (Carnie, 1990). Since little systematic information had been hitherto available concerning the attitudes of sentencers towards this relatively new penal option, the focus of the research extended beyond the national standards and their likely impact on sentencing.

The views of the sentencers who participated in Carnie's (1990) study were obtained through qualitative interviews. The interviews addressed a range of relevant issues, including sentencers' views as to the purpose and philosophy of the community service order; their perceptions and use of community service in relation to other sentencing options; their experiences of and attitudes towards the operation of community service schemes; and their views of and likely response to both the guidance contained in the national standards and the planned expansion of schemes.

29

A total of twenty-seven interviews (with forty-two respondents) were conducted between June and August 1989. The fieldwork took place, therefore, shortly after the introduction of the Social Work Services Group national standards in April 1989 but before the target date for the full implementation of the objectives and standards which had been set for June 1990.

The research involved interviews with 2 High Court Judges, 21 sheriffs, 5 District Court Clerks and 14 lay justices. The Sheriff Courts included in the study were served by the community service schemes that had participated in the prior evaluation of community service practice. The sample comprised both small and large courts from seven sheriffdoms which were located in both rural and urban communities.

The research was primarily focused upon the views of sheriffs, who have the greatest opportunity to make use of community service in Scotland. By contrast, the facility to impose community service orders had not been available to most District Courts, though some had expressed a desire for this sentencing option to be made available to them. Group interviews were conducted with court clerks and lay justices in five District Courts. Two of these courts were able to make use of community service as a disposal and the other three had expressed an interest in acquiring the facility. Of particular interest, in light of the objectives being pursued in the national standards and the already low level of custodial sentencing in the District Courts, was the manner in which lay justices would make use of the community service order were this option available.

A full description of the study and its findings and conclusions can be found in Carnie (1990).

Community service orders: assessing the benefit to the community

Rationale and objectives

The Scottish Office national standards clearly located community service as a sentence of the courts that punishes offenders while enabling them to make reparation for their wrongdoing by performing useful work for the community. Few studies had, however, sought to assess the value, in other than economic terms, of work carried out by offenders on community service orders.

Previous research in England (Godson, 1980) and in New Zealand (Leibrich et al., 1984b) had indicated that placement-providing agencies were broadly satisfied with the work that had been carried out on their behalf by community service offenders and believed that the work had been of benefit to the agency. A similar response had been received from beneficiaries in an unpublished local survey conducted by a Scottish community service scheme (Borders Social Work Department, 1987). This study alone included feedback from individual members of the public who had been recipients of work as well as from agencies that had provided placements for offenders on community service orders. The responses of the two groups were not, however, identified separately in the resulting report.

The SWRC study, which was conducted on the Centre's core-funding, was aimed at assessing the extent to which community service work was valued both by individual recipients and by voluntary and statutory agencies who made available placements for offenders to complete the work ordered by the courts. The research also sought to identify problems that had been experienced by individual beneficiaries and by agencies and to assess the extent to which agency placements enabled offenders to become integrated with staff and other volunteers while they were completing their community service work.

Research method and samples

Community service schemes in eight of the nine mainland social work departments participated in a questionnaire survey of individuals and agencies who had been the recipients of community service work during 1989. The questionnaires were addressed and dispatched by community service staff but returned directly to the SWRC in pre-paid envelopes. A covering letter stressed that the identity of potential respondents had not been disclosed by the schemes and emphasised that there was no need for respondents to identify themselves or their agencies.

The questionnaires were sent out during January and February 1990. Most schemes dispatched questionnaires to all potential respondents (except those who, in their judgement, would be unable to complete a questionnaire or who would be distressed by receiving one). Two schemes with a large number of team placements were unable, because of the time that would be required, to send questionnaires to all the individual beneficiaries for whom services had been provided during the relevant twelve month period. Instead, the schemes selected a sample of potential respondents who would be representative of the range of tasks that had been undertaken by the teams.

In total, 1602 questionnaires were dispatched by the participating community service schemes to individual beneficiaries and 567 completed questionnaires were returned. An identical response rate (35.4 per cent) was achieved for the agency questionnaires, with 172 completed

31

questionnaires being received from the 486 agencies to which they had been sent.

The questionnaires that were sent to individual beneficiaries were, by necessity, brief. Most questions required a fixed choice response, with some open-ended questions included to obtain more detailed, qualitative information where relevant. Information was sought about: the types of work carried out; the source of referral; the reasons why respondents could not have carried out the work themselves; satisfaction with the work performed; contact with the offenders; types of problems encountered; and respondents' willingness to have work carried out by offenders on community service in the future.

The agency questionnaires contained a mixture of (predominantly) fixed choice and open ended items. In addition to seeking information about the characteristics of the placement agency, the types of tasks undertaken by community service workers and their usefulness to the agency and its clients or users, the questionnaire explored: whether offenders had continued to contribute in a voluntary or paid capacity after completing their orders; the degree of integration of offenders with agency staff and other volunteers; the frequency and types of problems that had been encountered by the agencies when offering placements; the types of support from community service staff that were valued by the agencies; the willingness of agencies to offer further placements; and the types of offenders that agencies would be unwilling or reluctant to offer placements to. Examples of both sets of questionnaires can be found in McIvor (1990a).

Reconviction among offenders sentenced to community service

Rationale and objectives

The studies so far described sought to establish the extent to which various policy and practice objectives had been achieved by Scottish community service schemes. Rehabilitation is not generally regarded as being an explicit objective of the community service order. Some of the sheriffs interviewed in Carnie's (1990) study did, however, suggest that in some instances a challenging and constructive placement experience might have a positive impact upon offenders' attitudes and behaviour. Similar views were expressed by some of the individual and agency respondents in the survey of beneficiaries.

An association had, furthermore, been found in the evaluation of community service schemes between offenders' experiences on community service and their self-reported likelihood of re-offending. The predicted likelihood of re-offending was lowest among offenders who had found their experience of community service to be constructive and worthwhile (McIvor, 1989, 1991a).

Analyses of recidivism following community service have typically compared subsequent reconviction or re-arrest among offenders sentenced to this disposal with that among similar offenders who have received alternative sentences (usually custody). This was so, for example, in Pease et al.'s (1977) study of reconviction after twelve months among offenders made subject to community service orders in the English experimental schemes.

The absence of necessary comparative data precluded a comparison of reconviction among the earlier community service sample with that among similar groups of offenders who had received other custodial or non-custodial disposals. None of the existing reconviction studies had, however, examined the relationship between the perceived value to offenders of their community service experience and their subsequent reconviction. More specifically, were offenders for whom community service had proved to be particularly constructive and worthwhile less likely to be reconvicted or were they reconvicted less frequently than offenders for whom community service had been a less positive and rewarding experience?.

An analysis of reconviction among the questionnaire respondents from the earlier study was conducted using information derived from computerised police records. The objectives were:

1. To document the rates of reconviction during the four-year period following the imposition of the original community service order.
2. To examine the relative frequency and nature of reconviction prior to and following the imposition of the order.
3. To identify the factors associated with reconviction.
4. To assess the impact of offenders' experiences of community service on subsequent reconviction.
5. To examine the relationship between offenders' self-predicted likelihood of re-offending and actual reconviction.

Sample and methods

The reconviction study was conducted towards the end of 1991, some three and a half years after the original research. The Scottish Criminal Record Office (SCRO) provided statistical data relating to reconviction among 134 of the 136 questionnaire respondents from the earlier study (insufficient information was available to locate the police records of two offenders).

33

The relevant information was extracted by SCRO from their computerised records during November 1991. For each offender this included the number of new convictions since the date on which the original community service order had been imposed and the number of convictions in the two year period immediately preceding the community service sentence. For each recorded conviction SCRO made available the following information: date of sentence; the crime type/s (using the police classification system); the disposal/s; and the type of sentencing court (District, Sheriff Summary, High etc.). A marker was also included, where appropriate, to signify a breach of the community service order.

Owing to certain requirements regarding confidentiality, no information was provided by SCRO which would enable the identification of individuals from their computerised police records. For instance, names were replaced by community service scheme code numbers in order that the reconviction data, when computerised, could be linked with the earlier questionnaire responses and other data for the offenders in the sample.

Reconviction data enabling a three-year follow-up were available for the entire sample. In most cases complete reconviction data were also available for the fourth year from the date of sentence.

3 Offenders, offences, orders and outcomes

Introduction

The present chapter describes the characteristics of the 406 offenders sentenced to community service in the twelve schemes. The work carried out by the offenders is described, the levels of compliance and completion are examined and factors associated with an increased risk of breach are identified. Comparisons are also made with a further group of offenders who were referred unsuccessfully for a community service assessment and who received alternative sentences instead.

Who gets community service?

Gender, age, marital status and employment status

In common with other studies (e.g. Duguid, 1982; Pease et al., 1975) the offenders sentenced to community service were found to be predominantly young, male, single and unemployed. The average age of the sample was 23.4 years, with just over half (52.6 per cent) being under 21 years of age and three-quarters aged 25 years or younger. Most (95.6 per cent) were males, two-thirds were single and three-quarters were unemployed when their community service order was imposed.

Accommodation and family relationships

Just under half the sample (49.1 per cent) were living with their parents when sentenced and around a quarter (26.6 per cent) were living with a partner. Smaller percentages were living alone in their own tenancies (11 per cent); with other relatives (7.4 per cent); with friends (2.8 per cent); in bed and breakfast accommodation or lodgings (1.5 per cent); or in residential care (0.3 per cent). Five offenders were known to be of no fixed abode when made subject to a community service order.

In most cases (72 per cent) the offender's relationship with his or her immediate family was described in the social enquiry report as good. In around a fifth of cases (19.6 per cent) family relationships were said to be strained, often as a direct result of the person's offending behaviour. In the remaining cases, family relationships were described as poor or offenders were said to have no contact with their families.

Substance abuse

Just over a tenth of the sample (10.8 per cent) were described in their social enquiry reports as having problems related to the abuse of alcohol and a further 7.9 per cent were said to have experienced alcohol-related problems in the past. Approximately a quarter of the total sample (26.1 per cent) were known to have received their community service orders for an alcohol-related offence. Younger offenders were less likely to have had a history of alcohol-related problems or to have been convicted of an alcohol-related offence than offenders aged 21 years and over.

Three offenders were said to have ongoing problems related to the use of illicit drugs and a further eight had experienced difficulties with drugs in the past. Twenty-four offenders were known to have a history of solvent abuse, three of whom were said to be still abusing solvents at the time of sentence.

Social work history

Information about the social work histories of the offenders was obtained primarily from social enquiry reports. A little under half the sample (44.3 per cent) had been subject to some form of statutory social work supervision in the past, either as an adult (9.8 per cent), as a child (20.5 per cent) or both (14 per cent). Around a third of this group were subject to statutory supervision, in most cases probation, when sentenced to community service. A further 12 per cent had been subject to a statutory order in the twelve months prior to their community service sentence.

Offenders with a history of statutory social work supervision were more likely than other offenders to have a history of unsettled accommodation and alcohol abuse. They also tended to have a poorer history of employment and to enjoy poorer relationships with their families.

Criminal history

The offenders in the sample had, on average, 5.0 previous convictions and less than a fifth (18.3 per cent) were first offenders. Just under a third (29.9 per cent) had served at least one previous custodial sentence; 18.3 per cent had been subject to a probation order; and 11.8 per cent had previous experience of community service.

Women were more likely than men to have received their community service orders on their first conviction (50.0 per cent compared with 16.7 per cent). None of the women had previously been subject to community service and none had served a prior custodial sentence.

Young offenders (that is, those aged 20 years or less) had fewer previous convictions and were less likely to have experienced imprisonment than older offenders. Offenders with a history of statutory social work supervision had more previous convictions and had served more custodial sentences than those with no such prior social work involvement. Criminal history was also related to employment history and alcohol abuse: offenders who had a history of regular employment had fewer previous convictions and had less experience of custody, while those with a history of alcohol abuse had more previous convictions and had served more custodial sentences than other offenders in the sample.

Sentencing variables

The majority of the offenders had been referred for a community service assessment by the court: only 8.7 per cent of referrals had been initiated by the social worker preparing the social enquiry report. Most offenders (84.7 per cent) had been sentenced under summary proceedings in the Sheriff Court. The majority (84.5 per cent) were sentenced locally, while 12.8 per cent were sentenced in courts elsewhere in Scotland and 2.7 per cent had been sentenced to community service in England and Wales.

Around a sixth of the offenders (15.6 per cent) were in custody when referred for a community service assessment. Young offenders were more likely than those aged 20 years and over to have been remanded in custody prior to sentence (21.7 per cent vs. 8.9 per cent; $\chi^2 = 11.5$, 1 d.f., p < .001) and social work-initiated referrals were more likely to be in custody than those who were referred for a community service assessment by the court

(34.3 per cent vs. 14.0 per cent; $\chi^2 = 8.5$, 1 d.f., p < .01)

The offenders in the sample were most likely to have received their community service orders for offences involving dishonesty (55.9 per cent); offences involving violence (26.8 per cent); offences against public order (22.4 per cent); road traffic offences (12.8 per cent) or offences against criminal justice (11.6 per cent). Ten offenders (2.5 per cent) had been sentenced to community service for drug-related offences and four (1.0 per cent) for offences of a sexual nature. Young offenders were more likely to have received their community service orders for offences involving dishonesty and offences against criminal justice (such as breaches of bail) while older offenders were more likely to have been sentenced to community service for offences involving violence.

To summarise briefly, the 'typical' offender on a community service order was a young, single male who was unemployed, had at least one previous conviction (but no custodial experience) and had been sentenced to community service for an offence involving criminal damage or dishonesty, a minor assault or a breach of public order. Although almost half had previous experience of statutory supervision by the social work department, either as an adult or as a child, few were currently subject to other statutory requirements when their community service orders were imposed. Most offenders sentenced to community service had settled living arrangements and enjoyed good family relationships, and few were known to have had significant difficulties with alcohol, solvents or drugs.

Who is unsuitable for community service?

The profile outlined above is consistent with Carnie's (1990) observation that sheriffs regarded community service as being appropriate for a wide range of middle order offences and offenders. As one sheriff in his study indicated:

> I would say that you have the two extremes of the scale...but within these parameters the full range of offences and offenders in my book can be eligible for community service. Whether or not I would impose community service is a different matter.
>
> (Carnie, 1990, pp. 21-22)

Although the sheriffs interviewed by Carnie (1990) stated that they would not normally apply strict criteria when reaching decisions regarding an offender's suitability for a community service order, there was a broad degree of consensus that such a disposal would not be suitable for sexual offenders, for violent offenders, for offenders with a serious drug or alcohol related problem or for offenders who were deemed to be suffering from a psychiatric disorder. Reservations were also expressed by some sheriffs about the appropriateness of community service for first offenders, professional thieves, fire raisers, serious road traffic offenders and for cases involving an identifiable victim.

The community service staff in the twelve schemes similarly did not apply formalised criteria when assessing an offender's suitability for an order. Some noted that guidance on suitability (in the form of exclusion categories) had been adhered to more rigidly when schemes were in an experimental phase and staff were less reluctant to take risks (see also, Hoggarth, 1991; W. McWilliams, 1980). Now a range of factors would be taken into account and each case would be considered on its individual merits. As one community service officer commented:

> The suitability can vary and we don't really have exemptions. When the scheme started they would not take on very violent crimes or sexual offenders or folk who were addicted to alcohol or drugs. That no longer exists. Everyone is taken on an individual basis and folk would be either taken or refused because of the person themselves, not because of one particular thing that's wrong with them.

The characteristics of successful and unsuccessful referrals

How though, did the offenders who received community service differ from those were referred unsuccessfully for a community service assessment? In most respects the two groups were indistinguishable though they did differ according to marital status (unsuccessful referrals were more likely to be single) and remand status (unsuccessful referrals were more likely to be in custody when referred for an assessment). The successful and unsuccessful referrals had similar numbers of previous convictions and comparable percentages of the two groups had served at least one custodial sentence: the unsuccessful referrals had, however, served a higher number of prison sentences than those who were sentenced to community service (for further details see McIvor, 1989).

Offenders who were referred unsuccessfully for a community service assessment were more likely than those who received community service orders to have been sentenced for sexual offences, offences against public order and criminal justice offences (such as breaches of bail). If anything, the unsuccessful referrals appeared, as a group, to have been slightly more at risk of a custodial sentence than those who were sentenced to community service (see also Chapter 7).

Not all the unsuccessful referrals received alternative sentences because they were judged by the schemes to be unsuitable for a community service order: indeed two thirds of the unsuccessful referrals (65.7 per cent) had been assessed as suitable for community service and in most of these cases (around two-thirds) appropriate work could have been found for the offender to perform. Some differences were observed, however, between the unsuccessful referrals who were assessed as suitable for community service and those who were considered unsuitable for an order.

Offenders who were single were less likely to have been assessed as suitable for a community service order than offenders who were married, co-habiting, separated or divorced (66.6 per cent vs. 79.5 per cent; $\chi^2 = 4.0$, 1 d.f., p < .05) and those who were unemployed when referred were less likely to have been considered suitable than those who were employed (65.0 per cent vs. 83.5 per cent; $\chi^2 = 11.3$, 1 d.f., p < .001). Offenders who were already subject to some form of statutory social work supervision (such as probation) were less likely to be considered suitable (52.3 per cent vs. 72.4 per cent; $\chi^2 = 6.7$, 1 d.f., p < .01) and offenders who were in custody when referred were less likely than those who were at liberty to be assessed as suitable for an order (61.5 per cent vs. 73.4 per cent; $\chi^2 = 5.2$, 1 d.f., p < .05). Offenders who had been referred for an assessment by the author of their social enquiry report were more likely than court-initiated referrals to be deemed suitable for community service (89.8 per cent vs. 68.3 per cent; $\chi^2 = 8.7$, 1 d.f., p < .01).

Offenders who were assessed as suitable for community service had served fewer custodial sentences than those who were not, and those who had previously been on probation were less likely to be assessed as suitable than offenders who had no previous experience of this court disposal (57.1 per cent vs. 75.5 per cent; $\chi^2 = 7.3$, 1 d.f., p < .01).

A variety of reasons were given by community service staff to explain why particular offenders were, in their view, unsuitable for a community service order. As Table 3.1 indicates, offenders were most often thought to be unsuited to community service either because they lacked the necessary motivation to complete an order or because their personal or social circumstances would have made successful completion unlikely.

Certain factors were almost universally identified by schemes as contra-indicating community service. Failure to attend the assessment interview, substance abuse, unsettled accommodation and a poor response to previous social work supervision were cited by most schemes as reasons for offenders being assessed as unsuitable for an order.

Table 3.1
Why offenders were unsuitable for community service

Reason for unsuitability	Number of offenders	Percentage of offenders (n = 123)
Substance abuse	23	18.7
Previous response to cs/supervision	20	16.3
Failure to attend interview	19	15.4
Outstanding charges	11	8.9
Lack of motivation	11	8.9
Poor work history	10	8.1
Problematic behaviour or personality	10	8.1
Unfit for work	9	7.3
Needs support	9	7.3
Unsettled lifestyle	8	6.5
Accommodation	8	6.5
First offender	8	6.5
Commitments	7	5.7
Risk of continued offending	5	4.1
Lacks self-discipline	5	4.1
Refusal to consent	3	2.4
Other	5	4.1
Total	171	139.0

Young offenders were more likely than older offenders to have been judged unsuitable on account of their previous response to supervision, their first offender status or their lack of motivation. Older offenders were more likely than those under 21 years of age to have been considered unsuitable because of substance abuse or unfitness for work.

The community service order

Type and length of order

Although the Community Service by Offenders (Scotland) Act 1978 enabled community service orders to be imposed as a requirement of probation this facility was used on a regular basis by only two schemes. Two others had a few Section 7 orders during the period of the research but the remainder did not make this option available to the courts. The majority of community service orders imposed (96.3 per cent) were, therefore, straightforward orders to perform unpaid work imposed under Section 1 of the 1978 Act. The small number of Section 7 orders in the sample prevented any analysis of the relationship between the type of community service order imposed and the characteristics of the offenders in the sample.

The average length of community service order was 142.3 hours. The majority of orders were for between 81 and 200 hours (Table 3.2).

Table 3.2
Length of community service order imposed

Length of order	Number of orders	Percentage of orders
40-80 hours	47	11.6
81-120 hours	147	36.2
121-160 hours	94	23.2
161-200 hours	85	20.9
201-240 hours	33	8.1
Total	406	100.0

There was no difference in average length between Section 1 and Section 7 orders. The length of order imposed was similarly unrelated to previous sentencing history and to the category of offence for which the community service order had been made. Orders imposed under solemn proceedings in the Sheriff Court were, however, longer, on average, than those imposed under summary proceedings (171.6 hours versus 138.3 hours) presumably reflecting the more serious nature of offences dealt with in the former court.

In a study of community service in Northern Ireland, Jardine et al. (1983) found that unemployed offenders were sentenced to longer community service orders than offenders who were working when their community service orders were imposed. No such relationship was found in the present study: the average length of order received by unemployed offenders was 138.0 hours and by employed offenders was 143.4 hours. The lack of a clear relationship between employment status and length of order, even when the type of sentencing court was taken into account, is consistent with Carnie's (1990) conclusion that 'employment status might or might not have a bearing on the number of hours imposed depending upon which sheriff was hearing the cases'(p. 24). Although some sheriffs were inclined to take into account the amount of leisure time available to employed offenders when deciding upon the number of hours to impose, others considered it inappropriate for employment status to have a bearing upon order size: 'Most sheriffs subscribed to the view that it would be improper to penalise the unemployed offender simply because he could do the number of hours more readily' (Carnie, 1990, p. 25). Employment status was more likely to have an influence upon the likelihood of a non-custodial as opposed to custodial sentence being imposed. Sheriffs acknowledged that they tended to more actively explore the possibility of non-custodial options for offenders who might lose their employment if imprisoned. There was, on the other hand, 'a great deal of sympathy for the view that people who were unemployed were perhaps more 'deserving' of a place' (Carnie, 1990, p. 24).

Types of work performed

The schemes made use of placement provision of three broad types. All operated work teams in which small groups of offenders carried out practical work for individuals or groups in the community under the direction of a skilled supervisor employed by the community service scheme. Fewer schemes had workshop facilities: those that did employed offenders exclusively on joinery projects, such as furniture-making and repairing canoes.

Other offenders completed their community service orders by working for a range of voluntary and statutory agencies. In individual placements of this type, agency staff were responsible for issuing work instructions and for monitoring attendance at placement, the standard of the work and the offender's behaviour.

As Table 3.3. shows, most offenders were initially allocated to practical placements in workshops or (more usually) teams. The remainder were allocated to a variety of voluntary or statutory agencies, where just over half (53.3 per cent) were engaged exclusively in work of a practical kind.

Table 3.3
Community service tasks and placement setting

Type of work	Work team	Agency	Work shop	Total
Gardening	15	12	-	27
Painting & decorating	94	10	-	104
Joinery	1	1	21	23
Kitchen/domestic	-	61	-	61
Care duties	-	5	-	5
Teaching	-	5	-	5
Youth work	-	9	-	9
Audiovisual	4	1	-	5
Play assistant	-	10	-	10
Organising activities	-	2	-	2
Sport	-	2	-	2
Escorting/driving	-	2	-	2
Varied practical[1]	108	37	-	145
Other	-	1	-	1
Total	222	179	21	402[2]

[1] placements involving a variety of practical tasks
[2] four offenders were breached prior to allocation

There were wide variations across schemes in the proportionate use of team and agency placements (see also B. McWilliams, 1980). At one extreme, 88.5 per cent of offenders were allocated to team placements while at the other extreme team placements were used in only 15.5 per cent of cases. Schemes also differed in their relative use of voluntary and statutory agencies. In three schemes all agency placements were located in the voluntary sector and in two others the majority of individual placements were in statutory agencies. The remaining schemes tended to make equal use of placements in the voluntary and statutory sectors. The balance of placement provision reflected a number of factors such as the geographic characteristics of the area covered by the scheme, the level of demand for community service places and the supervisory resources available. In several schemes the mix of agency and team placements would depend upon the characteristics of the offenders on orders at any one time. As one community service officer, commenting on the uncharacteristically high use of team placements during the fieldwork period, explained: 'In my opinion it's the type of offender that we're getting from the court at the moment which tends to be younger, less experienced youth with very little work experience'.

A range of issues were taken into account by the schemes when allocating offenders to work placements. Staff were asked to select, from a list of factors, the three which were most influential in determining the choice of work placement. Two officers were unable to rank the factors in this way since they believed that each would be equally relevant to the allocation decision. The responses received from twenty organisers and officers are summarised in Table 3.4.

Table 3.4
The factors influencing the choice of placement

Factor	1st	2nd	3rd	Total
Present offence	8	5	1	14
Offender's attitude	7	1	2	10
Work/family commitments	3	2	5	10
Previous convictions	2	6	1	9
Wishes of client	-	4	4	8
Skills possessed by client	1	2	3	6
Therapeutic value of work	-	-	2	2
Availability of work	1	-	-	1

The relevant information was available in case records to identify the reasons underlying placement allocation in 264 individual cases. The offender's existing family commitments determined the choice of placement in five cases; transport was a major consideration in five cases; and in a further five cases the choice of placement appeared primarily to have been influenced by the nature of the offence for which the offender received his or her community service order. However, the most common reasons behind the choice of placement were: the interests expressed by the offender (38.2 per cent); the offender's attitude or personality, including the need for close supervision (21.7 per cent); the offender's work commitments (21.3 per cent); the skills possessed by the offender (14.1 per cent); and placement availability at the time (4.8 per cent).

There was a relationship between the reasons underpinning the choice of placement and the types of placements offenders were allocated to. Offenders' interests or skills were more likely to have influenced allocation to agency placements while allocation to team placements was more often influenced by the offenders' attitudes or by the assessment by staff that closer supervision was required.

The characteristics of offenders allocated to different types of placements likewise varied. Offenders aged between 16 and 20 years were more likely than those aged 21 and over to be allocated to group placements (70.3 per cent compared with 49.2 per cent; $\chi^2 = 17.3$, 1 d.f., $p < .001$). As a consequence, offenders who were allocated to work teams or workshops were younger, on average, than those allocated to work in voluntary or statutory agencies (22.3 years compared with 24.9 years; $t = 12.4$, $p < .001$). Within agency placements, however, the average ages of offenders engaged in practical as opposed to personal tasks did not differ significantly.

Offenders with a history of statutory social work supervision were more likely than other offenders to be allocated to group placements (71.1 per cent compared with 48.2 per cent; $\chi^2 = 15.3$, 1 d.f., $p < .001$) and within agencies were more likely to be allocated to practical work (69.2 per cent compared with 45.5 per cent; $\chi^2 = 5.2$, 1 d.f., $p < .05$). Only one woman (out of 17) was allocated to a work team, compared with 62.9 per cent of men and within agencies, women were more likely than men to be allocated to work involving the provision of a direct personal service (81.3 per cent compared with 42.7 per cent; $\chi^2 = 7.1$, 1 d.f., $p < .01$).

Placement allocation appeared, on the other hand, to be unrelated to the types of offences for which the sample were sentenced and to the number of hours of unpaid work that they were required to perform.

The majority of offenders completed their community service orders in the placements to which they were initially allocated. Eight offenders were involved in two placements concurrently and 65 had either one or two changes of placement while completing their court-ordered work.

The most common reason for a change of placement was a change in the offender's other work commitments (25 cases). There were 14 changes of placement because there was insufficient work for the offender to perform and 4 changes occurred through the unavailability of a supervisor.

In 7 instances a placement change occurred at the request of the offender, 8 placements were changed because of the offender's erratic attendance, 6 were terminated as a result of the offender's disruptive behaviour and 4 because the agency was accessible only with difficulty by public transport. In most cases, then, placement changes were necessitated by a change in the offender's circumstances or by an absence of supervision or work, rather than by problematic behaviour on the part of the community service worker. This may explain why offenders who experienced changes of placement were just as likely as other offenders to complete their community service orders successfully.

The outcomes of orders

Completion, revocation and breach

The majority of the 406 offenders (85.5 per cent) completed their orders successfully. Forty-five offenders (11.1 per cent) were returned to court for failure to comply with the requirements and had their orders revoked. A further six offenders who were breached for non-compliance were allowed to continue and subsequently completed their work. Twelve orders (3.0 per cent) were revoked in the interests of justice and two offenders were transferred to another area prior to their orders being completed.

Table 3.5
Reasons for breach

Reason	Number of offenders
Absences	23
Absences and failure notify change of address	11
Absences and failure to comply with instructions	5
Failure to notify change of address	3
Failure to comply with instructions	1
Behaviour at work	1
Absences and failure to complete work as instructed	1

The majority of breaches occurred as a result of repeated failure to attend for work as instructed, in some cases combined with a failure on the part of the offender to notify the community service officer of a change of address (Table 3.5). Community service orders were most often revoked in the interests of justice because the offender had been imprisoned for a new (5 cases) or old (2 cases) offence and would be unable to complete his or her order within twelve months. Three orders were revoked as a consequence of prolonged illness, two because offenders had obtained full-time employment which prevented then from competing their work and one as a result of continuing problems associated with alcohol abuse.

When only breached and completed orders were included, the overall success rate of the schemes was 88.5 per cent. Although the success rate differed across schemes (one scheme had a breach rate of almost 30 per cent while another had no breaches in the period covered by the research) this appeared to be attributable to the varying proportions of 'riskier' offenders in different schemes (for further details see McIvor, 1989).

Absences from placement

Three-quarters of the sample (74.9 per cent) had at least one absence from placement while completing their community service orders: around two-thirds (65.7 per cent) had at least one acceptable absence and almost half (48.5 per cent) had one or more unacceptable absences from work. Across the twelve schemes offenders had, on average, 2.97 acceptable and 2.03 unacceptable absences from placement.

Whether absences were defined by community service staff as acceptable or unacceptable was largely a matter of judgement in individual cases ('You have got to be flexible and everybody's situation is different...what's acceptable for one person is not acceptable for others'), though certain broad principles were adhered to. Generally speaking, absences would be considered acceptable if prior permission had been granted by community service staff or if, in instances of illness, a medical certificate had been provided. As one community service officer commented:

> We do have certain absences which we would consider were unacceptable and others which we would accept. Regarding sickness, well I think that's national - there are national guidelines from the Scottish Office about taking sick notes for a second and subsequent absence from community service. People have so many different reasons for not attending it is very difficult to be specific about what's acceptable and what's not...we would really be looking for prior agreement for non-attendance but we don't often get it.

In most regards the reasons broadly deemed acceptable by schemes were similar to those subsequently identified in the national standards, which include: certificated illness; the offender being in custody; and instances in which the request to miss a work appointment has been submitted to the community service officer in advance and approval granted, unforeseen requirements are placed upon the offender by his or her employer, or the offender is faced with a serious and unforeseen crisis arising from other responsibilities (Social Work Services Group, 1989).

Illness (certificated or otherwise) accounted for almost two-fifths of all absences (39.1 per cent). This was followed by: family commitments (7.5 per cent); other appointments (7.1 per cent); work commitments (6.3 per cent); attending court (6.3 per cent); in custody (5.5 per cent); personal problems (4.2 per cent); holidays (2.9 per cent); bereavement (2.5 per cent); and transport problems (2.0 per cent). In 7.2 per cent of absences no excuse was offered and in a further 3.0 per cent, work instructions had arrived too late or had been misinterpreted. A few absences occurred because the offender had over-slept and a few were attributed to a hangover. The manner in which the most common types of absences had been classified by the schemes is shown in Table 3.6.

Table 3.6
Percentage of absences considered acceptable by reason

Reason	Prior notification	No prior notification
Certificated illness	100.0	100.0
Uncertificated illness	84.7	35.3
Family commitments	98.3	61.7
Work commitments	95.8	54.0
Other appointments	91.4	30.9
Holidays	94.5	8.7
Personal problems	100.0	69.1
Court	100.0	84.1
Custody	100.0	98.1
Bereavement	100.0	100.0
Hangover	n/a	4.3

There was agreement across schemes with respect to how they would classify some types of absence. Certain reasons (such as certificated illness, court appearances, custody and bereavement) were almost universally accepted, regardless of whether or not prior permission had been given. Most other absences were generally regarded as acceptable so long as prior permission had been obtained.

This is further illustrated in Table 3.7a which summarises the views of community service staff towards different types of absence from placement. Staff were asked to indicate which reasons they would normally define as acceptable and which they would normally consider unacceptable if the offender had given notification of the absence in advance.

Table 3.7a
Normal classification of absences (prior notification received)

Reason	Classification		
	Acceptable	Unacceptable	Depends
Certificated illness	18	-	-
Uncertificated illness	8	9	1
Certificated illness in family	16	1	1
Uncertificated illness in family	10	5	3
Family bereavement	18	-	-
Work commitments	17	1	-
Family commitments	16	-	2
Other engagements	17	1	-
Transport difficulties	12	5	1
Holiday	17	1	-
Overslept	-	18	-
Hangover	-	18	-

With the exception of uncertificated illness and transport difficulties there was either unanimous or substantial agreement about how absences should be classified. Less consensus was found, however, in the way absences were regarded when no prior notification had been obtained (Table 3.7b).

Table 3.7b
Normal classification of absences (no prior notification received)

Reason	Acceptable	Classification Unacceptable	Depends
Certificated illness	18	-	-
Uncertificated illness	4	14	-
Certificated illness in family	10	5	3
Uncertificated illness in family	2	13	3
Family bereavement	18	1	-
Work commitments	8	8	2
Family commitments	4	12	2
Other engagements	6	10	2
Transport difficulties	6	11	1
Holiday	2	16	-
Overslept	-	18	-
Hangover	-	18	-

The greatest spread of opinion emerged in relation to absences arising from uncertificated illness, family illness, family commitments, work commitments, transport difficulties and other engagements. This is further illustrated in Table 3.8 which shows how, in practice, absences which were a result of uncertificated illness, family commitments and work commitments, and for which no prior notification had been provided, were responded to by eleven of the community service schemes (data for one scheme could not be readily classified).

Table 3.8
Percentage of absences deemed acceptable by schemes

Scheme	Uncertificated illness	Family commitments	Work commitments
1	45.4	50.0	37.5
2	53.3	50.0	n/a
3	73.7	-	-
4	50.0	28.6	25.0
5	7.1	54.5	n/a
6	13.4	100.0	100.0
7	36.8	-	-
8	16.7	33.3	100.0
9	20.0	100.0	100.0
10	42.9	66.7	-
11	n/a	100.0	100.0

Thus while there was, in general, a reasonable degree of consistency in the classification of absences across schemes, and practice was broadly in line with the national standards that were subsequently introduced, certain 'grey areas' emerged in which there was less consistency both between and within schemes. Similar findings have been reported by B. McWilliams (1980) and by Vass (1984) in their studies of enforcement practices in community service schemes in England and Wales.

Factors associated with non-compliance and breach

Although most offenders managed to complete their community service orders, some groups were more likely than others to be returned to court for failure to comply.

Offenders aged 16 and 17 years were slightly more likely to be breached than older offenders (19.0 per cent compared with 10.1 per cent), though this difference was not statistically reliable (p < .07). The likelihood of breach was also unrelated to the number of hours imposed: 10.2 per cent of offenders who were sentenced to orders of less than 100 hours were returned to court and had their orders revoked compared with 11.9 per cent of those sentenced to between 100 and 200 hours and 9.4 per cent of those given orders in excess of 200 hours. Several other factors were, however, found to be associated with an increased risk of breach.

Criminal history

Offenders whose community service orders were breached had more previous convictions than those who completed their hours (6.4 compared with 4.6; $t = 4.3$, $p < .05$). The former group had also served more previous custodial sentences than the latter (1.1 compared with 0.6; $t = 5.8$, $p < .02$). Offenders who had served two or more previous custodial sentences were more likely than those who had never been imprisoned or who had been imprisoned on only one occasion to have breached their community service orders (22.0 per cent compared with 9.6 per cent and 5.9 per cent; $\chi^2 = 11.4$, 2 d.f., $p < .01$). A similar relationship between criminal history and the completion of community service orders was found by Pease et al. (1975) in their evaluation of the experimental schemes in England and Wales.

Social work history

Offenders who had experienced statutory social work supervision as an adult or a child were more likely than other offenders to have been breached for failure to comply (19.0 per cent compared with 6.5 per cent; $\chi^2 = 9.8$, 1 d.f., $p < .01$). The incidence of breach was highest among offenders who were subject to statutory supervision when sentenced or who had been subject to such supervision in the previous twelve months (22.7 per cent).

Current offence

Offenders who were sentenced to community service for offences involving dishonesty were less likely to complete their orders successfully than those who received their sentences for other types of offences (15.7 per cent of the former and 6.4 per cent of the latter were breached; $\chi^2 = 7.2$, 1 d.f., $p < .01$). The higher breach rate among offenders sentenced for dishonesty offences appeared, however, to be attributable to the higher proportion of offenders with a history of social work supervision who were sentenced to community service for this category of offence.

Employment and accommodation

Offenders who had no previous work experience were more likely than others to be breached for failure to comply with the requirements of their community service orders (25.9 per cent compared with 9.6 per cent; $\chi^2 = 5.9$, 1 d.f., p < .02)) and a higher rate of breach was found among offenders who had a history of accommodation problems (21.7 per cent compared with 9.6 per cent; $\chi^2 = 4.9$, 1 d.f., p < .05).

A typology of risk

A discriminant function analysis was performed to assess the ability of these variables to predict whether an offender on community service would complete successfully or be breached. This analysis identified one function, of factor, which correctly classified 90.3 per cent of cases in the sample. This function was most closely associated with a history of social work supervision, the recency of such supervision and accommodation problems, suggesting that these variables were the most useful predictors of whether an offender on community service would succeed or fail.

Through a further series of analyses, which considered the effects of different variables, both singly and in combination, on the likelihood of breach, it was possible to classify offenders according to their risk of being returned to court for failing to comply with the requirements of their community service orders.

Low risk offenders were those who had not been subject to statutory supervision in the previous twelve months, who had no experience of residential supervision and who had no history of unsettled accommodation. Ninety-six per cent of offenders thus classified completed their community service orders successfully.

Offenders who were identified as having an *intermediate risk of breach* were those who had served fewer than two custodial sentences and had been subject to statutory supervision in the previous twelve months *or* who had experience of residential supervision or accommodation problems. Eighty-two per cent of offenders with these characteristics completed their community service orders.

Offenders who had been subject to social work supervision in the previous twelve months and who had one or more of the following characteristics were identified as having a *high risk of breach*: experience of residential supervision (List D); a history of unsettled accommodation; or two or more previous custodial sentences. Seventy-one per cent of this group completed their community service orders.

Summary

The offenders who were sentenced to community service were predominantly young, male, single and unemployed. Just under half had been subject to social work supervision as a consequence of their offending, either as an adult or as a child. Around a third of this group were subject to other statutory orders (mostly probation) when sentenced. Most offenders had settled living arrangements and few had problems related to the use of alcohol, solvents or drugs.

The sample were most likely to have received their community service orders for offences involving dishonesty or violence, for road traffic offences or for offences against public order. More than four-fifths had previous convictions (with an average of five previous convictions across the sample as a whole) and just under a third had experience of imprisonment.

Offenders who were referred unsuccessfully for a community service assessment were more likely than those who were sentenced to community service to have been single and to have been remanded in custody prior to sentence. The unsuccessful referrals had served a higher number of custodial sentences and were more likely to have been facing sentence for sexual offences, offences against public order and criminal justice offences (mainly breaches of bail).

Offenders who were assessed by community service staff as being unsuitable for a community service order were more likely than those who were considered suitable to have been single and unemployed. Unsuitable offenders were more likely to have been remanded in custody and to have been subject to some other statutory order, such as probation, when referred. Offenders were usually considered unsuitable on the grounds that they lacked the necessary motivation to complete a community service order or because their social or personal circumstances suggested that successful completion would be unlikely.

The majority of offenders who were sentenced to community service received Section 1 (stand alone) orders. While the proportionate use of group and individual placements varied across schemes, most of the sample were allocated to group placements in workshops or (more usually) teams. A little over half of those who were allocated to individual placements in voluntary or statutory agencies were employed throughout their orders on practical tasks. The factors that most often determined the choice of work placement were the offender's expressed interest in a particular type of work, the nature of the present offence, the offender's attitude, other work commitments and the offender's skills. Younger offenders and those with a history of statutory social work involvement were more often allocated to group placements while women were almost invariably allocated to personal tasks in an agency setting.

The majority of offenders completed their community service orders. Most of the breaches were prompted by a repeated failure on the part of the offender to attend for work as instructed. Three-quarters of the sample had at least one absence from placement while completing their community service orders. Illness, family commitments, other appointments, work commitments and attendance at court were the explanations most often offered for absenteeism. There was general agreement across schemes about whether different types of absence were acceptable or not when prior notification of the absence had been obtained. When no advance notification was provided by the offender, there was less consensus across schemes about how different absences should be defined. The greatest spread of opinion was found in relation to uncertificated illness, family illness, family commitments, work commitments, other appointments and transport problems.

Offenders whose community service orders were breached had more previous convictions and had more custodial experience than those who successfully completed their community service orders. The incidence of breach was higher among offenders who had been subject to social work supervision when sentenced or in the past. Offenders who had no work experience or who had a known history of accommodation problems were more likely to have been breached.

Some offenders are clearly more likely than others to be returned to court for failure to comply with the requirements of their community service orders, yet even those presumed to be most at risk of breach were more likely than not to complete their orders successfully. Certain factors might usefully serve as broad indicators of the risk of breach, but should not, in isolation of other considerations, automatically preclude the acceptance of an offender for a community service order.

The high completion rate attests to the overall success of these twelve community service schemes. But the schemes varied considerably in their organisation and practice, the classification of absences being but one example. The following chapter focuses upon the methods and procedures adopted by the schemes across a range of activities to establish whether some approaches were more effective, and more cost effective, than others.

4 Identifying effective practice

Introduction

Despite the early introduction by the Scottish Office of national guidelines for the operation of community service schemes (Social Work Services Group, 1980) the incremental development of community service across Scotland resulted in wide procedural variations between schemes. By the mid 1980s, community service staff in different parts of the country had begun to explore how some form of standardisation at the national level might best be achieved, in such ways as to optimise their practice.

The SWRC evaluation aimed to identify, from among the variety of procedures which were in operation at that time, those which were most likely to contribute to the achievement of high levels of completion and compliance. The comparative costing of different operational arrangements by colleagues at the Personal Social Service Research Unit at Kent University (Knapp et al., 1989, 1992) enabled additional comment to be made on the relative cost-effectiveness of different approaches to practice.

Assessing offenders' suitability

In the previous chapter, the criteria employed by schemes when assessing offenders' suitability for a community service order were explored. Here the interest is in the procedures adopted by community service staff to gain the necessary information about offenders and their circumstances upon which their assessments of suitability were based.

The national standards for community service schemes, which took effect from April 1989, introduced a requirement for authors of social enquiry reports to consult with community service schemes before reporting on community service to the court. On being contacted by a social worker preparing a social enquiry report, community service officers are required to offer a view on the appropriateness of the disposal as an alternative to custody, the suitability of the offender for an order and the availability of work. The author of the social enquiry report is responsible for explaining to the offender what community service will entail so that the offender's informed consent to the making of an order can be obtained. Only in exceptional circumstances should community service staff conduct a separate interview with an offender at the pre-sentence stage. According to Section 4.1.2.b of the guidelines (Social Work Services Group, 1989):

> Community service staff will not normally interview offenders pre-sentence unless, after consultation with report writers or for any other reason, they have continuing doubts about the risk to the agency or to the offender from accepting the offender on community service.

The research, of course, pre-dated the introduction of national standards and different approaches to pre-sentence assessment were found among the twelve participating schemes. Three of the schemes adopted the model prescribed by the national standards. Offenders were interviewed by the social workers responsible for the preparation of social enquiry reports and relevant information was conveyed to the community service scheme either through a face-to-face meeting or, more usually, by telephone. On the basis of this discussion with the social worker, the community service officer would reach a decision regarding an offender's suitability for community service and would establish whether or not appropriate work could be found. The resulting decision was incorporated by the social worker in the body of the social enquiry report and supplemented by a separate short statement from the community service officer, confirming his or her views as to the suitability of the offender and the availability of work.

In each of these three schemes, offenders would occasionally be interviewed by the community service officer. This would occur, for example, if a social enquiry report had not been requested by the court or if a community service assessment had been requested for a second continuation, in which case a social enquiry report would have previously been submitted and no further interviews by the social worker would be required. Usually, these pre-sentence interviews were conducted in the offender's home.

In the other schemes, virtually all offenders referred for a community service assessment would be interviewed for this purpose by community service staff. In most schemes, the community service interviews were office-based or, where necessary, were conducted in remand or other penal institutions. Only two schemes routinely carried out pre-sentence interviews in the offenders' homes. In some instances, offenders were jointly interviewed by the community service officer and the author of the social enquiry report. Joint interviews were, however, a significant feature in only one scheme.

Opinions were strongly divided about the value of separate pre-sentence interviews by community service staff. Those who conducted such interviews defended their practice on a number of grounds. The pre-sentence interview was said to yield more specific and relevant information than that which would normally be provided by the author of a social enquiry report who was, after all, attempting to assess the appropriateness of a range of sentencing options. Face-to-face contact with the offender prior to sentencing could, it was also argued, create a sense of continuity for the offender, help to establish rapport and facilitate the subsequent matching of offenders to appropriate work placements.

Carnie (1990) found that sheriffs generally held assessments by community service staff in high regard and some expressed concern about the procedural changes contained in the national standards:

> One sheriff in particular expressed grave doubts about this restriction on pre-sentencing interviewing of offenders by community service staff. He felt that this limitation would have a detrimental effect on the quality of the assessment he received. In this court much value was placed on the community service organiser's report and he argued that Paragraph 4.1.2.b hindered the organiser from carrying out their duties in an efficient and effective manner. Such was this sheriff's concern on the matter that formal representations had been made through the appropriate channels.
>
> (Carnie, 1990, p. 23)

On the other hand, community service staff who did not normally interview offenders at the pre-sentence stage tended to adopt the view that such interviews represented a duplication of effort because similar information was already being gathered by the social worker responsible for preparing the social enquiry report. They did not share the concern of their colleagues that the guidance contained in the national standards trivialised the assessment process and undermined the community service officer's assessment skills. Assessment by proxy was, it was argued, equally skilful, and perhaps more so, than assessment based on direct personal contact.

The research sought to establish whether interview-based assessments were, as their proponents suggested, a more effective means of establishing whether or not offenders were suitable for a community service order. If pre-sentence interviews were more effective as a screening mechanism then this might be evidenced by lower levels of absence and breach.

There was, however, no difference in the incidence of breach among schemes that conducted pre-sentence interviews and those that did not. The breach rate in the former schemes was 13.2 per cent and in the latter was 8.3 per cent, suggesting that the final outcomes of orders were not substantially affected by the method of assessment that was employed.

When the levels of unacceptable absences were compared, account was taken of the differing enforcement practices that were operational in the schemes. Separate comparisons were made between schemes that were defined as being strict in their enforcement practices and between schemes that were identified as being less strict (see p.70). Among the less strict schemes, those that conducted pre-sentence interviews had similar levels of both unacceptable and unacceptable absences to those that did not (3.1 compared with 2.7 unacceptable absences and 3.8 compared with 4.7 acceptable absences). The strict schemes that interviewed offenders for the purpose of assessment had fewer acceptable absences from placement than those that did not (1.7 compared with 2.6; $t = 5.2$, $p < .05$) but the method of assessment did not appear to have a bearing upon the levels of unacceptable absences sustained (1.4 compared with 1.0).

It is possible, of course, that pre-sentence interviews do provide for more effective assessments and that comparable outcomes were achieved because schemes that conducted such interviews, being more confident in their assessments, were as a result more willing to accept riskier offenders on community service orders. However this did not appear to be the case: similar types of offenders had been made subject to community service orders in schemes that interviewed offenders prior to sentence and schemes that did not and similar percentages of offenders in the two groups of schemes were assessed as having a high or intermediate risk of breach (31.5 per cent compared with 25.6 per cent).

There is also a possibility that different types of offenders were being referred to the schemes and that pre-sentence interviews enabled community service staff to more effectively select out offenders who would, in all probability, breach their community service orders. There were, however, no differences between the two groups of schemes with respect to the types of offenders referred for a community service assessment nor did they differ according to the characteristics of offenders deemed suitable for a community service order but subsequently dealt with in some other way by the courts.

There were, however, cost implications for schemes if they conducted interviews with offenders at the pre-sentence stage. Direct cost comparisons between schemes were complicated by the existence of different staffing structures which in themselves had implications for the costs of various activities: the cost of pre-sentence assessments would, for example, be influenced by whether the assessment was undertaken by an unqualified assistant, by a community service officer or by a scheme organiser. Three schemes did, however, have similar staffing arrangements but different pre-sentence costs. The lowest cost per assessment (£35.88) was found in the scheme whose assessments of suitability were based upon information provided by the author of the social enquiry report. Although the other two schemes normally interviewed offenders to assess their suitability, their costs per assessment were found to differ. The lower cost (£45.76) was obtained in the scheme whose pre-sentence interviews were office-based. In the other scheme, which covered a fairly large geographical area, most interviews were conducted in the offenders' homes and the cost per assessment of £81.78 reflected the additional travelling time and expenses involved.

To summarise briefly, it did not appear that the method of assessment employed had any significant bearing upon the characteristics of offenders judged to be suitable for a community service order or upon the subsequent levels of non-compliance and breach. Given the additional costs associated with pre-sentence interviewing by community service staff, this method of assessment would appear, according to these criteria, to be less cost-effective. Although it has been suggested that pre-sentence assessment interviews may facilitate the subsequent matching of offenders to work placements, this possibility could not be explored with the available data.

Matching offenders to work placements

It was shown in the previous chapter that schemes took into account a variety of factors when reaching decisions about the allocation of offenders to appropriate work placements and that the relevance of different factors varied according to the type of placement which was eventually selected.

The schemes differed according to the stage at which decisions were reached regarding placement allocation: while most schemes deferred the decision until after the offender had been sentenced to community service and at this stage explored with the offender the various options that were available, some allocated offenders to work placements largely on the basis of information gained prior to sentence. In these schemes, the offenders' own preferences for particular types of work were less influential in the matching process. This is illustrated in Table 4.1 for those cases for which the relevant information was available.

Table 4.1
Factors influencing placement allocation and method of matching

Main reason for allocation	Pre-sentence matching	Post-sentence matching
Offender's skills	15 (24.6%)	20 (9.9%)
Offender's interest	3 (4.9%)	92 (45.3%)
Current/previous offences	2 (3.3%)	3 (1.5%)
Attitude or personality	15 (24.6%)	39 (19.2%)
Practical considerations	26 (42.6%)	49 (24.1%)
Total	61 (100.0%)	203 (100.0%)

The schemes that matched offenders to work placements prior to sentence were more likely to allocate on the basis of the skills the offender possessed and with regard to practical considerations such as the availability of different types of work, the availability of transport or the offender's existing work or family commitments. The offender's expressed interest in undertaking a particular type of work was only rarely influential, though it was the most common reason underlying the choice of placement in schemes which interviewed offenders after sentence for the purpose of matching them to appropriate work. As one community service officer commented:

Following a court appearance when they are given community service I arrange an interview and again that's either in the office or at their home. I describe the variety of different placements available in more detail than in that first interview and normally I give the client the choice of the nature of work they would like to do...Sometimes people will just plump for practical work because it seems easier but if I think they would benefit more from a sort of individual placement I really try to encourage them, but no way would I force them to do that. It is basically their own choice, but again the nature of the offence for which they got community service and their previous convictions as well are taken into account.

All schemes would normally, when arranging an agency placement, contact the agency to establish their willingness in principle to offer a placement, then arrange a tripartite meeting between the offender, the community service officer and the potential supervisor to discuss the placement further and, if relevant, finalise the practical arrangements.

The national standards subsequently placed a requirement upon community service schemes to take into account the offender's interests and skills and to 'involve the offender in decision-making about the most appropriate placement' (Social Work Services Group, 1989; para. 4.3.3.c) as a means of maximising the value of community service for the offender. Was there any evidence, though, that involving offenders in the choice of work placements increased their compliance with the requirements of their orders?

The breach rate was found to be similar in schemes that actively involved offenders in the matching process (9.5 per cent) and those that did not (15.7 per cent). Nor, after controlling for the strictness of the enforcement procedures, did the two groups differ according to the number of acceptable and unacceptable absences that the offenders had. Among the less strict schemes, those that interviewed offenders post-sentence to allocate them to appropriate work had an average of 4.6 acceptable and 2.8 unacceptable absences per offender: this compared with an average of 3.2 acceptable and 3.2 unacceptable absences per offender in the schemes that reached a decision regarding placement allocation prior to sentence. Similarly, the strict schemes that involved offenders in the matching process had an average of 3.2 acceptable and 3.0 unacceptable absences while the scheme that did actively involve offenders in determining the choice of work had 3.8 acceptable and 2.7 unacceptable absences per offender.

To rule out the possibility that similar levels of compliance were achieved because the schemes that did not interview offenders after sentence to discuss the range of placement options were dealing with less risky cases, a comparison was made of the types of offenders subject to community service orders in the two groups of schemes. This revealed that 29.2 per cent of offenders in the schemes that involved offenders in the matching process could be classified as having an intermediate or high risk of breach compared with 27.8 per cent of offenders in the schemes that did not. It appeared, therefore, that the method of matching employed did not have a substantial impact upon offenders' subsequent levels of compliance with their community service orders.

It was possible, though, that offenders had got more out of their community service placements if they had had an active say in the type of work they carried out. The offenders' questionnaire responses were therefore analysed according to the method of matching adopted by the schemes. Offenders in schemes where placement decisions were made pre-sentence were not significantly less likely to say that they had been able to perform the type of work they wanted while on community service (77.1 per cent compared with 85.7 per cent); they were as likely to have found their experience of community service to be very worthwhile (51.1 per cent compared with 54.0 per cent); and they were as willing as offenders in the other schemes to undertake community service in the future (83.3 per cent compared with 90.6 per cent). Offenders in schemes that encouraged the offender's participation in the choice of placement were slightly more likely to have found their placements to be very interesting (44.7 per cent compared with 28.6 per cent; $\chi^2 = 2.8$, 1 d.f., p < .10).

The data on the costs of matching offenders to work placements were difficult to interpret not least of all because some schemes began the process of matching at the pre-sentence stage, combining it with the assessment of suitability. The costs of matching varied from scheme to scheme, but could not readily be explained in procedural terms. Nor were higher assessment costs offset by lower matching costs and vice versa. It did appear, however, that schemes with riskier caseloads (and correspondingly higher levels of absences) had higher allocation costs per placement, suggesting that these schemes were more prepared to take risks with the types of offenders they would consider suitable for an order, but in doing so devoted more time to placement allocation to ensure that a satisfactory match could be achieved.

The different staffing and organisational arrangements across schemes prevented any clear association between the method and costs of matching from being identified. Matching by means of additional post-sentence interviews should however, all things being equal, be more costly than allocation prior to sentence. These additional costs would be justified, though, if the involvement of the offender in the choice of work placement meant that future placement breakdowns were prevented. This did not appear, however, to be the case: offenders in the schemes that did not interview offenders to match them to placements were less likely than those in other schemes to have had a change of placement during their community service orders (10.6 per cent compared with 18.9 per cent; $\chi^2 = 3.9$, 1 d.f., $p < .05$).

The manner in which offenders were matched to their work placements did not appear, then, to have had a dramatic effect on their subsequent compliance with their community service orders nor were placement breakdowns more likely if offenders' interests were not taken into account by staff when deciding which type of setting or work to allocate them to. Offenders who were actively involved in the matching process tended, however, to express slightly more positive views about their community service work experience.

Time to complete

As community service became firmly established as a sentencing option in Scottish courts, several community service schemes found themselves faced with demands for orders from the courts which exceeded the capacity of the schemes. Some schemes responded by 'closing down' to all new referrals and others continued to assess offenders who had been referred by the courts but indicated in the resulting reports that appropriate work could not be made available. A few schemes operated a non-closure policy: even when the capacity of the scheme had been reached, offenders would continue to be offered places, but lengthy delays would often result before they could be allocated to appropriate work.

This situation was considered by the Scottish Office to be unsatisfactory. The temporary closure of schemes was seen as having the potential to undermine the credibility of community service with the courts. So too might excessive delays in starting offenders on their community service work. Lengthy delays could, moreover, adversely affect offenders' motivation and, possibly, their subsequent compliance with their community service orders, a view that was shared by sheriffs (Carnie, 1990).

The introduction of full central government funding was intended to ensure that schemes were adequately resourced in accordance with the likely demand for orders by the courts. Under the previous funding arrangements, additional resources could be provided to schemes only if this was agreed both by the local authorities, who were partly responsible for their financing, and by central government.

The national standards which were simultaneously introduced aimed to eliminate unnecessary delays in the time between an order being made and an offender being started on his or her community service work. The national standards required offenders to undertake their first work session within two weeks of their post-sentence interview by community service staff and no later than three weeks from the date of sentence.

There were marked differences between the schemes with respect to the delay in starting work and the average time taken by offenders to complete their community service orders (Table 4.2).

Table 4.2
Delay in starting work and time to complete by scheme

Scheme	Delay in starting work (days)	Days to complete work	Days to complete order
1	49.1	210.7	249.4
2	33.9	212.4	242.8
3	27.1	200.0	238.3
4	34.0	353.1	379.8
5	34.2	153.7	186.6
6	29.5	117.9	145.7
7	25.5	123.4	156.3
8	33.4	130.5	168.8
9	44.6	131.1	175.7
10	62.6	245.0	310.9
11	54.0	241.0	291.2
12	56.0	156.6	221.3
Average across all schemes	38.3	174.8	215.1

None of the twelve schemes had an average delay within the requirements subsequently laid down in the national standards. Four schemes, in particular, stood out as having a longer than average delay in starting offenders on their community service orders. In Scheme 1, one offender suffered a lengthy delay as a result of his other work commitments while another was delayed in starting work for several weeks because of illness. When these two offenders were excluded, the average delay in Scheme 1 was 37 days, which was in line with most other schemes in the study.

The longer than average delays in Schemes 10, 11 and 12, on the other hand, could be attributed to their operation of a non-closure policy which resulted in orders being 'stacked' and offenders allocated to a placement when a vacancy on an officer's caseload arose.

The schemes likewise varied in terms of the average time which elapsed between an offender's first work session and the completion of the work. Scheme 3, in particular, experienced lengthy delays in the completion of work. Indeed the average number of days required to complete a community service order was slightly in excess of the one year maximum required by statute. This scheme was highly reliant on the use of team placements and during the period covered by the research the team supervisor's illness resulted in the suspension of such placements for ten months. Some offenders were allocated to alternative agency placements, but others had their orders suspended until the team placements could resume. Extensions were sought and obtained from the sentencing courts.

There was no relationship between the delay in starting work and the final outcomes (breach or completion) of community service orders. Nor did schemes with longer than average delays have a higher level of non-compliance with the requirements. The lowest success rate (71.4 per cent) was, however, found in Scheme 3, suggesting that the lengthy suspension from placement may have adversely affected offenders' motivation to comply with their community service orders.

There was a moderate correlation between the time offenders took to complete their work and the levels of acceptable and unacceptable absences sustained. Partial correlations, with the length (in hours) of community service order controlled, revealed that the relationship between absences and time to complete could not be accounted for by differences in the lengths of orders imposed (acceptable absences, $r=0.38$; unacceptable absences, $r=0.43$). The time to complete the work, rather than the total numbers of hours imposed, appears to have had an influence on the levels of absences sustained.

These results suggest that lengthy delays in completing their community service work may have adversely affected offenders' motivation and their compliance with the requirements. It is also possible, however, that offenders took longer to complete their orders because they had absences from work. Offenders who had no absences, for example, completed their placements within an average of 124.7 days compared with those who had one or more absences who took, on average, 193.0 days from the first placement session to complete their community service work ($t=21.5$, $p<.001$).

Enforcement

In principle, each of the schemes adopted a broadly similar policy with respect to the enforcement of orders: three unacceptable absences, followed by written warnings, would be tolerated before an offender was returned to court. In practice, however, considerable variations emerged.

The schemes differed according to the average numbers of acceptable and unacceptable absences that were sustained by offenders while completing their community service orders. Differences also emerged with respect to the proportions of offenders in each scheme who had at least one acceptable or unacceptable absence from placement while completing their court-ordered work (Table 4.3).

Table 4.3
Acceptable and unacceptable absences across schemes

Scheme	Average number of acceptable absences	Average number of unacceptable absences	Offenders with at least one acceptable absence	Offenders with at least one unacceptable absence
1	4.4	4.7	83.3%	87.5%
2	2.9	1.3	85.3%	48.1%
3	3.9	3.0	76.9%	53.8%
4	2.8	3.4	63.9%	63.9%
5	4.5	2.7	66.7%	50.0%
6	4.8	2.7	89.2%	51.4%
7	1.7	1.0	52.2%	39.1%
8	2.6	1.0	69.0%	38.0%
9	4.3	1.6	68.8%	34.4%
10	0.6	0.6	20.0%	35.0%
11	2.7	2.1	73.9%	56.5%
12	0.5	1.8	30.0%	46.7%
All schemes	3.0	2.0	65.7%	48.5%

There were also variations between schemes in the average numbers of unacceptable absences that would be tolerated prior to a first official warning being issued and prior to an offender being returned to court for failure to comply (Table 4.4).

Table 4.4
Average number of unacceptable absences prior to first warning and breach

Scheme	Unacceptable absences prior to first warning	Unacceptable absences prior to breach
1	1.3	9.5
2	1.0	3.1
3	2.0	8.8
4	3.1	5.6
5	1.4	10.0
6	1.7	10.2
7	1.2	4.4
8	1.1	5.0
9	1.4	n/a
10	1.3	3.0
11	1.2	4.0
12	1.7	4.5
All schemes	1.5	5.9

Only three schemes had an average number of unacceptable absences prior to breach that was consistent with their enforcement policy and with the guidelines subsequently introduced by the Scottish Office (Social Work Services Group, 1989). The high number of absences tolerated by Schemes 5 and 6 was at least partly explained by their policy of counting absences over consecutive days as single absences for the purposes of enforcement and by their requirement that only corroborated absences could be included as grounds for breach.

To examine the impact of enforcement practices upon offenders' compliance, the following method was adopted to rank the schemes according to their strictness in enforcing the requirements of orders. First, the schemes were separately ranked according to the numbers of absences that would be tolerated prior to a first warning and prior to breach (Scheme 9, which had no breached orders during the period covered by the study was assigned the same ranked position on the two measures). The two ranked scores were then combined to obtain an overall ranked position for each scheme. This ranked position was found to be highly correlated with both the average numbers of absences prior to a first official warning ($r=0.86$) and the average numbers of absences prior to an order being breached ($r=0.88$).

On the basis of their composite ranking, six schemes were identified as being more strict in their enforcement practice and six were allocated to a grouping of less strict schemes. In their questionnaires, offenders had been asked to indicate how strict they thought the schemes had been in their enforcement of orders. Few offenders appeared to have regarded enforcement as very lax. As Table 4.5 indicates, however, offenders in the stricter schemes were more likely than those in other schemes to have described the enforcement practices as very strict ($\chi^2=11.0$, 2 d.f., $p<.01$).

Table 4.5
Offenders' views of how strictly requirements were enforced

Offenders views of enforcement	Strictness of enforcement	
	More strict	Less strict
Very strict	42 (51.2%)	11 (22.0%)
Fairly strict	35 (42.7%)	34 (68.0%)
Not strict at all	5 (6.1%)	5 (10.0%)

Twenty offenders who were interviewed explained on what basis they had formed a judgement about the strictness of enforcement in the schemes. In most cases, this was put down to staff having clearly conveyed their expectations ('They made a point that you had to be there and work. They should be strict - it's a punishment'), to personal experience ('I got a few warnings. It was fair.') or to their observations of what had happened to other people who had not turned up for work ('Two people were breached when I was there'). Offenders generally agreed that the enforcement process had been fair, and three thought that the schemes could be stricter in the way they responded non-compliance.

Despite differences in the strictness with which requirements were enforced, similar average success rates were achieved by the two groups of schemes (88.8 per cent in the stricter schemes and 88.1 per cent in the others). This could not be attributed to differences between them with respect to the characteristics of offenders on orders. Increased strictness of enforcement did not, therefore, result in higher proportions of offenders being returned to court for failure to comply.

There was, however, a moderate correlation between schemes' ranked position on the composite strictness variable and the average numbers of acceptable ($r=0.60$) and unacceptable ($r=0.67$) absences sustained by offenders while completing their community service orders. This apparent relationship between strictness of enforcement and compliance was confirmed by a comparison of absences in the more strict and less strict schemes. The stricter schemes had fewer acceptable (2.0 compared with 4.1; $t=32.2$, $p<.001$) and unacceptable (1.3 compared with 2.9; $t=27.7$, $p<.001$) absences per offender. They also had lower proportions of offenders with one or more acceptable ($\chi^2=11.4$, 1 d.f., $p<.001$) or unacceptable ($\chi^2=6.5$, 1 d.f., $p=.01$) absences while completing their community service work (Table 4.6).

Table 4.6
Strictness of enforcement and absence from placement

| | Strictness of enforcement | |
	More strict	Less strict
Percentage of offenders with acceptable absences	126/317 (58.1%)	138/185 (74.6%)
Percentage of offenders with unacceptable absences	92/317 (42.2%)	103/185 (55.7%)

Taken together, then, these results suggest that stricter enforcement produced increased compliance with the requirements. This is in accord with the finding by McWilliams and Murphy (1980) that a tightening up of the enforcement process resulted in improved attendance for work.

Higher levels of attendance at placement were, in turn, associated with lower costs. Knapp et al. (1992) found, in their comparative costing of schemes, a strong correlation between the average levels of absences and the hourly supervision costs (for community service staff) across schemes. Increased cost-effectiveness could, therefore, be achieved through a tightening up of the enforcement process which would reduce the level of absences without affecting the overall likelihood of breach. The resulting lower supervision costs would help to offset the additional costs which will arise from the more recent requirements in the Scottish national standards concerning the follow up and corroboration of absences.

A more consistently applied enforcement policy was welcomed by most of the sheriffs interviewed by Carnie (1990), though some expressed concern that a rigidly enforced policy might be open to abuse, with some offenders deliberately playing the system by having their full quota of three absences, knowing that in doing so they would not be returned to court. Even in the absence of rigidly enforced guidelines, however, it appeared that offenders were well able to gauge the tolerance of community service staff. This would explain why schemes achieved similar levels of completion despite wide variations in the levels of unacceptable absences from work.

Work placements and outcomes

As noted in the previous chapter, some community service schemes relied primarily upon the use of team placements while others made greater use of individual placements in voluntary or statutory agencies. Here the relationships between placement setting, the types of work offenders were required to perform and the outcomes of their community service orders are examined to assess whether different types of placement were associated with varying levels of compliance and breach.

The likelihood of breach was found to be related to the type of setting (group or agency) in which offenders completed their community service work. Offenders who completed their orders in work teams or workshops were more likely to be breached for failure to comply than those who completed their orders in voluntary or statutory agencies (14.4 per cent compared with 6.1 per cent; $\chi^2 = 4.7$, 1 d.f., p < .05). The small numbers of offenders in agency placements who were breached prevented further examination of the relationship between the outcome of orders and the types of work carried out in an agency setting.

It will be recalled from Chapter 3, however, that offenders who were more at risk of breaching their community service orders (that is, those with a history of social work supervision) were more likely to be allocated to placements in workshops and teams. This in itself might have accounted for the differential breach rate across placement settings. The relationship between placement setting and breach was therefore examined separately for two groups of offenders: those who had a current or previous statutory social work involvement (related to their offending) and those who did not. In neither case was the relationship between placement setting and outcome significant, suggesting that the different breach rates in group and agency placements were attributable to the higher percentage of riskier offenders who completed their orders in workshops or teams.

The levels of absences also differed according to the type of setting in which the community service work was carried out. Offenders in group placements had more acceptable (3.6 compared with 1.8; $t = 18.5$, $p < .001$) and unacceptable (2.6 compared with 1.0; $t = 19.6$, $p < .001$) absences than those who completed their orders in agencies. Higher levels of acceptable and unacceptable absences were found in group placements, both among offenders with no prior social work involvement and among those who were subject to statutory social work supervision when sentenced or who had been subject to such supervision in the past (Table 4.7).

Table 4.7
Absences by placement setting and social work history

	Group placement	Agency placement	
No prior supervision			
Acceptable absences	3.5	1.8	$t = 9.1$, $p < .01$
Unacceptable absences	1.8	0.9	$t = 4.6$, $p < .05$
Prior supervision			
Acceptable absences	3.6	1.8	$t = 8.5$, $p < .01$
Unacceptable absences	3.1	1.2	$t = 10.4$, $p < .01$

There is reason to suspect that these differences may at least partly reflect variations in the recording of absences by supervisors of group placements and by supervisors within agencies, particularly since the levels of acceptable absences also differed across placement setting. It is likely that agency-based supervisors exercised greater discretion as to whether or not to notify community service staff of an offender's failure to attend, allowing them instead, perhaps, to re-negotiate an alternative work session. This was the explanation offered by B. McWilliams (1980) for the differential attendance rates at team and agency placements. As one community service organiser in her study noted:

> Those placed within an agency negotiate their own working days etc. Some agencies are particular in making non-attendance returns whilst others tolerate absence and more often make little reference to absence in work returns. Those on work groups supervised by the service are expected every week. Every absence is immediately recorded.
>
> (B. McWilliams, 1980, p. 62)

Within agency placements, offenders who were employed on practical tasks had similar levels of acceptable absences to those who were engaged in personal work (1.9 compared with 1.7; $t=0.4$, $p=.50$). Exclusively practical agency placements were, however, associated with higher levels of unacceptable absences than were placements which offered an element of personal work (1.6 compared with 0.4; $t=9.7$, $p<.01$). As the following chapter shows, practical agency placements were considered by offenders to be less interesting, enjoyable and skilful than those involving work of a more personalised nature. Offenders in practical agency placements may, as a consequence, have been less motivated to attend their placements on a regular basis.

There was, indeed, a relationship between offenders' experiences of community service and the incidence of absenteeism. Offenders whose placements were said to have been very enjoyable had fewer unacceptable absences while completing their community service orders (0.7 compared with 2.0; $t=5.8$, $p<.05$) and this was also true of offenders who considered their experience of community service to have been very worthwhile (0.8 unacceptable absences compared with 2.4; $t=6.8$, $p<.01$).

The nature and impact of social work support

Offenders who have acute personal problems are not generally considered

74

suitable for a community service order if their problems are likely to adversely affect their ability to sustain a regular commitment to a work placement. For offenders such as these, probation is likely to be viewed by social workers and by community service staff as a more appropriate sentencing option. Nevertheless, as McIvor (1991b) has shown, many of the offenders in the research sample (65 of the 136 questionnaire respondents) experienced problems of one sort or another while they were completing their community service orders. Difficulties were most often encountered in relation to employment (in many cases lack of), finances, health and family. Offenders who experienced problems during their community service orders had higher levels of acceptable and unacceptable absences from placement.

In most instances, offenders had not informed community service staff when problems had arisen. Where staff did provide help or advice the intervention was likely to have been initiated by the community service officer rather than by the offender. As Table 4.8 indicates, community service staff had, in the course of their work, provided offenders with assistance in connection with a range of problems.

Table 4.8
Frequency of intervention by community service staff

Type of problem	Frequently	Occasionally	Never
Financial	1	17	1
Accommodation	2	16	1
Family	2	15	2
Employment	2	14	3
Health	2	14	3
Substance abuse	2	13	4
Legal	2	11	6

Usually, however, the assistance offered was of an immediate practical kind, such as advice or referral to another, more appropriate, source of help. When asked how they would respond to a client seeking help in connection with a family problem, for example, eight community service officers indicated that they would offer practical advice if it was a simple matter but would otherwise refer the offender to the social work department or suggest that he/she refer him/herself. Eight said that they would discuss the problem with the offender and offer basic counselling. If the scale or complexity of the problem suggested that longer term intervention was required, they would refer the offender to the local social work area team. Three community service officers (from two schemes), on the other hand, indicated that they would aim to deal with the problem themselves, regardless of its complexity, and would, if appropriate, work closely with any other social worker who might also be involved in the case.

These responses were consistent with regional policies, which in most areas discouraged community service staff from becoming unnecessarily involved in the provision of a social work service to offenders who needed help. Two schemes, however, aimed to provide a more comprehensive service to offenders on community service orders. As one officer commented, 'I would basically be prepared to offer whatever service in whatever area I was asked'.

There were relatively few instances of intervention (38 out of 406 offenders) referred to in case records which were, after all, primarily administrative tools. The two schemes which adopted a more proactive approach accounted for almost a quarter of the instances of intervention recorded in case files (9), even though they accounted for only an eighth of the offenders in the sample.

Since offenders were more likely to have absences if they had family or personal problems during their community service orders, and since absences were the most frequent reason for offenders being returned to court for failure to comply (see Chapter 3), lower levels of breach might have been expected among offenders whose problems were tackled and resolved.

To test this possibility, the combined success rate of the two schemes that offered a comprehensive social work service was compared with the completion rate for two schemes whose procedures were otherwise similar but who did not routinely offer offenders assistance, counselling and support (see McIvor, 1991b). The two pairs of schemes had similar success rates (85.4 per cent and 92.2 per cent respectively) but the schemes that provided a social work service (one of which had a high percentage of offenders on combined probation and community service orders) were found to have been dealing with higher proportions of offenders whose characteristics suggested that they were more at risk of breaching a community service order. When the completion rates of low, intermediate and high risk offenders in the 'social work' schemes were compared with those in other schemes in the study, the success rate for intermediate risk offenders was found to be slightly higher in the former schemes. These findings suggest, albeit tentatively, that the timely provision of appropriate advice, assistance and support may have enabled some offenders who would not otherwise have done so to complete their community service orders. While involvement of staff with offenders' problems can be relatively demanding of resources, it may be justified if it serves to increase offenders' ability to comply with the requirements of their orders and therefore reduces the amount of time spent on enforcement and on the costly process of breach.

Although offenders in other schemes may have received help from the local social work office when difficulties arose, offenders were not generally considered to be a pressing priority by already over-stretched social work departments unless child care issues were involved. Even if they sought assistance, therefore, there would be no guarantee that help would be forthcoming. This being so, was it reasonable to expect community service staff to offer a service instead?

Although only 17.7 per cent of the offenders who completed questionnaires indicated that they would be most likely to turn to community service staff for help if problems occurred while they were completing their community service orders, twelve of the 28 offenders who were also interviewed would have been prepared to approach staff if the need arose. Most of the interviewees (23) felt that community service staff would have been willing to help and most (22) thought it appropriate that they should do so, though seven offenders believed that intervention by staff would be warranted only if the offender had asked for help.

Most community service staff were keen to have greater scope to provide social work services to offenders on community service. Some felt that such an extension to their role would provide them with increased job satisfaction and some believed that they were often best placed to tackle any problems that arose:

> I think it is more satisfying to deal with it yourself. Maybe that's a selfish thought but at the same time hopefully you would have a relationship with the offender and to pass them on to someone else is a bit uncaring. If you are able to deal with it I think that it is appropriate and right for you to do so without just passing it on. I think it develops the relationship that you have with the offender.

> We find that because we are not designated social workers that clients who have gone through the whole spectrum of social work are more ready to talk to us. They don't see us as social workers which in a strange way allows us to intervene.

I think it would be an advantage for everybody. It would make the job more interesting as well because it's quite frustrating not to follow something through.

Difficulties were envisaged in some schemes where staff were unqualified and could not, therefore, be expected to take on a broader social work role without additional training and appropriate financial recompense. Lack of time was a further impediment:

In other areas they have smaller caseloads, perhaps 25 or 30. They probably do have time. We don't have time with a caseload of 40. Having said that, we would always try. If it's something fairly trivial that just needs a couple of minutes then we do our best.

Some staff expressed concern that too much emphasis on the social work aspect might undermine the credibility of community service and might lead to the distinction between community service and probation becoming blurred:

We do the best we can but we must remember that it's not our job and the chances are that if we are perhaps offering too much assistance the offender is actually going to forget that community service is a punishment. That's not to emphasise the punitive role of community service but we have found that if offenders begin to see it as just something to do when they can be bothered, then we are running into difficulties.

Given a community service scheme with qualified social workers there may be scope for more involvement but you must watch your levels because we would end up with community service just being a fringe activity to social work.

Since the research was conducted, the Scottish Office have introduced full central funding and national standards for all statutory social work services to the criminal justice system. In requiring that community service should be organised as an integral part of local authority social work services to offenders and their families, the Scottish Office further require that 'offenders on community service orders should have access to assistance with other problems in their lives when they request it' (Social Work Services Group, 1991b, para. 125.3). It is recognised in the national standards that while some issues will be readily and quickly resolved, others will require more extensive or intensive intervention. Community service schemes should, therefore, 'have the capacity to make an initial assessment of the offender's difficulties, make an appropriate early referral, and provide interim support' (Social Work Services Group, 1991b, para. 126.13). Social work managers are responsible for deciding who might most appropriately deal with requests which are likely to require a more intensive or long term involvement, taking into consideration the other activities and responsibilities of community service staff.

Summary

The twelve community service schemes differed in the procedures they adopted to assess offenders' suitability for a community service order. Some based their assessments upon information conveyed by the social worker who had interviewed the offender in the course of preparing the social enquiry report. Most, however, conducted separate interviews with offenders prior to sentence to establish whether they were suitable for community service or not. There was no reason to conclude that additional pre-sentence interviews by community service staff improved the quality of decisions that were made: similar types of offenders were sentenced to community service and similar levels of compliance and completion were obtained. Pre-sentence interviewing was, on the other hand, associated with higher assessment costs, especially if the interviews were conducted in the offenders' homes. While other benefits may accrue from community service staff having direct contact with offenders prior to sentence, this was beyond the scope of the research.

Schemes similarly differed in their approaches to placement allocation. Most interviewed offenders shortly after they had been sentenced to match them to an appropriate work placement. A few, however, decided which types of placement and which types of work to allocate offenders to on the strength of knowledge of the offender gained at the pre-sentence stage. Schemes that adopted the former approach took more active account of the offenders' own preferences for particular types of work. These schemes had similar levels of compliance and completion to those in which the offender was less actively involved in the matching process, but offenders tended to express more favourable views towards their work placements in schemes which actively engaged them in the choice of work.

Differences were found across schemes in the average amount of time that elapsed between an order being made and the first work session. The three schemes with the longest delays continued to accept further orders even when their capacity had been reached. Orders were 'stacked' and offenders were allocated to appropriate placements when vacancies arose.

The scheme with the highest breach rate also had, owing to the temporary suspension of work teams, the longest average time to complete a community service order. The longer the offenders took to complete their community service orders, the more acceptable and unacceptable absences they had.

Variations were found in the numbers of unacceptable absences that schemes would tolerate prior to issuing a formal warning and prior to returning an offender to court. Lower levels of acceptable and unacceptable absences were found in schemes that adopted a more stringent approach to the enforcement of orders, but these schemes resorted to breach proceedings no more often than others. Tighter enforcement, it seems, led to increased compliance without adversely affecting the success rate of schemes.

Group placements were associated with higher failure rates but this appeared to be attributable to the higher proportions of 'riskier' offenders who were allocated to placements of this type. The higher levels of acceptable and unacceptable absences in team or workshop placements could be accounted for by partly by the types of offenders who completed their community service orders in a group setting, but may also have reflected variations between paid community service supervisors and agency staff in the recording of absences. Offenders who were allocated to practical work in a voluntary or statutory agency had a higher incidence of unacceptable absences than those allocated to personal tasks and the level of unacceptable absences was lower among offenders who had found their placements to be very enjoyable and who considered community service to have been very worthwhile.

Even though community service schemes selected out offenders who had problems of such a nature or degree that they would adversely affect the completion of a community service order, many offenders had problems of varying seriousness while completing their community service work. Schemes generally offered advice or referral to a more appropriate source of help if they were aware that offenders had problems. Two schemes, however, endeavoured to offer a more comprehensive social work service and appeared to have achieved a slightly higher than expected completion rate with riskier groups of offenders. Most offenders indicated that they would be reluctant to approach their community service officer for help if problems arose. Most community service staff were, however, keen to extend the social work content of their work, though concern was expressed about the resource implications of doing so and some wished to guard against the distinction between community service and probation becoming increasingly blurred.

Since the research was conducted, much of the variation in practice across Scotland has been reduced by the introduction of national standards and objectives for community service schemes (Social Work Services Group, 1989, 1991). Pre-sentence interviews are no longer carried out by community service staff, but offenders have, within certain limits, a greater voice in determining the types of work they are allocated to. Delays in starting work should have been reduced, though in 1989 schemes were reportedly having difficulties, for a number of reasons, in meeting this new requirement (Social Work Services Group, 1990). Greater consistency should have been achieved with respect to the enforcement of orders, though some concern has been expressed by community service staff that the more recent reduction in the number of permitted warnings prior to breach (from four to three) to bring community service practice into line with probation may, at least in the short term, result in an increase in the numbers of offenders who are returned to court. On the other hand, the increased specialisation within social work departments in the provision of services to offenders and their families and the clearer integration of community service with the wider range of social work services to the criminal justice system should, in theory, engender a more flexible response to offenders who encounter a range of personal problems while they are completing their court-ordered community service work.

5 A worthwhile experience?

Introduction

From one perspective community service schemes may be judged to be successful if they are able to obtain high completion rates as well as high levels of compliance. To the extent that offenders do complete the work that they are ordered to perform, it can be argued that a major objective of the sentence is being achieved. The success of community service can, however, be assessed in other ways. In the following three chapters the value of community service work for the community is examined, the ability of the sentence to divert offenders from sentences of imprisonment is assessed and the impact of the community service order upon subsequent reconviction is explored. First, however, the present chapter focuses upon offenders' experiences of performing unpaid work and their attitudes towards community service.

Previous studies which have sought offenders' views about community service have generally found them to be positive. Most of the 20 offenders interviewed in Nottingham as part of the Home Office evaluation of the experimental schemes (Pease et al., 1975) believed that community service had been worthwhile and that the work they carried out had benefited the community in some way. Community service was also viewed as a more positive sentence than imprisonment and of more value to them than probation. In a survey of community service offenders in Warwickshire, 86 per cent of respondents felt that they had gained something from their experience of community service (Varah, 1981). Allen and Treger (1990), in their study of community service in Illinois, found that 67 of the 73 offenders who were interviewed considered community service to have been a positive experience, in most cases because it had offered them an opportunity to help other people. The offenders in Leibrich et al.'s (1984b) evaluation of community service in New Zealand similarly thought that they had benefited from the experience and that the recipients likewise had benefited from the work.

The views reported in the present chapter were derived from questionnaires completed by a self-selected sub-sample of offenders shortly before or after completion of their community service orders and by a smaller number of interviews which were conducted to obtain more detailed explanations of some of the responses provided in the questionnaires. But people who opt to participate in a research study are not necessarily representative of the wider population from which they are drawn. Without some knowledge of the characteristics of respondents and non-respondents it is difficult to ascertain the extent to which opinions and sentiments voiced by a minority are more widely shared.

For this reason, the questionnaire respondents and non-respondents were compared across a range of background characteristics. These included personal characteristics such as age, gender, marital status and employment history; social work history; previous convictions and sentences; type of sentencing court; remand status; offence for which community service was imposed; and length (in hours) of community service order. The sub-sample of questionnaire respondents were found in each of these respects to be indistinguishable from the larger sample from which they were drawn. The two groups did differ, however, in terms of their compliance with their community service orders: questionnaire respondents were less likely to have been breached for failure to comply with the requirements (3.0 per cent compared with 15.9 per cent; $\chi^2 = 13.1$, 1 d.f., p < .001). Questionnaire respondents who completed successfully, however, had similar levels of unacceptable and acceptable absences from placement to those among the wider sample who successfully completed their community service orders.

The under-representation of offenders who were breached is not wholly attributable to their reluctance to complete a questionnaire: some could not be traced and in a few cases community service staff did not send questionnaires to offenders whose breaches had been particularly acrimonious. It is likely, though, that had a higher proportion of offenders who had been breached been included in the sample, then slightly higher levels of dissatisfaction than those reported here would have been found.

Offenders' attitudes towards community service

The majority of the questionnaire respondents (87.4 per cent) believed that their experience of community service had been worthwhile and just under three-quarters (72.5 per cent) felt that they had gained something from being on community service. Most found the work interesting (87.9 per cent) and enjoyable (91.1 per cent) and would be willing, if necessary, to undertake community service again (88.0 per cent).

Just over four-fifths of the offenders (82.6 per cent) said that they had been able to carry out the type of work they wanted while on community service. The interviews revealed that offenders were usually interested in being given work that they had some prior experience of ('I'd done painting and decorating for two and a half years. So it was about the only thing I could do. That or welding, and they wouldn't give me welding'; 'Well, it was cleaning duties and I do all the housework in here anyway when my mum's at work'). Others had expressed an interest in working with particular groups of people ('I like helping the old folk...My grandfather's disabled. I just help them out'; 'Well, I like working with kids and other people and I said to the social worker that I'd like to do community work that involved children'.

Most offenders (74.6 per cent) believed that they had been able to make use of skills they already possessed during their work placements and just over two-thirds (68.7 per cent) had learned new skills, either of a practical or interpersonal kind:

> Everything to do with painting and decorating. How to put paper up, how to strip it, how to paint in window frames and all that, how to emulsion.

> Talking to people, understanding other people's problems. I thought I had a lot of problems but when you see people with alcohol problems and drug problems you know that you're lucky...I've found out that I can come to terms with other people's problems...I can understand how they feel.

Some of those interviewed did not consider that their placements had provided them with an opportunity to acquire new skills, either because the work was unskilful in itself ('It's not a new skill learning how to wash dishes!') or because their previous experience meant that there was little else to learn ('I'd done it before'). A few offenders explained that they had not learned new skills but had been able to brush up on those they already possessed ('I can hang paper a bit better now'). Just over a third of those who were unemployed (37.7 per cent) thought that their experience on community service had improved their future chances of obtaining paid work. Offenders were more likely to believe that community service had enhanced their work prospects the greater the extent to which their community service placements had enabled them to acquire new skills.

Most of the offenders (91.1 per cent) had at least some contact with the beneficiaries of the work they carried out and almost all (96.3 per cent) thought that the work would be of benefit to the recipients.

With no exceptions, the offenders reported that they had a good relationship with their placement supervisor: in most cases (77.3 per cent) the relationship was described as very good. The importance of the supervisor/worker relationship was widely recognised, with only five offenders considering it unnecessary for offenders on community service to get on well with their supervisors. As the interviews revealed, good relationships with their supervisors could help maintain offenders' motivation and commitment to their work (see also, Flegg, 1976):

I didn't feel as if, oh here we go again - I've got to go away down there. No, I quite looked forward to it.

He just made the atmosphere and the surroundings better to work with. If I didn't get on with a person I wouldn't have felt fine.

If you hadn't got on with your supervisor you wouldn't really want to go to your community service place. And then probably you'd do your work slovenly. I got on alright with her and everything was alright.

I seemed to enjoy it more, knowing I could get on with him.

It's important to get along with the members of staff at your placement because they make your order less of an ordeal.

Offenders who completed their community service orders in team placements and those who carried out tasks for voluntary or statutory agencies were equally likely to describe their relationships with their supervisors in positive terms.

Overall, then, most offenders appear to have found community service to be a reasonably constructive and rewarding experience. Attitudes did vary, however, according to their placement experiences.

Offenders' views of community service appeared to be affected by whether or not they were able to perform the type of work they wanted. Offenders who got the type of work they wanted were more likely than other offenders to have viewed their work placements as interesting (95.4 per cent compared with 60.9 per cent; $\chi^2 = 20.2$, 1 d.f., p < .001) and enjoyable (95.4 per cent compared with 73.9 per cent; $\chi^2 = 8.8$, 1 d.f., p < .01) and were more likely to have considered their experience of community service to be have been very worthwhile (59.3 per cent vs. 26.1 per cent; $\chi^2 = 7.1$, 1.d.f., p < .01).

Each of the offenders who had been able to make a great deal of use of their existing skills in their placements reported that they had been allocated the type of work they wanted, while this was true of only 56.3 per cent of those who had been able to make no use of their skills ($\chi^2 = 15.0$, 1 d.f., p < .001). Similarly, all those who believed that they had acquired many new skills while on community service indicated that they had got the type of work they wanted compared with 38.1 per cent of those who had acquired no new practical or interpersonal skills ($\chi^2 = 10.5$, 1 d.f., p < .01).

A degree of caution is, however, necessary in the interpretation of these findings. Whilst it is, indeed, possible that offenders' attitudes were influenced from the outset by the fact that they were required to undertake work that would be of little interest to them, it is equally possible that their views about whether or not they were able to perform the type of work they wanted were influenced retrospectively by their experiences on placement.

Contact with the beneficiaries

Offenders who had a great deal of contact with the beneficiaries of their work were more likely than other offenders to have found their community service placement to be very interesting and enjoyable and were more likely to have considered their experience on community service to have been very worthwhile (Table 5.1). Offenders who reported having had a great deal of contact with the beneficiaries were more willing than those who had less contact or no contact at all to be placed on community service again (95.6 per cent vs. 80.8 per cent vs. 75.0 per cent; $\chi^2 = 8.1$, 2 d.f., p < .05).

Table 5.1
Offenders' attitudes and contact with the beneficiaries

	Contact with beneficiaries	
Offenders' attitudes	A great deal	Some/none
Very interesting[1]	52.2%	19.2%
Very enjoyable[1]	49.3%	20.8%
Very worthwhile[2]	62.3%	40.4%

[1]$p < .01$
[2]$p < .05$

Acquisition of new skills

Offenders who had been able to acquire many new practical or interpersonal skills while completing their community service work were more likely than other offenders to have found community service to be very interesting, enjoyable and worthwhile (Table 5.2).

Table 5.2
Offenders' attitudes and acquisition of skills

	Acquisition of skills	
Offenders' attitudes	A great deal	Some/none
Very interesting[*]	68.0%	30.8%
Very enjoyable[*]	64.0%	31.5%
Very worthwhile[*]	84.0%	45.8%

[*] $p < .01$

Offenders who believed that the work they were required to perform while on community service would be of great benefit to the recipients were more likely to have found their placements to be interesting and enjoyable. They were also more likely to have thought that their experience of community service had been very worthwhile and were more willing, if necessary, to undertake community service again (Table 5.3).

Table 5.3
Offenders' attitudes and usefulness of work

	How useful	
Offenders' attitudes	Very	Fairly/ not at all
Very interesting[1]	48.9%	17.8%
Very enjoyable[2]	48.3%	17.8%
Very worthwhile[1]	65.2%	29.5%
Willing to be placed on CS again[2]	94.3%	75.0%

[1] $p < .001$
[2] $p < .01$

Community service workers who had been able to make use of skills they possessed during their orders and those who had acquired new skills were more likely to think that they work they had carried out would be highly valued by the recipients. There was no evidence, though, that work was thought to be more useful if it involved a greater degree of contact with the beneficiaries.

To summarise briefly, then, offenders found community service to be more rewarding if they were able to acquire skills during their placement, if they enjoyed a great deal of contact with the beneficiaries of their work or if they were engaged in work that they could perceive as being of considerable benefit to the recipients.

The views of the offenders in the sample differed somewhat according to their age when sentenced to community service. Young offenders (that is, those aged between 16 and 20 years) were less likely to have got on very well with their placement supervisors (68.7 per cent compared with 86.2 per cent; $\chi^2 = 4.8$, 1 d.f., p < .05) and were less likely to have found their experience of community service to be very worthwhile (50.0 per cent compared with 71.9 per cent; $\chi^2 = 5.0$, 1 d.f., p < .05). Younger offenders were, however, more likely to have acquired new skills through performing community service work (80.9 per cent compared with 55.4 per cent; $\chi^2 = 13.3$, 2 d.f., p < .01). The latter finding may partly reflect the higher proportion of young offenders allocated to group placements in which an element of practical training was often involved.

The following section explores whether offenders' attitudes and experiences varied according to the types of setting (team or agency) in which they completed their community service orders and the types of work (practical or personal) that they were required to carry out.

Offenders' attitudes and placement characteristics

The Wootton Committee (Advisory Council on the Penal System, 1970) stressed the potential value of having offenders work alongside other non-offender volunteers. Relatively few community service schemes have extensive provision for offenders to work with other volunteers. There is, though, a commonly held assumption that offenders are likely to benefit more from work which involves direct contact with the beneficiaries and work which is of a personal rather than practical kind. Such placements are assumed to be more fulfilling for offenders, more capable of enhancing their confidence and self-esteem and more likely, therefore, to effect a change in their attitudes and behaviour. Group placements tend, for these reasons, to be viewed as inherently inferior to placements in voluntary or statutory agencies. This is reflected, for example, in the use of group placements for assessment purposes and in the use of group placements for offenders considered unsuited to work in an agency setting (rather than vice versa).

An alternative viewpoint is that some offenders may respond better in a group situation and to practical work which is more familiar to them (West, 1976). Some offenders may be unsuited to personalised tasks and unwilling to engage in this type of work (Ralphs, 1980). According to this argument, the appropriateness of a placement for a particular offender is more important than the broad nature of the work or the setting in which it is carried out.

Team and agency placements

Offenders who were allocated to group placements, in teams or workshops, were as likely as those who were allocated to work in agency settings to have performed the type of work they wanted during their community service orders and they were as likely to have found the work they carried out to be interesting, enjoyable and worthwhile.

Group placements were found to be characterised by work which involved less direct contact with the beneficiaries than that undertaken in agency settings (34.4 per cent of offenders in the former and 79.2 per cent of those in the latter enjoyed a great deal of contact with the recipients of their work; $\chi^2=20.4$, 1 d.f., p<.001), but offenders in group placements were more likely than those in agencies to believe that the work they carried out would be highly beneficial to the recipients (75.0 per cent compared with 54.2 per cent; $\chi^2=4.4$, 1 d.f., p<.05). Offenders in team placements reported having made more use of their existing skills than did those who completed their placements in voluntary or statutory agencies (85.5 per cent vs. 62.5 per cent; $\chi^2=6.5$, 1 d.f., p<.05), but whether or not offenders acquired additional skills was unrelated to the placement setting in which their community service work was carried out.

There appeared, then, from the offenders' perspective to be no overall superiority of agency placements over placements in community service work teams or workshops. Although offenders who completed their community service orders in voluntary or statutory agencies enjoyed more contact with the beneficiaries of their work, offenders in group placements were better able to make use of their skills and regarded the work they performed as being of more direct benefit to the recipients.

The spectrum of work that was performed in agencies was, however, broad and encompassed a range of both personal and practical tasks. Comparisons were therefore made of the views of offenders who completed their community service orders in work teams or workshops and those who were engaged throughout their orders in performing practical tasks in an agency setting.

These comparisons revealed that offenders in team placements were more likely than those who undertook practical work in a voluntary or statutory agency to have acquired new skills during their community service placement (75 per cent compared with 45.5 per cent; $\chi^2=5.2$, 1 d.f., p<.05) and were more likely to regard they work they carried out as being very useful for the beneficiaries (75.0 per cent compared with 40.9 per cent; $\chi^2 = 7.1$, 1 d.f., p < .01) even though they were less likely to have had a great deal of personal contact with the people who would benefit from their work (34.4 per cent compared with 63.6 per cent; $\chi^2 = 4.6$, 1 d.f., p < .05).

Practical and personal work

It is often assumed that work which involves the provision of personal assistance to other people is more rewarding for offenders on community service orders than work which is comprised solely of practical tasks. By the very nature of the work, offenders who were employed on personal tasks during their community service orders were more likely to have had a great deal of contact with the beneficiaries than those who were engaged throughout their orders on practical work (78.4 per cent compared with 41.2 per cent; $\chi^2 = 13.3$, 1 d.f., p < .001). Practical and personal tasks were viewed as equally enjoyable and worthwhile and were equally likely to have enabled the offender to draw upon his or her skills or to acquire new ones. Placements with an element of personalised work were, however, more likely to be viewed as very interesting than those in which the work was exclusively of a practical kind (54.1 per cent compared with 32.2 per cent; $\chi^2 = 4.5$, 1 d.f., p < .05).

It has, of course, already been shown that offenders' experiences of practical work varied according to the type of setting in which it was carried out, with team placements being generally viewed as more constructive than those in voluntary or statutory agencies. None of the offenders who completed their community service orders in work teams or workshops were employed on personal tasks. Comparisons were therefore made of offenders' views of practical and personal work carried out within agencies. They revealed that offenders who had been engaged for at least part of their placement on personal tasks were more likely to have had a great deal of contact with the beneficiaries (92.3 per cent vs. 63.6 per cent; $\chi^2 = 4.3$, 1 d.f., p < .05); were more likely to have found their work very interesting (53.8 per cent vs. 31.8 per cent; $\chi^2 = 7.2$, 2 d.f., p < .05) and enjoyable (42.3 per cent vs. 31.8 per cent; $\chi^2 = 6.6$, 2 d.f., p < .05); and were more likely to have acquired new skills during their community service placements (80.8 per cent vs. 45.5 per cent; $\chi^2 = 5.0$, 1 d.f., p < .05).

The main differences between the three types of placement (group, agency personal and agency practical) are summarised in Table 5.4.

Table 5.4
Offenders' attitudes and placement type

	Placement type		
	Group	Agency practical	Agency personal
Great deal of contact with beneficiaries[1]	34.4%	63.6%	92.3%
Work very interesting	36.5%	31.8%	53.8%
Work very enjoyable	39.1%	31.8%	42.3%
Got the work they wanted	83.9%	68.2%	88.5%
Work very useful[2]	75.0%	40.9%	65.4%
Acquired new skills[2]	75.0%	45.5%	80.8%
Used existing skills[2]	85.5%	63.6%	61.5%

[1] $p < .001$
[2] $p < .05$

To sum up, then, it is clear that offenders' experiences and views of community service differed according to the types of placements that they completed their community service orders in. There was, however, no clear superiority of agency placements over group placements or of personal over practical work. While agency placements enabled offenders to have more contact with the beneficiaries of the work they were required to perform, the lower degree of contact in group placement appears to have been compensated for by the fact that the work tended to be more skilful and of greater potential value to the recipients. If anything, practical placements in voluntary or statutory agencies, which often involved tasks such as kitchen or cleaning duties, were less highly regarded by offenders than personal agency placements or placements in teams. But more important than the broad nature of the work undertaken or the setting in which it was carried out were the qualities of the work itself: offenders appeared to value most placements which maximised their contact with the beneficiaries, which enabled them to acquire new skills, and which engaged them in work that they could readily identify as being of benefit to the recipients.

What did offenders gain from community service?

Most offenders believed that they had gained something from their experience of community service. It is clear from Table 5.5 that offenders were most likely to believe that they had gained in a practical sense though acquiring work experience or skills ('I have found my community work placement to be very useful to myself and have brushed up on the painting and decorating skills that I already knew'; 'I thoroughly enjoyed the work I had in my placement because I learned a lot about joinery').

Table 5.5
What offenders gained from community service

	Number of offenders	Percentage of sample*
Skills	32	23.9
Work experience	26	19.4
Increased understanding of others	15	11.2
Increased confidence	13	9.7
Deterrence from offending	13	9.7
Increased self-awareness	8	6.0
A sense of usefulness/purpose	8	6.0
Retaining liberty	6	4.5
A chance to help people	6	4.5
A chance to meet people	2	1.5
Other	5	3.7
Total	134	100.0

*n = 134

A substantial proportion of the sample also believed that community service had, in some way, contributed to their personal development through increasing their understanding of other people ('Understanding of how to help the elderly'), giving them more confidence ('Confidence in dealing with strangers') or increasing their own self-awareness

('Selflessness'; 'Patience'; 'Knowledge that if you do wrong you must pay for it'). Some offenders believed that they had benefited through being able to retain their liberty while others felt that, as a result of their experience on community service, they were less likely to re-offend. A few offenders had valued the opportunity to help other people or had enjoyed the experience of feeling useful and appreciated ('The feeling of doing something for someone'; 'Feeling that someone cares') while some had welcomed the chance to meet other people though their work placements ('It was very enjoyable and gave me the chance to meet ordinary people who made my order a pleasure to do').

What offenders got out of community service was influenced to some extent by the types of placements they completed their orders in. Offenders in team placements were more likely to have gained useful work experience or skills while those in agencies were more likely to have benefited through helping people, meeting other people and, in the process, achieving an increased understanding of others.

Twenty-one offenders offered explanations as to why they had not gained anything from being on community service. In most instances, this was attributed to the fact that the work was unskilful or exposed them to nothing that was new (11 responses). In the experience of two offenders, community service was simply a punishment to be completed as and when instructed ('Only paying for crime') while two others could not see the benefit of the work they were required to carry out ('All I did was meaningless'). One offender disliked the work he had to carry out, one resented 'doing other people's dirty work', and one disliked the community service staff. One offender believed that community service 'will not get you anywhere' while another felt that the money spent on travel to placements could have been used instead to pay a fine. Finally, one offender had gained nothing from community service because he had been breached before commencing his placement and 'didn't get a chance to do any of it'.

The offenders were also asked to indicate what they had liked most and least about being on community service. As Table 5.6 shows, more than half had enjoyed the interpersonal aspects of their orders: contact with other people, whether it be the beneficiaries, their supervisors, agency staff or, in the cases of team placements, other offenders on community service. Just over a third had especially liked the work itself, either because it provided them with job satisfaction or because it offered them some additional work experience and skills.

Table 5.6
What offenders liked most about community service

	Number of of offenders	Percentage of sample[*]
The work	46	35.7
Meeting people	20	15.5
The beneficiaries	14	10.8
The supervisor	14	10.8
Helping people	12	9.3
Retaining liberty	10	7.8
Having something to do	7	5.4
The other offenders	7	5.4
Everything	6	4.6
Feeling useful	3	2.3
Community service staff	2	1.6
Other	3	2.3
Nothing	17	13.2

[*]n = 129

The work itself was also most often mentioned as the aspect of community service that the offenders liked least (Table 5.7). Complaints usually centred around the lack of interesting tasks ('Soul-destroying'; 'Washing the porridge pots out'; 'Meaningless jobs'). Several offenders disliked the commitment that being on community service required ('The lack of free time'; 'Getting up early') and the travelling or costs incurred in attending placements. Five offenders made specific reference to the lack of cleanliness of houses they were asked to work in, implying that the beneficiaries in these instances were unappreciative of and undeserving of their services:

> Over my placement I helped to decorate three houses. The first two were clean, respectable abodes but the third one was filthy and I do not enjoy working in filth and therefore didn't use my skills to their full.

A few offenders, who would have preferred to be more fully occupied, complained about the lack of work ('Sitting about when it rained';'Stopping for breaks'). For one offender, community service was a 'constant reminder of wrongdoing', while another was concerned about 'people knowing you're on an order'. More than a quarter of the sample, however, disliked nothing about their community service order.

Table 5.7
What offenders liked least about community service

	Number of offenders	Percentage of sample*
The work	23	19.4
The commitment required	12	10.1
Travelling	7	5.9
Everything	7	5.9
The cost	6	5.0
Dirty houses	5	4.2
Lack of work	4	3.4
The other offenders	4	3.4
The fact it is a punishment	3	2.5
The lack of responsibility or trust	3	2.5
Community service staff	2	1.7
The supervisor	2	1.7
The rules	2	1.7
Not being paid	2	1.7
Other	5	4.2
Nothing	33	27.7

*n = 119

While most offenders did not think that community service could be improved, fifty-nine (45.0 per cent) thought that it could. The suggestions they offered are summarised in Table 5.8.

Table 5.8
How community service could be improved

	Number of offenders	Percentage of responses
Better or more varied placements	16	23.2
Travelling expenses paid	9	13.0
Better staffing	9	13.0
Different work hours	8	11.6
Could help the community more	5	7.2
More resources	4	5.8
Better matching/preparation	4	5.8
Provision of transport to placement	4	5.8
More say in choice of placement	3	4.3
Follow-on employment/references	3	4.3
Other	4	5.8
Total	69	100.0

Since the work itself was most often the aspect of community service that the offenders mentioned as having liked least, it was not surprising to find that the provision of more skilful, interesting or varied placements was the most frequently suggested way in which community service might be improved. Several offenders believed that fares to placement or lunches should be provided, while a few thought that transport could be provided or existing arrangements improved:

> Some expenses (bus fares at least) should be refunded. This is a common complaint from each individual serving an order.

> It cost me up to £2 per day to get to the community service placement. So count that up at 240 hours community service at 8 hours every Saturday and it comes to a great deal of money and I have never had a penny back.

> I think they should collect you from the house. I don't think we should have to pay the first £2 each week.

They should provide a general meeting point rather than collecting people from home.

Comments about staffing ranged from requests for more contact between offenders and community service staff (offenders who were 'doing well' tended to be left by staff to get on with their orders while they devoted their energies to dealing with others who were causing problems in their placements or otherwise failing to comply; this was sometimes misinterpreted as signifying a lack of interest on the part of the community service officer) to the suggestion that schemes could employ ex-offenders to supervise teams. Three offenders suggested that community service staff might help offenders find employment after finishing their orders or 'provide a certificate or reference for future employment'.

Several respondents thought that community service could be improved by changes to the way in which the hours were worked. But while some offenders would have preferred to have completed their orders by working more often than they did ('I think that my order dragged out too much just getting one day per week'), others felt that the working day was too long.

Continuing on a voluntary basis

Anecdotal accounts can frequently be found of offenders who, having become enthusiastically involved in the work of an agency, have continued their involvement on a voluntary, and sometimes paid, capacity after completing the hours of work ordered by the court (e.g. Morgan and Ruffles, 1980). While the issue of continued participation was not addressed directly in the questionnaire, a few offenders spontaneously commented on the fact that they had continued to attend their placements or intended to do so:

> I completed my 240 hours in October and now continue on a voluntary basis.

> I found it very interesting and educational and now do voluntary work at this home.

> It was a good laugh. I got on with everyone and will be going back to help them when my community service is finished as I found it very interesting.

I would do community service on a voluntary basis when my present employment expires.

The question of continued involvement was further explored in the interviews. Half of those who were interviewed indicated that they would, if it were possible, be prepared to continue the work they carried out in their placements on a voluntary basis. Three members of this group had continued to attend their placements ('I'm doing that just now...usually every day...because I enjoy it so much. The children's faces light up as soon as you walk in the door. I think that's what I enjoy most about it') and one other was in the process of applying, on the encouragement of the agency staff, for a paid post as a handyman in the children's home in which he had completed his community service order. Others were willing in principle to continue: a few had intended doing so but had not followed up on their initial intentions and three were willing but unable to do so because of their other work commitments. For example:

It's a good place. You get to know the people and all that. I'd do it for voluntary. I'm not doing anything else anyway.

I actually thought about it. I was going to go back but I never got round to it.

I was going to and should have started the next week but I didn't go for a week and felt a bit funny. The woman's been asking for me to go back.

Maybe if I didn't have the job I've got just now, but not on a Friday...I quite enjoyed it when I was up there and I would do it again if I was unemployed.

I'd like to but I'm not saying I would turn up every time. But maybe on a Sunday when I've got nothing else to do I'd appear and give them a hand. I work Monday to Friday full-time.

Five offenders were undecided about whether they would be willing continue or not:

I don't know. I've not really thought about that much. I wouldn't mind going in and seeing the staff periodically but I don't know if I'd go in voluntary because I'm usually quite busy.

Eight offenders, on the other hand, were clear that they had no interest in continuing their community service work. A variety of reasons were given:

I was asked but I didn't like the kids at the youth club.

I didn't like getting up in the mornings.

I don't like working for nothing.

It was a boring job.

The possibility of continuing their involvement was clearly more realistic for offenders who had been placed in voluntary or statutory agencies. The extent to which offenders do carry on working for agencies after they have completed their community service orders is examined further in the following chapter.

Is community service punitive?

The offenders' responses suggested that in most instances community service was regarded as a rewarding and worthwhile experience. Although community service is intended to be of value to offenders as well as to those who benefit from their work, a primary objective is, nevertheless, to punish offenders for their wrongdoing by depriving them of their leisure time. Is it possible, then, for a measure to fulfil what appear to be rather disparate penal objectives?

The simple answer is yes. Three-quarters of those who were interviewed believed that community service was punitive because of the inconvenience it caused, the commitment it required, or the fact that the work was unpaid. None of the offenders regarded the work itself as having been punitive:

It's a punishment because if you're working you've got to do it at the weekends. You've got no time for anything else. And it's still hanging over you. Even if you're not working you've still got to get out of your bed in the morning, go over there, work eight hours and get nothing for it.

It's there to inconvenience you. Not so much in my case but in other cases when they need to be there on a Saturday. They can't go to the football and they can't go to the pub with their pals. They've got to be there.

It's an easy option but a punishment as well. If you're working all week the last thing you want to do on a Saturday or Sunday morning is go away and paint someone's house. It's an easy option because it means you're still working, you still go to the pub or whatever at the end of the week and you're not inside.

It was easy for me because I knew what I was doing. It was hard if you didn't. You had to get out of bed, be there, do as you were told to a high standard. But they didn't treat you as criminals.

It's not as bad as jail but it put me out a wee bit.

The other seven offenders thought that community service was an easy option and saw no aspects as punitive. Some, however, engaged in 'syllogistic thinking' similar to that reported by McDonald (1986): prison is equated with punishment and since community service is not prison then it cannot be a punishment ('It's better than going to jail'; 'It's easier than doing time'). Others, because they had enjoyed their placements, had not experienced community service as a particular inconvenience and found it difficult to conceptualise in punitive terms:

It's better than jail. I enjoyed it. Perhaps other placements are punitive.

It's not really a punishment because you're learning something.

Although the interview sample was small, it appears from this group of offenders that community service was fulfilling the requirement in the subsequently introduced national standards that it should:

...present a challenge to the offender. The punitive element in the penalty is contained in the time which offenders must devote to community service work, in the essential disciplines of regular attendance, prompt time-keeping, and satisfactory work performance, and in the prompt application of disciplinary procedures for non-compliance.

(Social Work Services Group, 1991b, para. 10)

Summary

The views presented in this chapter have shown that community service was, for many offenders, a rewarding and constructive experience. Most found their placements to be interesting, enjoyable and of value to the beneficiaries, many acquired new practical or interpersonal skills and most felt that they had gained something from being on community service and that their experience had been worthwhile. Most offenders acknowledged the importance of their relationship with their placement supervisors.

No clear preferences emerged for group or agency placements or for practical or personal work, though placements in voluntary or statutory agencies that engaged offenders exclusively on relatively unskilled practical tasks were regarded as less rewarding and worthwhile. More generally, the specific features of placements were more important than the broad nature of the work or the setting in which it was carried out. Offenders expressed more favourable views towards placements which offered a great deal of contact with the beneficiaries, placements in which they were able to develop new skills, and placements in which they could recognise the work they performed as being of direct benefit to the recipients. Several offenders had continued to attend their agency placements after completing their orders and others were willing, in principle, to do so. At the same time, community service was not widely viewed as an easy option. Most offenders had felt inconvenienced by the restrictions that community service placed upon their leisure time and by the regular and sustained commitment that it required. Although some had disliked the work they carried out in their placements, none of the offenders who were interviewed regarded the work itself as punitive or harsh.

These conclusions are further reinforced by the additional comments offered by offenders in the questionnaires. While a few were critical, either of particular aspects of community service (such as the non-payment of travelling expenses) or of community service more generally ('Sometimes you're better off in jail than doing community service'; 'It was a waste of time going there'; 'It was pretty shitty'), most took the opportunity to comment positively on their experience of completing a community service order:

> It was beneficial to me as I was doing something useful within the community and I enjoyed it as much as the kids. And as an added bonus on my part I got to see and visit places with the kids that I normally wouldn't have otherwise. I would thoroughly recommend it to anyone.

In my opinion community service gives people a chance to prove that they are willing to change their ways and for minor offences is a good alternative to prison.

Quite enjoyable. There was nobody on my back and I only got out of it what I put into it.

I just did my work. The people I was working for were really good to get on with. The hours were good and there was a lot of things I learned. I made friends with the people staying there. I learned and enjoyed it.

I enjoy working with old people and the supervisor and staff were very pleasant to be with.

I found the work very interesting and the supervisor very helpful and patient with my work. I also have praise for all the staff of the community service scheme whom I found did everything they possibly could to settle you into the work placement and if you had any problems they were always there to help if possible.

Two offenders in particular appeared to encapsulate the spirit and ethos of the community service order:

I found that I benefited more than I would have if I had been sent to prison as I found something I really like doing. I wouldn't have got a chance to work for the elderly in prison. For minor crimes, community service would be a more beneficial sentence to both criminal and society.

It is a very good thing to do because you are doing good for the community as well as your punishment.

6 A worthwhile service?

Introduction

Since its introduction in England and Wales was first recommended by the Wootton Committee, a primary objective of the community service order has been for offenders to 'perform service of value to the community or to those in need' (Advisory Council on the Penal System, 1970, para. 41). Benefit to the community is emphasised in the national standards for community service in England and Wales (Home Office, 1988b) and in the Scottish Office guidelines. The latter place an obligation on community service schemes to provide work placements 'which are seen to be of value to the community, the agency and the offender alike' (Social Work Services Group, 1991b, Part 2, para. 1.6.2). Community service work should, moreover, 'be seen by both the community and the offender to be constructive and enable the offender to make reparation to the community for the offence' (Social Work Services Group, 1991b, Part 2, para. 11).

In the previous chapter it was shown that the majority of offenders found community service to be a rewarding experience. Many acquired new skills (of either a practical or interpersonal nature) while performing the work ordered by the courts and most found their experience of community service to be constructive, enjoyable and worthwhile.

More pertinently, almost all the offenders (96 per cent) believed that the work they had carried out would have been of value to the beneficiaries. Relatively few studies have, however, attempted to assess the benefit to the community of community service work. Some (e.g. McDonald, 1986) have documented the economic contribution of unpaid work by offenders on community service orders. Others have explored the experiences of placement-providing agencies and have generally reported high levels of satisfaction with the work carried out (e.g. Allen and Treger, 1990; Berk and Feeley, 1990; Leibrich et al., 1984b).

Among the even more limited amount of British research which has addressed the beneficiaries' perspective is Godson's (1980) study of 35 agencies that offered community service placements to offenders in Hampshire. Much of the study focused upon practical issues, such as the criteria employed by agencies with respect to the types of offenders to whom they would make placements available, the types of work carried out, methods of supervision and level and type of contact with community service staff during the order. The agencies were, however, also asked to indicate how satisfied they were with the offenders' performance. In most cases agencies were reported to have been satisfied with the effort made, the standard of work and its usefulness, although concern about the level of absences was widespread, with the attendance of workers being described as unsatisfactory in 39 per cent of placements.

In Scotland, the Borders Community Service Scheme conducted a survey of those directly involved in the operation of the local scheme: the courts, social workers and agencies and individuals who had benefited from community service work (Borders Social Work Department, 1987). Responses were received from fifty-one agency and individual recipients, relating to more than seventy jobs. Dissatisfaction with the work was expressed in only six cases.

The Borders survey, as far as the author is aware, is the only one of its kind to have sought the views of individual members of the public (as opposed to agencies) who had had work carried out on their behalf by community service work teams. Unfortunately, the responses of individual beneficiaries were not distinguishable from those of voluntary or statutory agencies in the resulting report.

There has to date been little systematic information, then, about the extent to which the work provided by community service schemes in Britain is valued by its recipients. The SWRC study documented the views and experiences of both individuals and agencies throughout Scotland who had benefited from community service work. The present chapter reports the findings of that survey, beginning with the responses of members of the public who had been in receipt of work by teams of offenders on community service orders.

Individual beneficiaries

The respondents

The majority of the 567 survey respondents (84 per cent) were elderly and/or suffered from an illness or disability which had prevented them from carrying out the work themselves. Twenty-eight beneficiaries were single parents, 8 responses were received from young people who were moving from care into independent accommodation and 7 questionnaires were completed by adults with learning difficulties living in supported accommodation in the community.

Lack of financial resources to pay for necessary work was mentioned as a factor underlying referral to community service in 18 cases and a further 23 people made use of their local community service work team to receive or deliver furniture being donated by or to the local social work department.

Just under half the beneficiaries (49.0 per cent) had initiated the request for assistance themselves and almost a third (31.1 per cent) had been referred to the scheme by a social worker. Other sources of referral included: family members (7.0 per cent); friends (3.4 per cent); neighbours (2.7 per cent); and health visitors (2.7 per cent). Referrals had also been initiated in a few instances by home helps or homemakers, by representatives of other voluntary or public agencies, by general practitioners and by the church.

Approximately a quarter (25.5 per cent) of the recipients had had work carried out by offenders on community service on a previous occasion. This had, therefore, been most people's first experience of community service work.

Types of work carried out

The types of work that had been carried for the beneficiaries are summarised in Table 6.1. Clearly, the services offered by the community service teams were predominantly of a practical nature. Painting and decorating and gardening tasks accounted for the vast majority of the work that had been carried out, with over 97 per cent of the respondents having been provided with one of these services. With the exception of furniture removal, the relative incidence of other types of work was low.

Table 6.1
Types of work carried out for individual beneficiaries

Type of work performed	Number of beneficiaries	Percentage of cases*
Painting and decorating	287	50.7
Gardening	264	46.6
Furniture removal	84	14.8
Joinery/damp-proofing/alarms	30	5.3
Varied manual labour	14	2.5
Window/car washing	12	2.1
Carpet fitting	5	0.9
Domestic (including shopping)	5	0.9
Fuel delivery/splitting	4	0.7
Other	4	0.7

* n=565

Seventy-seven people thought that, had community service been unavailable, the work could still have been completed. The alternative sources of assistance included: paid contractors (22 respondents); neighbours, family or friends (18 respondents); or other volunteers (15 respondents). Seven people believed that they could have carried out the work themselves and six thought that the services might otherwise have been provided by the local authority.

Although 22 people believed that paid contractors could have performed the tasks conducted by the community service teams and seven suggested that they could have carried out the work themselves, this may have been only with considerable difficulty or financial hardship. Since respondents were asked to indicate whether or not the work *could* otherwise have been carried out and not whether it *would*, there is little reason to suspect that community service schemes were, to any significant extent, depriving contractors of work.

Recipients' experiences of community service work

Most beneficiaries (79.1 per cent) had at least some contact with the community service team while they were carrying out the work. In just over a fifth of cases (21.3 per cent) people indicated that they had enjoyed a great deal of contact with the team. As Table 6.2 shows, the majority of people who came into contact with the offenders on community service indicated that they had got along well with them: only three beneficiaries described their relationship with the community service workers as poor.

Table 6.2
Beneficiaries' experiences of community service

	Responses		
	Very	Fairly	Not at all
How well got on with workers	79.1%	19.6%	0.7%
How well work was supervised	81.9%	14.1%	4.0%
How happy with standard of work	77.2%	19.0%	3.8%
How beneficial work was	87.3%	11.0%	1.7%

Table 6.2 also confirms that most people's experiences of having work carried out by offenders had been positive. Most believed that the work had been carried out to a high standard, that it had been very well supervised and that it had been of considerable benefit to them.

Painting and decorating tasks entailed the greatest amount of contact between the recipients and the community service work teams and were most highly valued by them. Each of the four main categories of work (painting and decorating, gardening, furniture removals and 'other') were, on the other hand, thought to have been equally well performed.

However, not everyone was happy with the work that had been carried out. Twelve people reported that the work had been sloppy or had been carried out with too much haste ('They made a balls up of it and left streaks everywhere'). Eight others complained that tasks had not been completed ('The decorating was fine considering the boys were not professionals. The gardening was disappointing because I was told they would do a lot more. All they did was to clear rubble and cut the grass') and three that the work had taken too long ('The only thing that disappointed me was the amount of time it took to do the job'). The offenders' attitudes were criticised by two respondents ('The ones that helped could not care less') while two others said that although the work had not been carried out to the standard that they would have wished, they were nonetheless appreciative of the service that had been provided ('Not the way I would have done it had I been able however I am very grateful for what they did').

Problems encountered

Most people (95.2 per cent) encountered no problems while having work carried out by offenders on community service. Where problems had arisen, damage (to carpets, flowers etc.) was most common, being mentioned by nine beneficiaries ('Purposeful damage to tin of paint - three holes punched into bottom of paint tin - causing paint to leak out over floor'; 'As I have already said, my rhubarb was ruined by grass cutter').

Six people voiced complaints about the unreliability of teams ('I was never sure if they were coming as they often did not turn up when they said. They telephoned to say they could not make it. That happened several times'). Other less frequently mentioned problems related to poor supervision, messy work, apparent lack of skills, delays in the completion of the work and offenders' poor attitudes ('Spoke to gardening boys - got a lot of cheek'). The most serious incident concerned an elderly woman who had been the victim of theft by a community service team member who was subsequently convicted of the offence ('Money went missing from my bag and I had to go to court eventually when he was charged').

Recipients' attitudes towards community service

Given that most of the beneficiaries had described their experience of community service in favourable terms, it was not surprising to find that most (96.0 per cent) said that they would be willing to have work carried out by offenders on a future occasion. Only thirteen people were unwilling to make use of community service again. The explanations provided included: the poor standard of the work; their reluctance to trust offenders around their homes; and the unreliability of the team.

Table 6.3
Why beneficiaries would make use of community service again

Reasons	Number of beneficiaries	Percentage of cases*
Good standard of work	170	49.9
Work would not otherwise get done	109	32.0
Generally happy with service	75	22.0
People friendly/helpful	62	18.2
Service free of charge	36	10.6
No problems/well supervised	27	7.9
Good for the offenders	19	5.6

* n=341

As Table 6.3 shows, people most often attributed their willingness to make further use of their local community service scheme to their satisfaction with the standard of the work that had been carried out by offenders on community service orders:

> They were very willing, good workers and made a very good job of it.

> I could find no fault with the work done in my home and the way it was carried out and would be most willing to have this service in the future.

> I was delighted with the standard of workmanship and the efficient way it was carried out. My entire house was decorated. I could not have managed this on my own.

> Work very well done, no time wasted, very well supervised, excellent time-keeping, no noise during working, no mess, very pleasant to deal with. First class.

> The standard of work was high and to my complete satisfaction.

Just under a third of the beneficiaries indicated that they would make use of community service again because unless they did so, certain types of work would not get done. Others said that further help from the community service scheme would be valued since they could not afford to pay for certain essential services or would suffer financial hardship if they did:

> As I am 86 years of age and have had six major surgeries I am unable to concentrate to do very much.

> Because I worked hard to make a lovely garden. It was my hobby and joy. I hated to see it full of weeds and neglected.

> I am unfit to do my garden myself so was very grateful when community service did it. I also will be very grateful to have them back again.

> I am a single parent and suffer MS. I could not have paid a professional painter and decorator to carry out the same work.

> We are pleased and grateful for work already done. Being senior citizens just having to pay for materials and not labour was a great help to us financially.

Around a fifth expressed general satisfaction with, or gratitude for, the service provided and just under a fifth commented on the helpful or friendly attitudes of the team:

> I can wash my windows and hang out my washing in comfort without having grass up to my waist.

> I would be quite willing to have the community service workers any time. Although the work was only done in the evenings, giving the lads a cup of tea and biscuits was a small price to pay for the service I received.

> I tried other services and could not get any help. In fact they told me my house was not dirty enough to get done. I am most grateful for the work they carried out.

> In my experience I found them to be friendly, willing and co-operative. A letter to this effect was sent to the overall team leader to show my appreciation.

They did a good job and were a happy bunch of people who were trying to make good a wrong.

Since I so seldom see anyone it gave me great joy to be able to speak to the supervisor and the 'offenders'. Even more, though it took hours to prepare they always treated me with courtesy and never failed to thank me for the lunch I provided.

Smaller numbers of beneficiaries attributed their willingness to make further use of community service to the absence of problems while the work was being completed, their observation that the work was well supervised or their belief that performing unpaid work for the community would be beneficial to the offenders themselves:

The supervisor was most efficient and they all worked cheerfully and well.

I had not trouble whatsoever. They could not do enough to help. They laid the carpet for me and placed all my furniture back in place.

I feel that community service gives purpose and a sense of self worth to those who carry it out seriously.

Everyone deserves to have the opportunity to help.

The people who participated in the survey were given an opportunity to provide additional comments on their experiences as recipients of community service work. Some offered suggestions as to how community service might be improved or suggested ways in which the services currently available might be extended. For instance:

This is not a criticism but it would be helpful to know on a regular basis how individuals are placed on the waiting list to give them time to save up for the paper/decorating materials. I was also unaware of the scope of the work and thought it was only confined to decorating. It was a pleasant surprise when they offered to do other wee jobs about the house. We are delighted with their help and indebted to them.

During the winter when it's snowing it would be a great help if they had a list of people who use community service and arranged to clear snow from stairs and garden paths.

Some people suggested that it would be helpful if certain types of work (especially gardening) could be carried out on a more regular basis and a few thought that community service might be usefully extended to include various types of environmental improvement work. However, most took the opportunity to voice their support for community service or to further express their appreciation for the work that had been done:

> In my opinion I feel that rewards, in some instances, are gained by the community service workers themselves i.e. a sense of responsibility and possibly the awareness of carrying out a task for one in less fortunate circumstances than oneself.

> All I can say is thanks for this type of service, plus it does not overcrowd the prisons for minor offences and I think it does the lads good to let them know we trust them in our homes. I used to go out and leave them to it, telling them to help themselves to whatever they wanted to eat and take a cup of coffee anytime and left soup for them. They did not abuse this. Thank you.

> To widows such as myself it serves as a lifeline as I have no-one to turn to for help. Please keep up the good work which is much appreciated.

> The lads who made the concrete base worked very willingly, at least one of them was experienced in this kind of work. The end product was excellent. The paper-hangers tried hard but were not suited for that kind of work. We treated them well and they responded in the same spirit. There was a good relationship between the supervisor and the workers and we all parted as friends.

> I approve in general of the 'spirit' behind community service.

> Just many thanks to the men (and woman) who decorated my house and did my garden. It would be a pleasure to have them again.

To summarise briefly, it is clear that the work undertaken by the community service teams was highly regarded by the majority of recipients. The responses revealed high levels of satisfaction with the standard of work provided. Most people reported that the work had been of considerable benefit to them, few had encountered problems when the work was being carried out and people were, with only a few exceptions, willing to make further use of their local community service scheme.

113

The agency perspective

The characteristics of the agencies and their clients

The voluntary and statutory agencies that took part in the survey offered services to a wide range of client/user groups or to the community in general (Table 6.4).

Table 6.4
Client/user groups served by the agencies

Client/user group	Number of agencies	Percentage of agencies[*]
Elderly	54	31.6
Children/teenagers	41	24.0
Mentally handicapped	21	12.3
Physically handicapped	18	10.5
Families/single parents	15	8.8
Substance abusers	6	3.5
Mentally ill	4	2.3
Unemployed	1	0.6
Mixed user group	24	14.0
Community in general	18	10.5

[*] n = 172

Some agencies provided services for more than one category of client. In Table 6.4 the term 'mixed user group' is applied to those agencies who provided services to three or more identifiable groups of clients or users. The term 'community in general' is, on the other hand, applied to those agencies whose services were available to anyone in the community who wished to make use of the resource.

A third of the agencies described themselves as community projects or resources and a quarter were residential facilities. Some offered a range of services, such as a combination of day care, residential facilities and advice.

Most agencies were able to make community service placements available during weekdays (90.6 per cent) while just over half (52.6 per cent) could offer placements in the evenings and a similar proportion (50.9 per cent) could provide work for offenders at the weekend.

The agencies had supervised, on average, nine community service offenders in total and three in the previous twelve months. However, there were wide variations in placement provision and experience. Sixty per cent of the agencies had supervised between one and six offenders in total but six had offered placements to between 40 and 70 offenders on community service orders. Likewise, although three-quarters of the agencies had supervised four or fewer offenders during the previous twelve months, four had offered placements to between 15 and 20 offenders during that period.

The types of offenders agencies were willing to accept

Forty-one agencies (23.8 per cent) indicated that there were no categories of offenders that they would normally exclude from consideration. Some were prepared to consider each case on its own merits ('Prepared to give a chance to any offender within reason'), some were happy to leave it up to community service staff to select appropriate offenders for them ('No qualms about anyone - happy to take anyone on the recommendation of community service') and others would tailor the work according to their knowledge of individual offenders ('Nobody really providing we knew what the offences were and could place the people in places where they will not be subjected to temptation or repeat their offences').

Most agencies did, however, exclude certain types of offenders. The 'other' category in Table 6.5 includes offenders convicted of wilful fire-raising, drunk drivers, teenagers, the physically unfit and various other undefined groups who would put the agency's clients or users at risk or 'spoil the agency's fabric'.

As Godson (1980) similarly found, the agencies were clearly most intent on excluding offenders who may pose a threat to their clients/users, with explanations such as 'clients vulnerable to exploitation' being offered by 88 respondents. The work on offer in three agencies was said, by its very nature, to exclude certain types of people while three other agencies indicated that their policy of refusing to accept particular categories of offenders was guided by a concern for the safety of staff.

Table 6.5
Types of offenders/offences that agencies would exclude

Type of offence or offender	Number of agencies	Percentage of agencies[*]
Sexual abuse/offences	51	29.6
Violent/aggressive	51	29.6
Dishonesty	46	26.7
Offences against children	31	18.0
Substance abuse/offences	19	11.0
Offences against the elderly	5	2.9
Offences against women	3	1.7
Other	14	8.1

[*] n = 172

The agencies were also asked to indicate whether there were any other categories of offenders that they would have reservations about offering placements to. Reservations were generally expressed by agencies about accepting the types of offenders that others would automatically exclude. Reservations were expressed additionally about: persistent offenders; people convicted of vandalism; unclean people; people living locally; people who might boast about their offences to teenagers; and people who are HIV+ (depending on the type of activity involved). Again, potential risk to clients/users was most often cited as the reason underpinning such reservations.

Overall, 68 agencies excluded or had concerns about offering community service placements to aggressive offenders or those convicted of offences involving violence. Sixty-three agencies would not accept offenders convicted of offences involving dishonesty or would have reservations about doing so, while this was true of 57 agencies in relation to sexual offences or abuse. Just over a fifth of the agencies (37) were unwilling or reluctant to offer placements to individuals convicted of offences against children (sexual or otherwise) and 22 excluded or had concerns about accepting people who had been convicted of alcohol or drug related offences or who were known to have problems related to the use of alcohol or drugs.

The types of work that had been carried out by offenders are summarised in Table 6.6. Most had employed offenders on more than one type of work and in some agencies (thirty in total) offenders had been engaged in as many as six or seven different types of task.

Table 6.6
Types of work performed in agencies

Type of work	Number of agencies	Percentage of agencies[*]
Handiwork	76	44.2
Domestic duties	73	42.4
Painting and decorating	65	37.8
Gardening	63	36.6
Group activities/sport	61	35.5
Care duties	59	34.4
Serving meals	39	22.7
Driving/escorting	32	18.6
Befriending	31	18.0
Tutoring/teaching	9	5.2
Administrative/journalistic	7	4.1
Artwork/graphics	5	2.9
Other	13	7.6

[*] n = 172

Practical tasks, such as domestic work (kitchen and cleaning duties), painting and decorating, general handiwork and gardening clearly predominated. Certain types of personalised work, such as care duties, organising and participating in sports or group activities, driving/escorting and befriending were also fairly common. The 'other' category in Table 6.6 includes publicity distribution, furniture removal, thrift/craft shop work, work with animals and craftwork.

Eighty-six agencies described the work undertaken by offenders as being solely or mainly of a practical kind. In 66 agencies offenders were engaged in a mixture of practical and personal work. Only 19 agencies claimed to employ offenders exclusively or primarily on personalised tasks.

Most of the agencies (89.4 per cent) said that the work offenders were engaged in brought them into direct contact with the their clients/users. Not surprisingly, offenders who were involved in work of a personal nature had higher levels of such contact than those employed on practical tasks.

Most agencies also believed that the assistance provided by offenders on community service was of direct benefit to the individuals or groups for whom the agency provided services. Only eight agencies stated that their clients or users would not benefit directly from community service work. Personal tasks were seen as being of more benefit in this respect than was practical work.

Agencies' experiences of community service work

Almost two-thirds of the respondents (65.5 per cent) believed that the work carried out by offenders on community service had been very useful for their agency and only one person thought that the assistance they had received had been of no benefit. Most agencies (59.1 per cent) were very happy with the standard of work provided by offenders and only two thought that the standard of work had been poor.

Practical and personal tasks were said by the agencies to have been of equal benefit to them and the two broad categories of work were considered to have been equally well performed. However, offenders were less well integrated with staff, and where relevant with other volunteers, in agencies that placed a particular emphasis upon practical work (Table 6.7).

Eighty-five agencies indicated that at least one offender had sought to continue attending his or her placement after completing the hours ordered by the court and 71 agencies had invited offenders to continue their involvement in either a voluntary or paid capacity once they had competed their community service work. In total, offenders had carried on working beyond their required hours in 99 of the agencies that took part in the survey.

It was shown in the previous chapter that offenders who completed their community service orders in voluntary or statutory agencies expressed more favourable attitudes towards placements that enabled them to engage in tasks of a personalised nature. There was no clear evidence from the agency survey, however, that offenders had more often sought to continue their involvement with agencies that offered this type of work. Although 43 per cent of agencies offering only practical work and 57 per cent of those offering varying degrees of personal work reported that one or more offenders had offered to continue, this difference was not statistically reliable (p = 0.13).

Table 6.7
Offenders' integration into agency, invitation to continue involvement with the agency and type of work carried out

	Type of work		
	Solely/mainly practical	mixed	Solely/mainly personal
Offenders very well integrated[1]	31 (37.8%)	44 (67.7%)	12 (63.2%)
Offenders invited to continue[2]	23 (31.3%)	37 (59.7%)	11 (61.1%)

[1] $p < .001$
[2] $p < .01$

There was, on the other hand, a relationship between the types of work that offenders carried out and the agencies' likelihood of inviting offenders to continue on a voluntary or paid basis after completing their community service orders. Agencies that had employed offenders solely or primarily on practical tasks were less likely than others to have encouraged the continued participation of offenders once they had carried out the work required by the courts (Table 6.7).

Problems experienced by agencies and support received

Sixty-four agencies considered that their experience of offering placements to offenders on community service orders had been very satisfactory, 75 thought that it had been fairly satisfactory and nine indicated that it had not been satisfactory at all. Slightly more than half the agencies (52.4 per cent) had experienced problems relating to the supervision of community service placements (Table 6.8).

Table 6.8
Problems experienced by agencies

Type of problem	Number of agencies	Percentage of agencies*
Poor attendance/punctuality	58	33.7
Lack of effort or skill	13	7.6
Poor attitude/bad influence	10	5.8
Offending against agency	8	4.6
Unsuitability for agency	5	2.9
Offenders' problems/commitments	4	2.3
Lack of support from CS staff	4	2.3
Confidentiality	3	1.7
Alcohol abuse	2	1.2

* n = 172

Attendance and punctuality were most often identified as problematic ('Failing to turn up, usually due to illness. Contact with agency is not always made'; 'In one case only lack of regularity proved to be time-consuming in follow-up').

Several agencies complained that some offenders who had been placed with them had shown a lack of motivation, effort or skill ('Lack of commitment - not working, erratic attendance etc.') and five others felt that offenders had sometimes been inappropriately placed ('We've had an odd person who didn't settle in the establishment but considering the amount of CSO we have had most has been successful').

Ten agencies were critical of some offenders' attitudes ('On starting they come with a chip of their shoulder but as the hours go by they see what we do for the community and attitudes start changing') or believed that in some cases community service workers had had a negative influence on their clients or users ('Lack of basic manners when dealing with teenagers i.e. encouraging swearing, sexist talk etc.'). Eight agencies were reported as having been the victims of offences committed by offenders on community service, either during or after their orders. In one instance, however, the respondent believed that the community service worker had been unfairly blamed for an incident that had occurred:

> On one occasion items went missing and suspicion fell on the individual on community service, although I am of the opinion that it was not her that was responsible. We asked for her to be removed to avoid any possible repercussions from the group she was involved with. The blame lay with our group for loose storage of money which allowed it to walk. This has now been sorted out.

Most of the agencies that experienced problems (62.9 per cent) were said to be very happy with the support they had received from community service staff, though six felt that the level or quality of support offered had been poor. Two agencies had decided not to notify the community service scheme when problems had arisen.

In more general terms, most agencies (70.6 per cent) felt very well supported by community service staff when they offered placements to offenders on community service orders. Only five complained that the support provided by the community service scheme was unsatisfactory.

Table 6.9
Types of support valued by agencies

Type of support	Number of agencies	Percentage of agencies
Contact/communication	52	30.2
Pre-placement arrangements	35	20.3
General advice and support	29	16.9
Responsiveness and flexibility	24	13.9
Supervision/monitoring	23	13.4
Enforcement	18	10.5
Accessibility of CS staff	17	9.9
Clarification of objectives	3	1.7

It is clear from Table 6.9 that good ongoing communication, by telephone or by placement visits by community service staff, had been valued by many agencies ('Personal visits and telephone communication. A good backup service'; 'Ongoing contact to see things work out okay'). Agencies had also appreciated the pre-placement work undertaken by schemes. This included the provision of adequate information about offenders who might be placed in the agency and the opportunity to meet with them prior to a decision being reached ('...bringing each person along to introduce to staff and situation').

A number of agencies had valued the general support, information and advice provided by their local community service scheme ('Answering queries and just being there for support if needed') while others were appreciative of the community service staff's flexible approach and their responsiveness to the agency's needs ('Finding people who will fit in well to the agency').

Several agencies were grateful that the community service staff had provided overall monitoring and supervision of offenders while they completed their orders ('Backup service for individual while individual is with this organisation'). Others valued the fact that community service staff had assumed responsibility for enforcing orders and dealing with instances of non-compliance ('Liaison with workers following non-arrival at site').

A few agencies commented positively on the accessibility of community service staff ('All staff are very accessible - never any problems in contacting for support') or their responsiveness if problems arose ('Their immediate response to problems experienced by either the worker or the agency and their ability to deal with it sensitively and directly'). Three appreciated the clarity with which the community service staff had communicated their expectations of the agency and their objectives ('Clarity about the conditions they wanted for and wanted from their clients').

Most of the agencies (135) were satisfied with the support they already received from the local community service scheme and could identify no other additional types of support they might value. Seventeen agencies said that they would welcome more contact with community service staff while offenders were completing their orders and four said that they would appreciate more background information about offenders before deciding whether or not they were prepared to offer them a place. Six agencies were keen to have more offenders placed with them while six said that they would be happier if community service staff had direct responsibility for the supervision and recording of work. Two agencies thought that offenders might benefit from additional support and advice from community service staff while completing their orders, one agency believed that placement preparation or induction could be improved and three sought increased clarity regarding the objectives of community service and their responsibilities in offering placements to offenders on orders. Although most agencies (103) said that they were very clear about their obligations and responsibilities when providing placements for offenders on community service orders, thirteen agencies admitted that they were not at all clear what the local scheme's expectations of them were.

Agencies' attitudes towards community service

Almost all the agencies (96.5 per cent) were prepared to continue offering work placements to offenders on community service orders. Only five agencies would not make placements available in future. In two cases this was attributed to their unsatisfactory experience of supervising community service offenders. Three agencies, on the other hand, were willing in principle to continue offering placements but felt that they could provide insufficient work to keep offenders usefully occupied for the duration of their orders.

Table 6.10
Why agencies would offer further placements

Reason	Number of agencies	Percentage of agencies[*]
Benefit to agency	43	37.4
Benefit to offenders	40	34.8
Previous experience	36	31.3
Benefits to client/community	21	18.3
Work still to be done	21	18.3
Agency philosophy/policy	8	7.0
Mutual benefit	6	5.2
Good support from CS staff	3	2.6

[*] n = 115

Agencies were most likely to cite benefit to the agency, benefit to the offenders or the fact that their previous experience of offering placements had been positive as their reasons for continuing to accept offenders from their local scheme (see Table 6.10):

> They do jobs for us we really would have difficulty getting done in any other way.

> If placements are constructive they can complement the work of the agency - added resource.

> They have been enthusiastic and effective members of a team of helpers and instructors, obviously deriving a good deal of pleasure from the work and for some of the younger offenders it is their first experience of being 'needed'.

> To respond as a community to offenders who are willing to compensate - hopefully to assist offenders enjoy working for the community.

> Long-term contact with our staff and clients can help alter outlook of offenders.

> The people have all been very helpful and willing and have integrated well.

> The service given by clients on community service to say the least has been admirable. The assistance given to our organisation has been very helpful in many ways.

Some agencies were attracted to community service because their clients/users or the wider community benefited from the work undertaken by offenders on orders. For others, further placements would be much appreciated since there were still plenty of tasks that needed to be carried out:

> We feel that the participants have given great benefit in terms of experience, skills, counselling, advice, practical skills to our customers.

> Residents benefit greatly as staff do not always have the time to spend long periods with individuals who are very attention seeking.

> It is seen as a valuable resource and at the same time a helpful way of working in the community and for the community.

Most clubs for the physically disabled are dependent upon volunteer helpers. Fewer and fewer volunteers are willing to make a commitment of five hours per week.

A few respondents indicated that offering placements to offenders on community service orders was consistent with the agency's principles, objectives or philosophy ('As a believer in the concept of community service I feel able to offer a worthwhile placement'), some highlighted the fact that community service placements were of mutual benefit to the agency, to its clients/users and to the offenders performing unpaid work ('So far, everyone has gained from the experience') and three made explicit reference to the quality of support they had received from community service staff ('Very satisfied with the person who was carrying out the order. Good support and liaison from the community service staff').

The agencies were given an opportunity to volunteer additional comments about their experience of offering community service placements. Three were divided in their opinions as to whether or not it was advantageous to accept offenders from the immediate local community. Two thought that the familiarity of the offender could be a bonus. As one agency commented:

The residential unit is based in a small community and the individual who worked here was well known to the residents. This, perhaps, made things easier for all concerned. It may not have worked so well with a strange face.

The third agency suggested, however, that the placement of local offenders might have its drawbacks:

There is often an expectation that local people will carry out their orders in our premises. This, I feel, is counterproductive as 'hard men' still have their reputations to keep up and cannot be seen to be helping elderly ladies by their mates. While the local venue is convenient and can save on travel it keeps the offender's potential experience limited to his own environment. I have often suggested that a person already known to us is not taken by us on a community service order.

A few agencies pointed out that through accepting offenders of community service, additional work could be created for agency staff. For instance:

It's very difficult to offer them support to the extent that they require. If the community service offender has no specific skills then increased involvement is required by full-time staff and part-time volunteers and staff to give them direction and give them enthusiasm.

Some agencies referred to administrative difficulties, such as the time and effort involved in dealing with absences from placement. The additional comments provided by most, however, reinforced the generally positive views about community service that had been expressed elsewhere in the questionnaires:

We have no complaint to make about either the placements we have had nor the service provided by the community service staff. We have been very grateful to them.

We are very happy with the people who have worked with us. They have been well chosen for their aptitude to our particular work and we have encountered no major problems. We operate a reciprocal trial basis for one month i.e. four visits during which either side can opt out. We have a very good backup service from the social work department. We have found that sometimes it takes a while for people to adjust to our type of work but having done so the benefits to both sides can be immense.

We have been delighted with the work done and personal contact. Community service people have responded well and always seem to get a lot out of the placement.

The placements seem to have been of at least as much benefit to the offenders as to the organisation. Members of the organisation who come into contact with the offenders relate to them very well and often improve the offenders' social skills, particularly communication with people of different age groups and sex. The work gives the offenders confidence in coping with an entirely new situation as well as showing them how some of the less fortunate members of the community cope with their difficulties - sometimes a very humbling experience! It also seems to benefit some offenders to be in a position where they do not feel inferior or threatened by other people and know after the first few sessions that they can fill a need in other people's lives. Community service staff are very helpful and knowing 'backup' is available if problems arise enables the group to be more venturesome in the type of offender it accepts.

We have had a great response from the placements at this centre. Built up confidences and relationships and they always visit after they leave. They have (some with more help than others) become good team members and are able to use their own initiative a great deal. This has worked out to be of great value to us as well as to the placement.

Summary

Most of the individual beneficiaries of work performed by community service teams were elderly or suffered from an illness or disability that prevented them from carrying out the work themselves. Most people had contacted the community service scheme themselves or had been referred by their social worker and almost all had received help with painting and decorating or gardening tasks. With few exceptions, satisfaction was expressed with the services they received. Most people believed that the work had been completed to a high standard, that it had been well supervised and that it had been of benefit to them. The majority of the beneficiaries had some contact with the offenders while they were carrying out the work and relationships with the teams were usually reported as having been good. Few problems were encountered while the work was being carried out and the majority of beneficiaries were willing to make use of their local community scheme again. The attitudes of the community service workers were frequently praised and several people suggested that undertaking unpaid work for the community would be of benefit to the offenders themselves.

The responses received from a range of placement agencies in the voluntary and statutory sectors confirmed that offenders on community service were providing a valued and worthwhile service. In most agencies the work was regarded as being of a high standard and as being of benefit both the agency and to its clients or users. Most offenders were engaged in work with at least some practical elements and agencies appeared to value equally practical and personal tasks. While most agencies placed some restrictions on the types of offenders they would accept and many had experienced problems as a result of supervising offenders on community service orders these were usually of a relatively minor nature and the perceived benefits to the agency, to its clients/users and to the offenders themselves appeared in most cases to have outweighed the costs. Agencies generally felt well supported by community service staff, many had encouraged offenders to continue their involvement after their orders were completed and they were with very few exceptions willing to offer further work placements to their local community service schemes.

7 Community service and custody

Introduction

The Wootton Committee (Advisory Council on the Penal System, 1970) regarded the proposed community service order as being an direct substitute in certain cases for short sentences of imprisonment but did not preclude its use in a wider range of situations. Community service could, according to paragraph 37 of the Wootton Report, be:

> ... a welcome alternative in cases in which at present a court imposes a fine for want of any better sanction, or again in situations where it is desired to stiffen probation by the imposition on the offender of an additional obligation other than a fine. If might also be appropriate as an alternative to imprisonment in certain cases of fine default.

The subsequent legislation, both in Scotland and in England and Wales, enabled the courts to impose community service orders upon offenders who had been convicted of offences that were punishable by imprisonment, as long as the offender had been assessed as suitable for a community service order, arrangements could be made for the offender to perform unpaid work and the offender agreed to an order being made. In this way, the scope of the community service order was broadened, permitting its use, in accordance with the views of the Wootton Committee, as an alternative to other non-custodial sentences.

Arguably the greatest debate and uncertainty surrounding community service concerns whether this option should be construed as an alternative to imprisonment (that is, as an explicit tariff measure) or as a sentence in its own right. Even in the experimental schemes in England and Wales opinions were divided on this issue (Pease et al., 1975). Thus while three of the six chief probation officers regarded community service solely or primarily as an alternative to custody, the other three considered it as having a potentially wider use. The 167 probation officers interviewed by Pease et al. were likewise divided in their opinions: fewer than half regarded community service only as an alternative to imprisonment. Similarly divergent views were expressed by the probation officers in Vass's (1984) study: ten officers believed community service to be primarily an alternative to custody, four considered it to be a sentence in its own right and five regarded it both as an alternative and as a sentence in its own right. Lewis (1981) noted that even within a community service scheme different grades of staff may 'identify with different objectives of the scheme and fail to establish a corporate view of what they are aiming at'(p. 12).

Variations in the use of community service across courts have been documented by Young (1979) who concluded that 'there was no consensus, either within or between areas and courts, on the types of offenders for whom the sentence was appropriate, the reasons for which it should be imposed, or the way in which it should be administered.' (p. 135). This Young attributed partly to the Wootton Committee's lack of clarity in articulating the objectives of the community service order and to the Home Office's failure to rectify the resulting confusion.

Opponents of the view that the use of community service should be determined more by the needs of individual offenders than by explicit tariff considerations have expressed concern that 'probationisation' of the community service order would result both in a decline in its overall use and in a decrease in the proportion of offenders who are diverted from custody by this measure (McWilliams and Pease, 1980). Others have cautioned that an individualised approach to community service might lead to its use even when the offence for which the order has been imposed does not merit such a substantial intervention (West, 1977) or might result in a reduction in the credibility of community service as a relatively demanding sentence (Bryant, 1983).

The case for increased consistency in the use of community service has perhaps been most convincingly articulated by Pease (1978, 1980b) who highlighted the adverse implications for offenders of existing variations in sentencing practice. Pease emphasised in particular the risk that 'tariff escalation' could occur on breach or on a subsequent court appearance if the intentions of the sentencer who imposed the original community service order were unknown.

Given the confusion about its intended aims and the failure of legislation to specify that community service orders should be imposed only if the offender would otherwise be dealt with by means of imprisonment, it is hardly surprising that a number of studies have highlighted the limited diversionary impact of this popular penal measure. The first attempt to assess the extent to which community service functioned as an alternative to imprisonment was made by Pease et al. (1977) in their evaluation of the experimental English schemes. Three of the four methods used - judgements by probation officers, the outcomes of breaches and the alternative disposals received when a community service order was recommended but not made - produced estimates that community service was replacing custody in between 45 per cent and 50 per cent of cases. The fourth estimate, which suggested that 19 per cent of offenders on community service orders had been diverted from custody, was based on the disposals received by offenders who were referred for a community service order by the court but who subsequently received an alternative sentence.

Willis (1977), on examining sentencing trends in England and Wales, questioned the extent to which the use of community service orders had increased at the expense of imprisonment. He also concluded that the majority of offenders on community service had been convicted of 'those types of offences for which a term of imprisonment would not normally be regarded as inevitable and might not even be deemed appropriate' (pp. 124-5). Godson (1981), on the other hand, estimated on the basis of their offending and sentencing histories that around 70 per cent of community service offenders in his study were at a high risk of receiving a custodial sentence. He also observed that 76 per cent of offenders who were breached received, on revocation of their orders, a sentence of imprisonment for the original offence. However without further information about the characteristics of offenders who were breached and the likelihood of high risk offenders actually being sentenced to a term of imprisonment, conclusions about the diversionary impact of community service cannot readily be drawn from these data.

There is evidence that in Scotland community service has, over the years, become increasingly used as an alternative to other non-custodial options. In his study of the five experimental Scottish schemes, Duguid (1982) attempted to assess, by both indirect and direct methods, the manner in which community service was being used by the courts. A total of 498 offenders who had been referred by the courts or by social workers for a community service assessment subsequently received an alternative sentence. Approximately a third of this group were directly sentenced to imprisonment. When only those cases in which the final outcome was known were considered (that is, those on whom sentence was, for whatever reason, deferred were excluded), 42 per cent of the sample were found to have received a custodial sentence.

The unsuccessful referrals were not in all probability comparable with those who were made subject to community service orders. However Duguid employed a more direct method of estimating the extent to which community service had replaced sentences of imprisonment. During the first year of operation of the experimental schemes, sheriffs agreed to indicate, on a case by case basis, what alternative disposal would have been imposed had community service not been available. In 71 per cent of the 147 cases, the sheriffs indicated that the offender would have received an immediate custodial sentence. Social workers who were responsible for the preparation of social enquiry reports on offenders who received community service orders were also asked to indicate for each offender which alternative disposal they thought would have been most likely. In the first year, 78 per cent of offenders on community service were thought by social workers to have been diverted from custody by this new measure. No data relating to individual cases were available from sentencers during the second year of the experimental schemes, however only 58 per cent of offenders in this year were judged by social workers to have received their community service orders in lieu of imprisonment.

Assuming that the social workers' assessments were not any less accurate in the second year (and there is no prima facie reason to believe that they were) it appears that the use of the community service order may have been quickly extended to include higher proportions of less serious offenders or offences. There is, indeed, some evidence that since their introduction, community service orders have increasingly been imposed in Scotland on offenders who are less likely, on the basis of their prior sentencing histories, to receive a custodial sentence. Whereas in 1981 54 per cent of all orders were imposed on offenders who were classified, on the basis of sentencing history, as having a high or intermediate risk of custody, this was true of only 48 per cent of offenders given community service in 1985 and 42 per cent of those so sentenced in 1989 (Social Work Services Group, 1988, 1990).

The present chapter examines more closely the way in which the community service order had been used by Scottish courts.

The sentencing of unsuccessful referrals

One indirect method of estimating the tariff position occupied by the community service order is to examine the sentences received by offenders who are referred for a community service assessment but who subsequently, when they appear for sentence, receive an alternative disposal.

The characteristics of the 482 offenders who were unsuccessfully referred for a community service order during a six month period in 1987 were described in Chapter 3. In most cases (378) details of the alternative sentences imposed were available: where the final court outcome was unknown this was usually because sentence had been deferred to enable the offender to demonstrate his/her intention to be of good behaviour or to address specific problems on a voluntary basis. The sentences received by the unsuccessful referrals are presented in Table 7.1.

Table 7.1
Sentences received by unsuccessful referrals

Sentence	Number of offenders	Percentage of offenders
Custody	165	43.7
Monetary	151	39.9
Probation	36	9.5
Admonished	7	1.9
Custody & monetary	7	1.9
None/absolute discharge	4	1.1
Probation & monetary	3	0.8
Admonished & monetary	2	0.5
Probation & custody	1	0.3
Suspended sentence & monetary	1	0.3
Custody & admonished	1	0.3
Total	378	100.0

Overall, 46 per cent of those who were unsuccessfully referred for community service (and whose final disposal was known) received an immediate custodial sentence, while 54 per cent were dealt with by means of some other non-custodial sanction. Custodial sentences ranged in length from 7 days to 21 months, with an average of 4.75 months and a standard deviation of 4.46 months. The majority of prison/YOI sentences (84 per cent) were for six months or less and only 5 per cent were for over one year.

Although less than half the unsuccessful referrals had received sentences of imprisonment, this tells us little about the extent to which those who were sentenced to community service had been diverted from custody. It was previously shown in Chapter 3 that the unsuccessful referrals differed from the successful referrals in several notable respects: the former were more likely to have been remanded in custody prior to sentence, to be single and to have been convicted of criminal justice offences (primarily breach of bail). The unsuccessful referrals also had, on average, more experience of custody.

A number of factors, such as age and previous sentencing history, were associated with an increased risk of custody. However, the factors that appeared best able to predict the risk of custody were: remand status (offenders who were remanded in custody prior to sentence were more likely to be imprisoned); number of previous convictions (offenders who received custodial sentences had, on average, more previous convictions); and employment status (unemployed offenders were more likely to receive a custodial sentence). If anything, then, the unsuccessful referrals appear, as a group, to have had a higher risk of custody at the outset, suggesting that slightly *fewer* than 46 per cent of the community service sentences were likely to have replaced imprisonment.

It is also possible, of course, that the level of custodial sentencing among the unsuccessful referrals would differ according to whether or not they had been assessed as suitable for a community service order and whether or not appropriate work could be made available for them to perform. However, this proved not to be the case. Among the offenders assessed as suitable for a community service order, 44 per cent of those for whom no work was available and 44 per cent of those for whom work could be provided were given a custodial sentence. Similarly, 49 per cent of offenders who were considered unsuitable for community service received an alternative sentence of imprisonment.

The outcomes of breaches and other revocations

A second indirect way of estimating the diversionary impact of community service is to examine the sentences received by offenders whose orders are revoked, either as a result of failure to comply or for other reasons, such as ill health or imprisonment.

It will be recalled that the majority of the 406 offenders on community service completed their orders successfully. Forty-five offenders were, however, returned to court for failure to comply with the requirements and twelve orders were revoked in the interests of justice. The reasons for revocation and breach were detailed in Chapter 3. Table 7.2 outlines the alternative sentences imposed upon the 50 offenders for whom this information was known.

Table 7.2
Alternative sentences imposed following premature termination
of an order

Alternative sentence	Number of offenders	Percentage of offenders
Custody	28	56.0
Fine/compensation order	11	22.0
None	7	14.0
Probation	2	4.0
Admonished	1	2.0
CSO	1	2.0

Overall, then, just over half the offenders whose orders were terminated before the requisite number of hours had been completed were awarded a custodial sentence for the original offence. However, the types of alternative disposals imposed differed according to the reasons for the offender's return to court. Offenders who were breached for failure to comply with the requirements were more likely to be imprisoned than those whose orders were revoked in the interests of justice: while 26/40 of the former group received custodial sentences this was true of only 2/10 of the latter.

The amount of the order that had been completed when the offender was returned to court also had some bearing upon the outcome. Offenders who received custodial sentences had completed, on average, 24.5 per cent of their hours while those who received non-custodial disposals had completed, on average, 42 per cent.

How, then, might these findings be interpreted? For various reasons, the percentage of breaches resulting in the imposition of a custodial sentence is a poor indicator of the extent to which community service orders were originally imposed in place of imprisonment. It is possible, on the one hand, that more severe sentences were imposed than would have been warranted by the original offence as an additional punishment for failure to comply with an order of the court. This, for instance, may account for the differential treatment of offenders according to the reasons for their community service orders being revoked. It also appears, on the other hand, that some offenders may have been dealt with less severely when the order was revoked in recognition of the fact that they had completed a substantial part of their sentence. Further evidence that considerations such as these were influential in determining which alternative sentence would be imposed has been provided by sentencers themselves. The majority of sheriffs interviewed in Carnie's (1990) study were of the view that, unless convincing arguments were presented in mitigation, offenders who were returned to court for failure to comply with the requirements of a community service order would almost certainly be imprisoned for the original offence:

> The prevailing view was that if an offender had been given the chance to do community service, having had it clearly explained that this was the last opportunity before imprisonment, and he has not availed himself of this advantage, then custody should inevitably follow.
>
> (Carnie, 1990, p. 33)

A range of factors were nevertheless taken into account when determining the most appropriate sanction following a breach, with the offender's commitment to community service and the proportion of the order completed being particularly influential:

> They saw this as one way of differentiating between the offender who was doing his best, but had gone off the rails, and the offender who, from the outset, had never made a serious effort to comply with the conditions imposed. While a certain measure of sympathy was reserved for the former, no quarter was given to the latter.
>
> (Carnie, 1990. p. 33)

The other factors taken into account by sentencers when dealing with breaches of community service were the nature of the original offence and the reason for revocation being sought. It is impossible, then, to use the re-

136

sentencing of offenders who have been breached or whose orders have been for some other reason revoked as a reliable benchmark against which the diversionary impact of the community service order might be assessed.

Risk of custody and custodial sentencing

A more accurate estimate can be obtained by examining the rate of custodial sentencing among comparable groups of offenders and extrapolating from this figure to the community service sample. The classification system developed by the Scottish Office (see, for example, McIvor, 1990b) was used to assess the custody risk of offenders sentenced to community service and those referred unsuccessfully for a community service assessment. According to this system, offenders are judged to have a high risk of imprisonment if they have served a previous custodial sentence or if they have been subject to supervision as an adult and have had at least one other non-custodial disposal. The risk of custody is deemed to be intermediate if the offender has previously been sentenced to community service or has been subject to statutory supervision as an adult or child and low if the individual has no previous convictions or has received only non-custodial, non-supervisory sentences in the past. Insufficient data were available to classify all the offenders in the two samples in this way. The resultant percentages of high, intermediate and low risk offenders are presented in Table 7.3.

Table 7.3
Custody risk and research sample

| | Research Sample | |
Custody risk	Community service	Unsuccessful referral
High	147 (45.8%)	164 (58.8%)
Intermediate	21 (6.8%)	17 (6.1%)
Low	153 (47.7%)	98 (35.1%)

The unsuccessful referrals were more likely to have received custodial sentences if their risk of custody was assessed as being high. Thus 60.6 per cent of high risk cases, 50.0 per cent of intermediate risk cases and 28.8 per cent of low risk cases were sentenced to periods of imprisonment instead of community service. Overall, 48.8 per cent of the unsuccessful referrals whose custody risk could be assessed in this way received custodial sentences, a figure which is not dissimilar to the 46 per cent imprisonment rate for the entire sample.

On the assumption that a similar conversion rate would apply to the offenders sentenced to community service, then it is estimated that, overall, 44.8 per cent could have expected to receive a custodial sentence had community service not been made available when they were sentenced. This estimate assumes that 89.1 high risk offenders (60.6 per cent of 147), 10.5 intermediate risk offenders (50.0 per cent of 21) and 44.1 low risk offenders (28.8 per cent of 153), or 143.7/321 in total, would have been diverted from custody by their community service sentence.

The accuracy of this method is, of course, limited by its failure to take account of the seriousness of the offence or offences for which the samples were sentenced. The likelihood of the unsuccessful referrals receiving a prison sentence appeared, however, to be largely unrelated to the types of offences of which they were convicted, with the exception that custody was more likely if they were sentenced for offences against criminal justice, such as attempting to pervert the course of justice or (more usually) breaches of bail. These types of offences were more prevalent among the unsuccessful referrals than among the offenders sentenced to community service, suggesting that, if anything, the latter were, on the basis of their offences, at slightly less risk of imprisonment. As such, it can be reasonably concluded that community service orders had replaced sentences of imprisonment for slightly fewer than 45 per cent of the offenders on orders.

Sentencers' views

How consistent, then, are these findings with sentencers' views of how they use community service? The sheriffs in Carnie's (1990) study sat in the courts that were served by the community service schemes in the earlier research. The majority believed that community service orders should be imposed primarily in cases where a custodial sentence would otherwise be warranted but were prepared, on occasion, to extend its use to offenders for whom imprisonment was not an appropriate option. A fifth of the sheriffs, on the other hand, adopted a more individualised approach, regarding the community service order as a sentence in its own right to be matched to the needs of the offender. These sheriffs contested the view that community service was ever intended to be solely an alternative to custody: 'this was 'a complete fiction'...indeed, one which had been 'engendered knowingly by social workers over the last ten years" (p.12). One sheriff summarised this viewpoint as follows:

> If you are strictly speaking to regard community service as only available as an alternative to custody then in my book it would be very, very, seldom used. Imprisonment should be very, very seldom used in the Sheriff Court sitting certainly as a summary criminal court. I think sheriffs generally became so attracted by the idea of community service after having been born and brought up in this wholly negative sentencing world that we welcomed this very much when it arrived and we are certainly straining at the leash to use it, quite apart from as an alternative to custody.
>
> (Carnie, 1990, p. 13)

Similar views were expressed by the magistrates and clerks to the justices in Vass's (1984) study, who regarded community service as an alternative to custody but believed that it could also function as an alternative to other non-custodial sanctions or as a sentence in its own right. As one magistrate commented:

> In my view at least 60 per cent of orders made are not alternatives to imprisonment. Many of these people are diverted from fines. We have to consider whether fines can be paid. If we think that there is a risk of default, then community service can prove a useful alternative.
>
> (Vass, 1984, p. 73)

The introduction of full central funding and national standards for community service was intended to increase the numbers of offenders who would be diverted from custody by this measure. The new funding arrangements facilitated the allocation of additional resources to schemes to expand the number of places available to the courts. But, as Carnie (1990) found, there was no guarantee that these additional places would be used in the way the Scottish Office intended to divert more people from prison sentences. Only a quarter of sheriffs indicated that they would make use of the increased provision to divert more offenders from custodial sentences. A quarter did not believe that the increased availability of places would influence their sentencing practice, since more places did not necessarily mean than more people would be suitable for a community service order. A further quarter thought that the increased provision would increase the credibility of community service, by locating it more firmly among the range of sentencing options and encouraging its increased use. The remaining quarter admitted that they would be:

...very tempted to use the increase in availability of places in some instances where they might otherwise be considering a fine...There was a stark recognition that the majority of offenders had very limited income and were not in a position to pay even a modest fine, let alone one which the public might want.

(Carnie, 1990, p. 35)

This view was clearly articulated by one sheriff who explained:

The difficulty is dealing satisfactorily with someone who is unemployed, where they are dependent on state benefit, when there is no reason to put them on probation and no particular reason to defer sentence and the fine you can impose is inappropriate. There is no doubt in my mind there will be a great temptation to make community service orders rather than impose fines on the unemployed.

(Carnie, 1990, p. 35)

Through a concern that the tariff position of community service should, as far as possible, be preserved, the facility to impose community service orders had not been widely extended to the District Courts. Several had, however, made it clear that community service would be a welcome addition to their repertoire of sentencing options. The fear that the extension of community service to the District Courts would erode its position in relation to custodial sentences was, as Carnie (1990) found, well grounded: 'District Court Justices undoubtedly saw community service as a mechanism to be utilised where the imposition of a financial penalty was unrealistic, inappropriate or had failed in the past' (p. 42). As one lay justice commented:

The financial penalty is more and more difficult to operate. We would welcome another disposal rather than a financial penalty at District Court level and we would like to implement community service orders not as an alternative to a custodial sentence but as an alternative to a financial sentence.

(Carnie, 1990, p. 42)

The District Court Justices were aware that by using community service in this way, inconsistencies across courts of different levels could result. Because of their limited sentencing powers and the relatively minor nature of offences dealt with by the District Courts, most community service orders would be towards the bottom end of the scale. One justice suggested that the minimum limit of 40 hours might be abolished so that very short orders could function as alternatives to fines. So long as community service was promoted as an alternative to custody, the District Courts would have little opportunity to use it. The lay justices' case, according to Carnie (1990) 'rested on the argument that community service should stand as a sentence in its own right' (p. 46).

Community service staff, by contrast, were firmly of the opinion that community service was an alternative to custody ('Basically, the overall philosophy is as a direct alternative to custody') and this view was embodied in local policy ('The regional policy would be to try and maintain community service as an alternative to an immediate custodial sentence'). Staff also recognised that community service was not always used in that way by the courts. As one officer commented: 'Well, theoretically all our assessments should be for clients who face the likelihood of receiving a custodial sentence - in practice that is not the case'. Schemes were reluctant to classify offenders as unsuitable simply on the basis that they did not appear to be at risk of imprisonment, believing that it was inappropriate for community service staff to step beyond their responsibilities and pre-empt the decision of the courts. Several schemes would, nevertheless, indicate to the court that an offender was suitable for community service only if he or she would otherwise be imprisoned for the offence ('We should always say in the report that we consider the person suitable if the court was considering a custodial sentence'). One scheme, faced with a high number of seemingly inappropriate referrals, including first offenders convicted of relatively minor offences, was more direct in its approach:

> We would probably draw the court's attention to the fact that we didn't think they should be getting community service because a custodial sentence was not likely in our view. But that wouldn't stop us from saying they are not suitable for community service. Because although we have a policy of alternative to custody we have to bear in mind that the Act does not say that and that we cannot read the court's mind all the time. It would be a sad day if we actually got it wrong because we raised it.

When, on the other hand, it was felt that the offender was clearly at risk of imprisonment, some schemes would make an extra effort to encourage the imposition of a community service order, either by emphasising the offender's suitability ('If he was very likely to be getting a custodial sentence and was very suitable, then I think I would try to sub-paragraph the report as to why I thought he could cope with community service') or by highlighting the likely consequences of a period of imprisonment ('I think I would perhaps dwell more in my report on the effects of a custodial sentence on that individual if it was very likely that they were going to get a custodial sentence').

Several community service schemes, aware of their limited resources, expressed concern that the acceptance by the courts of community service as a sentence in its own right would lead to its overuse and place unacceptable demands upon schemes. As one officer explained:

> I've tried to acquaint sheriffs with the fact that if they are going to use it for obviously non-custodial cases then they are going to kill the scheme because the scheme can't expand to meet that kind of demand.

The increased clarity about the objectives of the community service order as detailed in the national standards was no doubt welcomed by community service staff though, as we shall see later in this chapter, the impact of these guidelines upon sentencers was, at best, minimal.

Tariff escalation

Community service staff were especially concerned about the risk that tariff escalation might occur when offenders were sentenced to community service in place of other non-custodial sentences. As one community service officer commented:

> Recently I have been interviewing offenders who are either very young or appearing before the court for the first or second time. Now if we accept that community service is not for first offenders we have to look pretty closely at these cases and ask why is the sheriff asking for this assessment? We have to be very careful. We don't want to push an offender up the ladder of criminality too quickly.

Staff also perceived a risk that offenders who were not initially sentenced to community service instead of custody might nevertheless be imprisoned if their orders were subsequently revoked:

I don't feel it's right that someone should have the threat of a custodial sentence hanging over them if they weren't going to receive a custodial sentence to start with because in this area when someone has been breached in all except one extreme case they have received a custodial sentence. The person who didn't receive a custodial sentence was a breach that had been outstanding for just over two years and the person had remained out of trouble for these two years and had a full-time job. He got a hefty fine - £900. I don't like to put someone in the position of going to jail if they weren't going in the first place.

The sheriffs interviewed by Carnie (1990) believed that it was possible, in theory, that the imposition of a community service order might have the effect of moving some offenders prematurely up the sentencing tariff. It was also asserted, however, that this was unlikely to occur in practice, especially if, in the event of breach, offenders were dealt with by the sheriff who had imposed the original community service sentence and who was therefore in a position to recall his or her original sentencing intentions. Thus according to one sheriff: 'You go back to the original offence; instantly you would have a clear idea as to whether this was one of the majority of cases, a straight alternative to custody, or whether one of the minority where you thought this might be a useful disposal in its own right' (Carnie, 1990, p. 36). Even if the original sentencer did not deal with the breach it could, argued one High Court Judge, be dealt with appropriately since 'the papers of the case tell you what the reason for the order has been' (Carnie, 1990, p. 36).

There was more risk, it seems, that offenders might be prematurely sentenced to imprisonment on a subsequent court appearance, particularly in the larger courts. Even in the case of breaches, however, most sentencers held the view that imprisonment should be the appropriate response to an offender's failure to comply with an order of the court.

It did appear from the research that some offenders who were breached may have been re-sentenced to periods of imprisonment, even though their community service orders had initially replaced other non-custodial penalties such as fines. The rate of custodial sentencing following breach (65 per cent) was higher than the estimated rate of diversion from custody. However, as Table 7.4 shows, offenders who were assessed as having a high or intermediate risk of custody were more likely to breach their community service orders than offenders whose risk of custody was low ($\chi^2 = 4.2$, 1 d.f., p < .05).

Table 7.4
Outcome of community service order by custody risk

Outcome of order	Custody risk		
	High	Intermediate	Low
Successful completion	116 (84.7%)	17 (85.0%)	141 (92.8%)
Breach	21 (15.3%)	3 (15.0%)	11 (7.2%)

If 60.6 per cent of the high risk, 50.0 per cent of the intermediate risk and 28.8 per cent of the low risk breaches would have been imprisoned if they had not received a community service order, then 49.7 per cent of offenders who were breached for failure to comply were likely to have been diverted from custody when initially sentenced. This figure, while higher than the estimated diversion rate for the entire sample, is 15 per cent lower than the actual rate of custodial sentencing of offenders whose orders were breached, suggesting that in a few cases offenders had subsequently been sentenced to terms of imprisonment even though such a sentence was unlikely when they were initially sentenced to community service.

Informed consent

The precise extent to which community service orders were replacing custodial sentences may be difficult to quantify. It is clear, however, that many of the offenders, and perhaps even more than half, who had been sentenced to community service would not have been imprisoned had this alternative option not been available. This was not the impression gained by the offenders themselves, most of whom (88.6 per cent) believed that their community service orders had been imposed in lieu of custodial sentences. This is consistent with Pease's (1985) observation that 'whenever offenders on community service are asked what sentence they would have received if community service had not been available, they estimate custody more often than is realistic' (p. 70).

The smaller sample who were interviewed explained how they had reached an opinion about which sentence community service had replaced. In most cases (17), and in line with the explanation offered by the National Association of Probation Officers (1977), views had been formed primarily on the basis of comments made in court:

> The judge at the trial recommended custody but it was a different judge when I got sentenced.

> The judge told me when I was getting sentenced, 'I'm thinking about a custodial sentence for you'.

> The sheriff said I would get six months if I didn't complete it. No doubt about it for the offence.

> The judge more or less told me it was my last chance. I've got a big record.

> The sheriff at the time said that if I did re-appear up in front of him that he'd put me in jail. He said he'd better not see me back in court.

> I thought I was going to detention centre for three months. I was asked by the judge if I was prepared to do community service and he told me the alternative was three months detention. So there was no doubt in my mind about what the choice was going to be.

Eight offenders believed that a prison sentence was likely because of the severity of the offence or their previous criminal record:

> My friend was up with me and he was sentenced to detention.

> Because I was up for police assault and if that hadn't been available I'd probably have got put in jail.

> Because of my previous convictions.

Three based their views on information or advice from their solicitors:

> As far as my lawyer was concerned, I could think about going to prison. There would be a very strong possibility. So I had my mind set on that. When I got the community service order I was relieved.

My lawyer said they didn't have enough evidence to put me away. But if they did have enough evidence I would have been imprisoned without being recommended for community service.

These findings raise important questions about the issue of informed consent. Consent clearly cannot be informed if it is based on a misunderstanding of what the alternative would be (though Willis, 1978, has suggested that consent given under the correct fear of imprisonment cannot be real consent). Given the lack of consistency in the use of community service by the courts, community service staff were not in a position to offer a realistic and reliable indication of what sentence the community service order would replace. Had the offenders been made aware of the alternatives it is likely that many would have been less willing to consent to an order being made. Although most offenders appeared to derive some satisfaction from their experience on community service, the fact that it was an onerous and intrusive sanction was not widely disputed and other non-custodial disposals would in many cases have seemed preferable to the discipline and commitment required by community service.

The comparative costs of community service and custody

Consistency and clarity of sentencing practice is clearly desirable if inequities are to be avoided and if consent is to be fully informed. On economic grounds too, there is reason to be concerned about the limited diversionary impact of community service. In their comparative costing of community service and custody, Knapp et al. (1992) estimated that, when both the direct and indirect costs of the alternative sentences were included, community service was not as cheap as is commonly thought. Nevertheless, the cost of an average community service order (at £1044) compared favourably with the equivalent costing of alternative custodial sentences (£2268).

But community service will be a comparatively cheap penal option only if it is used consistently to replace sentences of imprisonment and not if it frequently replaces other less costly non-custodial sanctions, such as fines. There are, therefore, good economic reasons too for ensuring that community service is used, to a greater extent than has hitherto been the case, as an alternative to custodial sentences.

Enhancing consistency of practice

When the Scottish Office introduced national standards for community service schemes, it was with the hope that increased consistency of practice, in ways that were likely to maximise the credibility of community service as a demanding but constructive sentencing option, would, in turn, increase the consistency of its use by the Scottish courts. One sheriff interviewed by Carnie (1990) clearly thought that greater consistency and clarification was required:

> I feel that sentencers are a bit in the dark as to how to apply community service, in particular how many hours to order. I think that's a real difficulty and it would help in a way if there was possibly some standard tariff giving a different scale for solemn and summary cases. Even if that was laid down clearly it would give us some sort of guidance as to what sort of order was thought to be appropriate. What might also help is if some indication were given as to the appropriate alternative if community service wasn't carried out. This is all very difficult to reconcile and I think that these are problems which sentencers are floundering about with.
>
> (Carnie, 1990, p. 38)

The national standards were unlikely in themselves to promote increased consistency of sentencing practice. As Carnie (1990) noted:

> Although every sheriff interviewed claimed to be aware of the 'existence' of the new national standards, only 3 out of the sample of 21 had in their personal possession a copy of the document. And even these 3 sheriffs, while viewing the contents with interest, admitted that they had not devoted any length of time to reading the document assiduously. It's impact, therefore, could not be said to be widespread, or indeed influential, amongst the sentencing fraternity. As one sheriff remarked candidly: 'I don't think the courts to be honest will pay much attention to the national standards. Indeed I wonder if it's appropriate that they should do. The courts are here to administer the law and the law is what is expressed in Acts of Parliament. It doesn't seem appropriate to me that we should start allowing our sentencing policies to be influenced by documents put out by Central Government'.
>
> (Carnie, 1990, pp. 40-41)

Sentencers were equally dismissive of the notion of legislative reforms which would restrict their sentencing options and most sheriffs were 'not fired with much enthusiasm' for judicial guidelines from the High Court (Carnie, 1990, p. 40). The proposition that sentencers be required to state the alternative sentence when imposing a community service order was generally viewed as unnecessary, undesirable and unworkable.

It was against this backdrop of opinion and the recognition by central government that the national standards in themselves would have a limited influence on increasing the courts' use of community service as an alternative to custody that legislative changes were introduced. Section 61 (3) of the Law Reform (Miscellaneous Provisions) (Scotland) Act 1990 amended the original legislative basis of community service in Scotland by requiring that courts impose community service orders only in those cases where they would otherwise sentence the offender to a period of detention or imprisonment. This legislative reform came into effect on 1 April 1991 and it is too early yet to tell what its influence has been. But, as the sheriffs in Carnie's (1990) study indicated, there will always be ways to get round artificial boundaries. The obvious concern is that, in spite of the well-intentioned motives of policy-makers, anomalies might be further perpetrated rather than reduced if some sentencers continue to use community service as they have done in the past.

Summary

In common with previous studies, it was estimated that fewer than half the offenders who were sentenced to community service had been diverted from a sentence of detention or imprisonment. Sentencers confirmed that they did not regard community service exclusively as an alternative to custody. They were likely, nevertheless, unless other factors were presented in mitigation, to impose custodial sentences if offenders were returned to court for failing to comply with the requirements of their community service orders. Although sheriffs thought it unlikely that offenders could be placed prematurely at risk of imprisonment as a consequence of inconsistencies in the use of community service across courts, it did appear in a few cases that tariff escalation was likely to have occurred: more offenders were imprisoned as a result of breach than would have been predicted on the basis of their assessed risk of custody when initially sentenced.

Although fewer than half the sample were likely to have been diverted from custody when their community service orders were imposed, most offenders believed that their orders had replaced a sentence of imprisonment or detention, usually because of comments made by the sentencer in court.

Community service was found to be a less costly option than imprisonment, though not so cheap as is commonly supposed. The relative cheapness of community service would be increased if it were used more consistently as an alternative to custody.

However sentencers were generally opposed to the introduction of various methods which might encourage greater consistency in the use of community service orders, but which would, at the same time, limit their autonomy and discretion. The national standards had had a minimal impact upon sentencing practice and would continue to do so. The legislative changes which were introduced to restrict the use of community service to those offenders who would otherwise receive custodial sentences would not have been welcomed by sheriffs who suggested that ways could be found to side-step legislative reforms.

8 Offenders' experiences and subsequent reconviction

Introduction

The community service order is not generally considered to be an explicitly rehabilitative sanction, although the Advisory Council on the Penal System (1970) was attracted by the possibility that the undertaking of unpaid work might in some instances effect 'a changed outlook on the part of the offender' (Para. 34). Several of the agencies and individuals who had work carried out by offenders from Scottish community service schemes (see Chapter 6) shared the view that the experience of performing unpaid work may have a longer term impact on some individuals' offending behaviour and while most of the sentencers in Carnie's (1990) study regarded punishment and reparation as their primary sentencing objectives when imposing a community service order, it was often suggested that a challenging and constructive placement experience might have a positive impact upon offenders' attitudes and behaviour:

> Working with those less fortunate than themselves, such as the disabled and the handicapped, even for a short time, could give some offenders a fresh perspective on the scope and scale of their own perceived problems. Through helping others their sense of self-worth and self-respect could improve. This was considered vital to the success of any rehabilitative process and was repeatedly endorsed.

One sheriff managed to convey this sentiment rather eloquently, 'from my point of view I am looking for the offender to glimpse his own dignity and for the community to say that it was fitting; that's the ideal'... An inspired placement could have positive effects in helping the offender to complete his order and in the longer term it might even help prevent re-offending.

(Carnie, 1990, p. 30)

Although some authors (e.g. Bucknell, 1980; West, 1976) have emphasised the rehabilitative potential of the community service order, Harland (1980) has argued that 'all claims about its rehabilitative efficacy continue to be perpetrated by impressionistic and anecdotal accounts by judges and probation officers, more than by the results of rigorous evaluation' (p. 457).

Comparatively few studies have examined the impact of community service upon subsequent offending behaviour. Of those that have, most have typically compared recidivism following community service with that following other sentences such as imprisonment. There is no evidence to suggest that community service is any less effective in this respect than the other sentences against which it has been compared. Several studies (e.g. Berk and Feeley, 1990; Bol and Overwater, 1986 - cited in Bishop, 1988; Leibrich, 1984; McDonald, 1986; Schneider, 1986) have shown that offenders ordered to perform unpaid work were no more likely to be re-arrested or reconvicted than those who had been imprisoned or made subject to probation orders while others (e.g. Ervin and Schneider, 1990; Schneider and Schneider, 1985) have found lower levels of recidivism among offenders sentenced to community service.

Two British studies have examined reconviction rates for offenders sentenced to community service orders. In their evaluation of the experimental schemes in England and Wales, Pease et al. (1977) found that approximately 44 per cent of offenders on community service were reconvicted within twelve months compared with 35 per cent of a comparison group who were imprisoned and 31 per cent of a second comparison group who received alternative non-custodial penalties. Since the comparison groups were not, in fact, fully comparable with the community service group (the latter were significantly younger and age was shown to be associated with reconviction) Pease et al. (1977) concluded that 'there was no evidence of any reduction in reconviction rates following community service' (p. 18).

The second study, published by the Home Office (1983), examined reconviction for 'standard list' offences among offenders in England and Wales who were sentenced to community service orders in January and

February 1979. Just over a third (36 per cent) of the sample had been reconvicted within twelve months of their original sentence, 51 per cent had been reconvicted within two years and 59 per cent had at least one further conviction in the three years from the date of imposition of their community service orders. Age was again found to be associated with reconviction, with higher proportions of younger offenders (those under 21 years of age) being reconvicted in each time period. Although no comparative data were available for groups of offenders sentenced to other court disposals, it was suggested that the levels of reconviction after two years were similar to those for corresponding groups of incarcerated offenders in Phillpotts & Lancucki's (1979) study.

These Home Office reconviction studies are now somewhat dated and the distinctive nature of the Scottish criminal justice system - and, in particular, the differing sentencing options available to the courts - prevents any conclusions being reached about the likely level of reconviction following community service in this country. The present chapter describes the rate of reconviction after three years of a sample of 134 offenders who completed their community service orders between September 1987 and May 1988. In the absence of comparative data for similar groups of offenders sentenced to other disposals, the nature and frequency of reconviction before and after sentence are examined.

Previous studies of reconviction have sought to identify the factors which are associated with an increased likelihood or frequency of reconviction, but with few exceptions have failed to explore the relationship between specific features of criminal justice interventions, such as their content and quality, and recidivism. While it is important to ascertain whether a particular sanction influences reconviction, it is equally important to establish why that might be so. A wide range of tasks are undertaken by community service workers in a wide range of settings and work placements with certain features appear to be more rewarding for offenders than others. The extent to which community service has an impact upon reconviction, if at all, might be expected to vary according to the characteristics of work placements in which offenders complete their orders. If a relationship between the characteristics of work placements and reconviction can be identified, then there is greater scope for gaining some insight into the reasons why some offenders are less likely than others to be reconvicted following their community service sentences.

The methods employed in the reconviction study, the sample of offenders on whom it was based and the specific research questions it addressed have been outlined in Chapter 2. The issue of recidivism was, however, first explored in the evaluation of the community service schemes and it is to some of these earlier findings that we first turn.

Predicted likelihood of re-offending

The 136 offenders who returned questionnaires on completion of their community service orders were asked to indicate how likely it was that they would re-offend. Ninety-seven offenders (72.9 per cent of those who responded to this question) said that they were unlikely to commit further offences while 25 (18.8 per cent) thought it fairly likely and 8 (6.0 per cent) considered it very likely that they would re-offend. Three offenders were unsure what the likelihood of their re-offending was.

Some groups of offenders were more likely than others to predict that they would re-offend. Offenders who were subject to some form of statutory social work supervision when sentenced to community service or who had been subject to such supervision in the previous twelve months were more likely than other offenders to indicate that it was either very likely or fairly likely that they would commit further offences (50.0 per cent compared with 20.3 per cent). Similarly, offenders who were known to have problems relating to the use of alcohol when sentenced were more likely than other offenders to predict that they would re-offend (50.0 per cent compared with 21.4 per cent).

Younger offenders (that is, those aged between 16 and 20) were no more likely than older offenders to predict that they would continue to offend. However, offenders who thought that they would re-offend had, on average, more previous convictions than those who thought that further offending was unlikely (7 compared with 4) and first offenders were less likely than those with one or more previous convictions to predict that they would re-offend (4.2 per cent compared with 28.9 per cent).

There was no apparent relationship between the types of placements (team or agency) in which offenders completed their community service orders and their predicted likelihood of re-offending. Nor was the predicted likelihood of re-offending related to the types of work (practical or personal) that the offenders had carried out. It did vary, however, according to how interesting, enjoyable and useful offenders found their placements to be and offenders who believed that they had gained something from being on community service were less likely to predict that they would re-offend than those who felt they had gained nothing from the experience (20.7 per cent compared with 41.2 per cent).

None of the offenders thought that they were more likely to re-offend after completing their community service orders than they were before. Most (65.2 per cent) thought that they were now much less likely to commit further offences and a further 26 (19.7 per cent) believed that they were slightly less likely to do so. Twenty offenders (15.2 per cent) indicated that they were as likely to re-offend as they had been prior to commencing their community service sentence, although six of this group thought it unlikely that they would offend again.

This initial examination of the potential relationship between offenders' experiences on community service and subsequent recidivism provided interesting, if inconclusive, findings. In particular, the causal direction of the relationship between the quality of placement experience and predicted re-offending was unclear. It was possible, that is, that offenders who were, in any case, likely to re-offend were less motivated to gain something from their experience on community service. The possibility, on the other hand, that placements with certain characteristics might have had a positive impact upon offenders' attitudes and behaviour, prompted a more detailed examination of reconviction among this group of offenders.

The rate of reconviction

As previously noted in Chapter 2, reconviction data for up to four years from the date of their original community service sentences were available for the majority (134) of the offenders who had participated in the earlier research. Since complete reconviction data were available for all offenders for the first three years following sentence, most of the analyses were based upon the three year data. Where relevant, however, information relating to reconviction in the fourth year is also reported.

The cumulative percentages who were reconvicted over time are presented in Figure 8.1. Approximately two-fifths (40.3 per cent) of the sample had been reconvicted within twelve months and just under three-fifths (57.5 per cent) had been reconvicted by the end of the second year. After three years, 63.4 per cent had been reconvicted on at least one occasion, and 66.4 per cent were known to have been reconvicted within four years.

It is clear that the likelihood of being first reconvicted was highest in the first two years after sentence and thereafter decreased. Indeed no offenders were reconvicted for the first time between the 43rd and 48th months following the imposition of their community service orders. The period of greatest risk appears to have been in the first six months after sentence, during which time 29.1 per cent of the sample were reconvicted (43.8 per cent of those who were reconvicted at least once in the four-year follow-up period). This figure may, of course, be inflated to an unknown extent (and to a greater extent than in subsequent periods) by the presence of convictions for offences that pre-dated the community service order. However only six offenders who were reconvicted within six months had no further reconvictions during the follow-up period. If it is assumed that each of these six offenders were reconvicted only for old offences, then an adjusted reconviction rate of 59 per cent after three years is achieved, which is not substantially dissimilar from the rate of 63.4 per cent which is based on the assumption that all reconvictions were for offences that were committed after offenders were sentenced to community service.

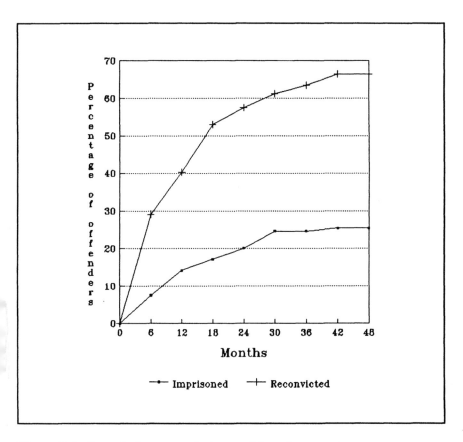

Figure 8.1: Cumulative reconviction and imprisonment

The offenders had an average of 2.4 new convictions for 3.7 offences in the three years after sentence. They were most likely to have reconvictions for offences against public order, such as breaches of the peace and malicious damage (41.8 per cent); offences involving dishonesty, such as housebreakings or thefts (34.3 per cent); offences involving violence (24.6 per cent); and offences against criminal justice (usually breaches of bail - 24.6 per cent). None of the sample were reconvicted of sexual offences and

155

only one was reconvicted of an offence in the firearms/explosives category.

Offenders tended to be reconvicted on only one or two occasions of offences within a given category. This was so, for instance, for 30 of the 46 offenders who were reconvicted of offences involving dishonesty; for 41 of the 56 offenders who were reconvicted of offences against public order; and for 28 of the 33 offenders who were reconvicted of offences involving violence. On the other hand, small numbers of offenders tended to account for the majority of new convictions involving dishonesty and the majority of new convictions for offences against criminal justice. For instance, more than half the new convictions for offences involving dishonesty (71/133) were attributable to nine offenders and four offenders accounted for almost one third (43/133) of convictions in this category.

Offenders were most likely to be first reconvicted for offences involving dishonesty (34.8 per cent of those reconvicted), for breaches of public order (31.5 per cent) or for offences involving violence (16.8 per cent). Two-thirds had been convicted of similar types of offences in the two years prior to sentence. The relationship between previous offences and the type of offence on first reconviction was most marked for offenders first reconvicted of offences involving dishonesty, 83.9 per cent of whom had been previously convicted of a similar type of offence.

The percentages of the sample who had been imprisoned after differing periods of time are also shown in Figure 8.1. Overall, 14.2 per cent of the sample had received a custodial sentence within twelve months and 20.1 per cent had been imprisoned within two years. By the end of the third year, 24.6 per cent of the sample had received at least one custodial sentence and 25.4 per cent were known to have been imprisoned within four years. Almost two-fifths (33) of the 85 offenders who were reconvicted within three years received a custodial sentence during that period.

Offenders were more likely to have been imprisoned on at least one occasion the more quickly they were reconvicted after being made subject to a community service order. Thus half of those who were reconvicted within twelve months received at least one custodial sentence compared with approximately a quarter of those first reconvicted in months 13-24 and only one of the eight offenders who were first reconvicted in the third year after sentence.

Reconviction while completing community service

The offenders whose reconviction data were analysed had been asked in the earlier study to provide details of further convictions and outstanding charges that related to offences that had been committed or that they were alleged to have committed while they were completing their community service orders. Twenty-four admitted to having been reconvicted during this period and 22 had been charged but not yet convicted. Eight offenders claimed to have had both further charges and convictions. In total then, 38 offenders stated that they had either been charged with or convicted of an offence that they had committed or had been accused of committing during their period on community service. Eleven offenders admitted to having been imprisoned before completing their orders.

The reconviction data revealed that 39 offenders (29.1 per cent of the sample) were reconvicted at least once while subject to community service. This group had an average of two convictions and were convicted, on average, of three offences during this period. Most (28) were, however, reconvicted only once or twice. By contrast, more than half of the new convictions that were sustained while offenders were completing their community service orders (43/79) were attributable to eleven offenders. Fifteen offenders were sentenced to periods of imprisonment while undertaking unpaid work for the community.

It is impossible to estimate how many of these new convictions were for offences that were committed while the offender was subject to a community service order and how many were for offences that had been committed prior to the community service order being imposed. Likewise, an unknown number of convictions that were recorded after the order was terminated will have been for offences that were committed while the offender was still completing his or her community service work.

The self-report data provided by the offenders offer no further illumination. Indeed, their unreliability is simply highlighted by the official reconviction data. For instance four of the 24 offenders who said that they had been reconvicted had no further convictions recorded against them in the relevant period. Another 19 offenders who claimed not to have been reconvicted were found to have sustained convictions while completing their orders: whether or not these new convictions were for old (i.e. pre-community service) offences is impossible to determine.

The nature and frequency of conviction before and after community service

The data so far discussed offer no basis for assessing whether the rate, frequency or seriousness of reconviction among the sample were different following their community service sentences than they were before. To do so requires a comparison of the level reconviction, its frequency, the types of offences committed and types of disposals received before and after the offenders were made subject to a community service order.

Relative rate and frequency of reconviction

Overall, the sample were equally likely to be have been convicted in the two years following the imposition of their community service orders (57.5 per cent) and in the two years before (61 per cent). The frequencies of conviction before and after the community service sentence were also comparable, although there was a slight trend towards offenders being less frequently reconvicted over time, especially in the third year following sentence (Table 8.1).

Table 8.1
Average numbers of convictions and offences before
and after community service

	Months				
	13-24 before	0-12 before	0-12 after	13-24 after	25-36 after
Convictions	0.93	0.92	1.00	0.75	0.62
Offences	1.30	1.32	1.47	1.46	0.95

Relative seriousness of offences

It seems, then, that offenders were no more likely to be reconvicted after being sentenced to community service than they were before and there was no evidence that they were convicted more often: if anything, the frequency of conviction was slightly lower after sentence than in the two years before.

There did appear, however, to be a change in the types of offences committed by the sample after being made subject to a community service order. Offenders were less likely to be convicted of offences involving dishonesty, offences involving violence and offences against public order in the three years after being sentenced to community service than in the two years before (including the offences for which the community service orders were imposed). Thus while 68 per cent of the sample had previous convictions for offences involving dishonesty, only 34.4 per cent were convicted of dishonesty offences after being ordered to perform community service (Table 8.2). Likewise, 41 per cent of the sample had at least one prior conviction for an offence involving violence while 23.9 per cent were reconvicted of violent offences in the subsequent three-year period.

Table 8.2
Offences committed before and after community service

Offences	Neither	Before only	After only	Both
Dishonesty	26.1%	39.6%	26.0%	28.4%
Violence	48.5%	27.6%	9.7%	14.2%
Sexual	97.0%	3.0%	-	-
Drugs	94.8%	1.5%	3.0%	0.7%
RTA	70.1%	11.9%	12.7%	5.2%
C.Justice	59.0%	16.4%	14.2%	10.4%
Conduct	38.1%	20.9%	11.9%	29.8%
Fire/explosives	98.5%	0.7%	0.7%	-

n = 134

The change in the percentages convicted of offences against public order was less marked, with 50.8 per cent of offenders having received their community service orders for this type of offence or having had other previous convictions for offences of this nature and 41.7 per cent being reconvicted for offences against public order in the three years after the date on which they were sentenced to community service.

There does appear to have been a trend towards the commission of less serious offences following the imposition of a community service order. Ideally, however, before and after comparisons should be made for similar time periods. Table 8.3 shows the most serious offences committed by the sample in each of the two years before (including the community service conviction) and after being sentenced to community service. In the absence of more specific information, offence seriousness was determined with consideration to the type of offence, the type of court and the type of disposal.

Table 8.3
Most serious offences before and after community service

Offence	Most serious old offence (n = 134)	Most serious new offence (n = 77)
Dishonesty	48.5%	39.0%
Violence	32.1%	28.6%
Sexual	2.2%	-
Drugs	1.5%	2.6%
RTA	4.5%	1.3%
Criminal Justice	4.5%	7.8%
Conduct	6.7%	20.8%
Total	100.0%	100.0%

The data in Table 8.3 suggest that there was indeed some shift towards the commission of less serious offences. Thus while 80.6 per cent of the sample had offences involving dishonesty or violence as their most serious previous offence, these were the most serious types of new offences for only 67.6 per cent of those who were reconvicted within two years, with the decrease in the incidence of dishonesty offences being most marked. Conversely, public order offences, such as breaches of the peace or malicious damage, constituted the most serious previous offences for only 6.7 per cent of the sample, while representing the most serious offences for 20.8 per cent of the offenders who were reconvicted.

Relative severity of sentences

A crude estimate of the relative seriousness of offending prior to and following community service can also be made by comparing the patterns of sentencing before and after the imposition of the orders. The sentences received by the offenders in the two years prior to the community service sentence and in the three years after, which are illustrated in Table 8.4, were broadly similar, except in one significant respect: offenders were more likely to have been imprisoned in the three years after receiving a community service order (24.6 per cent) than in the two years before (14.9 per cent).

Table 8.4
Sentences before and after community service

Sentences	Neither	Before only	After only	Both
Admonished	66.4%	14.2%	14.2%	5.2%
Monetary	29.1%	14.2%	17.9%	38.8%
Probation	88.1%	4.5%	6.7%	0.7%
CSO	87.3%	6.0%	5.2%	1.5%
Custody	67.2%	8.2%	17.9%	6.7%

n = 134

Table 8.5, on the other hand, compares the severity of the sentences received by the sample for convictions in the two years up to (including the community service conviction) and two years after the date on which the community service order was imposed, thereby equating the time period over which the comparisons are made.

The data in Table 8.5 confirm that offenders were more likely to be imprisoned following their community service sentences than before. This could be interpreted as indicating that offenders tended to commit more serious offences after they had been sentenced to community service. Although this may have been true in some cases, the higher incidence of custodial sentences in the follow-up period may also reflect progression up the sentencing tariff, so that a custodial sentence becomes more likely for less serious offences once an offender has been made subject to a community service order.

161

Table 8.5
Severity of sentences before and after community service

	Most severe old sentence (n = 134)	Most severe new sentence (n = 77)
Admonished	-	2.6%
Monetary	-	46.8%
Probation	-	6.5%
CSO	85.1%	2.6%
Custody	14.9%	41.6%
Total	100.0%	100.0%

Although offenders were more likely to be imprisoned in the two years after being sentenced to community service, more than half of those who were reconvicted during that period received sentences less severe than community service or imprisonment. This suggests that in many cases the new convictions were for offences judged to be less serious than those for which these offenders had originally been sentenced to a community service order.

To summarise briefly, there was no evidence that the offenders in the sample were more likely to be reconvicted or were more frequently reconvicted after being sentenced to community service. They were less likely to be reconvicted of more serious offences and more likely to be reconvicted of less serious offences, and although they were more likely to be imprisoned following community service than before, most of those who were reconvicted were, at worst, placed on probation or community service, admonished, given compensation orders or fined.

Factors associated with reconviction

Previous studies (e.g. Pease et al., 1977; Phillpotts and Lancucki, 1979) have identified a relationship between reconviction and certain characteristics of offenders, such as age and previous criminal history. Before the association between features of the community service sentence and reconviction is examined, the relationships between the personal characteristics of offenders, their previous offences and sentences and the rate and frequency of reconviction in the three years after being sentenced to community service are explored.

Personal characteristics and reconviction

In common with previous studies, the likelihood of reconviction was found to be related to the age of the offender when sentenced. Offenders who were reconvicted were, on average, younger than those who had no further convictions (21.8 years compared with 26.6 years; $t = 13.6$, $p < .001$). Offenders who were under 21 years of age were most likely to be reconvicted and those aged 30 years or older were least likely to be reconvicted in the three years after being sentenced to community service (Table 8.6).

Table 8.6
Reconviction and age

	16-17	18-20	21-30	30+
			Age	
% reconvicted[*]	76.2	77.1	54.5	38.1
Average number of reconvictions	5.2	3.7	3.5	1.9

[*] $\chi^2 = 12.6$, 2 d.f., $p < .01$

Although 16 and 17 year olds were as likely as 18-20 year olds to have been convicted at least once, the younger offenders tended, on average, to have more new convictions during the three-year follow-up period. The difference between the different age-groups in the frequency of reconviction was not, however, statistically reliable though the weak negative correlation between the frequency of reconviction and age ($r = -.22$) suggests that as the age of the offender increased, the number of convictions they sustained during the follow-up period tended to decrease.

The small number of females (six) in the sample precluded a detailed analysis of the relationship between reconviction and gender. Marital status and employment history were, however, associated with reconviction. Single offenders were more likely to have been reconvicted than offenders who were married, co-habiting, separated or divorced (70.2 per cent vs. 52.0 per cent; $\chi^2 = 3.7$, 1 d.f., p = .05) and offenders who had no previous employment experience were found to have, on average, more new convictions than those who were employed when the order was made or who had had some employment experience in the past (7.0 vs. 3.4; t = 6.7, p < .02).

Offenders who had a history of statutory social work supervision, either as an adult or a child, were more likely than other offenders to be reconvicted within three years of being sentenced to community service. Whether offenders were reconvicted and how often they were reconvicted was also related to how recently they had been subject to statutory social work involvement as a result of their offending. Thus while 42.1 per cent of those with no prior social work supervision were reconvicted, this was true of 77.8 per cent of those whose most recent period of supervision had been more than two years prior to the imposition of their orders and 94.4 per cent of those who were subject to statutory supervision when sentenced or who had been subject to such supervision in the preceding two years ($\chi^2 = 19.4$, 2 d.f., p < .001).

Offenders who had a recent or current social work involvement (such as probation or supervision through the children's hearing system) were, in addition, more frequently reconvicted: the average of 6.5 new convictions among this group compares with an average of 3.3 convictions for offenders whose social work involvement was less recent and 3.2 convictions for offenders who had never been subject to statutory supervision by the social work department (f = 3.5, 2,51 d.f., p < .05).

It will be recalled that when questioned four years previously about their likelihood of re-offending, offenders who were known to be experiencing alcohol-related problems when sentenced were more likely to predict that they would re-offend. There was found to be a slight, though not significant, association between alcohol abuse and reconviction. Offenders who were known to have alcohol-related problems when sentenced to community service were somewhat more likely to be reconvicted on at least one occasion in the three years after sentence (80.0 per cent vs. 60.0 per cent; $\chi^2 = 2.1$, 1 d.f., p = .15)

Criminal history and reconviction

Reconviction was also found to be associated with a number of factors related to the offenders' criminal histories and most notably with the level of previous convictions in the two years prior to sentence (Table 8.7)

Table 8.7
Previous convictions and reconviction

	Previous Convictions			
	0	1	2-4	5+
% reconvicted[*]	39.2	70.4	75.6	100.0
Average number of reconvictions	2.4	3.5	3.8	5.6

* $\chi^2 = 24.7$, 3 d.f., $p < .001$

Offenders who were reconvicted had more previous convictions in the two years prior to their community service sentences than those who were not (2.5 vs. 0.6; $t = 20.0$, $p < .001$). Both the likelihood of reconviction and the number of new convictions increased the higher the number of convictions the offenders had sustained in the two years preceding the community service order. Indeed, all of the 15 offenders who had five or more previous convictions were reconvicted within three years of being sentenced to community service and this group were reconvicted more often, on average, than offenders who had four or fewer convictions in the preceding two-year period (5.6 new convictions compared with 3.3; $t = 4.4$, $p < .05$).

The risk of reconviction was also related to how recently offenders had been convicted prior to being sentenced to community service: the shorter the gap between the community service conviction and the most recent previous conviction, the greater the likelihood of reconviction. Thus 88.6 per cent of offenders who were convicted six months or less prior to their community service sentence were reconvicted, compared with 71.4 per cent of those most recently convicted between seven and twelve months prior to sentence, 61.7 per cent of those most recently convicted between 13 and 24 months prior to sentence and 39.2 per cent of those with no convictions in the two years prior to their community service orders being imposed ($\chi^2 = 25.6$, 3 d.f., p < .001).

The likelihood of offenders being reconvicted also varied according to their previous sentencing histories. Offenders who had previously been sentenced to community service were more likely than other offenders to be reconvicted (100 per cent vs. 60.6 per cent; $\chi^2 = 4.6$, 1 d.f., p < .05) and offenders who had served at least one custodial sentence in the two years prior to their community service sentence were more likely than others to be reconvicted on at least one occasion in the following three years (95.0 per cent vs. 57.9 per cent; $\chi^2 = 8.6$, 1 d.f., p < .01).

Reconviction appeared to be largely unrelated to the types of offences for which offenders were sentenced to community service and to the types of offences for which they had sustained convictions in the past. However, offenders with one or more previous convictions for criminal justice offences (primarily breaches of bail) were more likely than other offenders to be reconvicted in the three years after being sentenced to community service ($\chi^2 = 6.4$, 1 d.f., p < .02).

Offenders who received their community service orders for an offence or offences committed in the company of one or more co-accused had a higher number of new convictions than those who had committed the offence/s which resulted in the imposition of their community service orders alone (5.0 vs. 2.7; t = 7.8 p < .01). Finally, offenders who had been sentenced to community service under summary proceedings had slightly more new convictions in the follow-up period than did those who had been sentenced under solemn proceedings in the Sheriff Court (3.9 vs. 1.8; t = 2.7, p = .10).

The factors identified here as being associated with reconviction are broadly similar to those identified in previous studies of reconviction following a range of sentences. Younger offenders and those with more extensive and serious criminal histories were most likely to be reconvicted and tended also to be reconvicted more often. The relationship between reconviction and other variables, such as marital status, employment history and offending-related social work supervision has been less frequently examined. The association between risk of reconviction and marital status most likely reflects the fact that younger offenders were more likely to be single. The younger offenders in the sample were also more likely to have had no prior work experience when they were sentenced to community service.

The association between reconviction and a recent statutory social work involvement could easily be misinterpreted as indicating that social work intervention makes people more likely to re-offend! A more likely explanation is that these offenders had been made subject to such statutory social work involvement precisely because their risk of re-offending was deemed to be high and they had been identified as experiencing a range of social or personal problems which were contributing directly or indirectly to their offending behaviour. For example although the number of offenders who experienced accommodation problems while completing their community service orders was small, this group were, on average, more often reconvicted in the three years after sentence (7.6 times compared with 3.4 times; $t = 5.6$, $p < .05$).

It is not immediately obvious why offenders who were convicted alone were less often reconvicted than those who had been convicted along with one or more co-accused. However, offenders who had co-accused were younger than those who had offended alone (22.1 years compared with 24.9 years; $t = 4.44$, $P < .05$) and were more likely to be under 21 years of age when sentenced (63.8 per cent compared with 41.4 per cent of those who were convicted alone; $\chi^2 = 5.49$, 1 d.f., $p < .02$).

Persistent offenders: a profile

The offenders sustained a total of 318 convictions in the three years after being sentenced to community service, more than half of which (163 or 51.2 per cent) were amassed by only 15 individuals. Three offenders had 14, 18 and 19 new convictions respectively in the follow-up period and two others had been reconvicted 13 times. Most (11/15) of these more persistent offenders (that is, those with seven or more further convictions) had been reconvicted within six months of being sentenced to community service and all had been reconvicted within 18 months. Each offender in this group was reconvicted on at least one occasion for offences involving dishonesty and most had further convictions for offences against public order (14), criminal justice offences (12), offences involving violence (11) and road traffic offences (9). Ten were sentenced to at least one custodial sentence in the three year follow-up period. What, then, distinguishes this group of more persistent offenders from other offenders who were reconvicted less frequently or who had no further convictions at all?

The relevant comparative data, which are summarised in Table 8.8, suggest that persistent offenders were significantly younger than others in the sample and more likely to be single, to have been subject to some form of statutory social work supervision in the previous two years and to have experienced personal problems while completing their community service orders. They had, on average, more previous convictions in the two years prior being sentenced to community service and were more likely to have served at least one previous custodial sentence. This group were also more likely than other offenders to have previous convictions for offences against criminal justice (largely breaches of bail) and were most likely on completing their community service orders to have thought it probable that they would re-offend.

Table 8.8
Offenders characteristics and number of reconvictions

| | Number of new convictions | | |
	0	1-6	7-19
Average age (years)[1]	26.6	22.5	18.9
16-20 years[1]	16/49	41/70	12/15
Single[2]	25/49	46/70	13/15
Unemployed	33/49	54/70	14/15
No employment experience	2/49	4/70	4/15
Male	46/49	68/49	14/15
Current/recent SW sup.[1]	1/38	10/42	7/12
Family problems during CS[2]	4/48	8/68	5/15
Accomm. problems during CS	-	2/67	3/12
Average no. of PCs[1]	0.6	2.3	3.7
Previous custody[1]	1/49	14/70	5/15
Previous CJ offences[1]	4/49	24/70	8/15
Likely to re-offend[1]	4/47	20/68	7/14

[1] $p < .01$ [2] $p < .05$

The profile which emerges, then, is of a young, single, unemployed male with several previous convictions, including breaches of bail, and other family or personal problems who commits a variety of offences and is either unmotivated or unable at least in the short term to change his pattern of offending behaviour.

Offenders' experiences of community service and reconviction

The reconviction study was prompted by the earlier finding that offenders' predictions of how likely it was they would re-offend varied according to how rewarding they had found their experience of performing unpaid work to be. The present section, therefore, examines the relationship between reconviction and the offenders' experiences of community service.

The likelihood and frequency of reconviction were unrelated to the types of placements (group or agency) in which the offenders completed their orders and the types of work (practical or personal) that they performed. There was, however, a relationship between subsequent reconviction and extent to which offenders had found community service to be worthwhile. The offenders who had found community service to be very worthwhile had, on average, fewer new convictions (2.9 compared with 4.6; $t = 4.4$, $p < .05$) and were slightly less likely to be reconvicted (56.9 per cent vs. 70.5 per cent; $\chi^2 = 2.1$, 1 d.f., $p = .15$) those who had found it less worthwhile or not worthwhile at all.

It is possible, of course, that those offenders who most valued their experience of community service differed from other offenders in other important respects and that these differences, rather than the perceived quality of the community service experience, may have accounted for these differences in reconviction.

The two groups were, indeed, found to differ in terms of age (those who found community service to have been more worthwhile were more likely to be aged 21 or over) and marital status (single offenders were under-represented in the group who believed community service to have been very worthwhile). Neither of these variables were, however, significantly related to how often people were reconvicted in the three years after being sentenced to community service. The apparent relationship between the quality of experience and frequency of reconviction cannot, it seems, be wholly attributable to other mediating factors.

Although the likelihood of reconviction was not strongly related to how much offenders had valued their experiences of unpaid work, some sub-groups of offenders were less likely to have been reconvicted if they had found community service to be very worthwhile. Offenders who were unemployed when sentenced to community service were less likely to be reconvicted if they had found community service to be very worthwhile than if they had found it less worthwhile or not worthwhile at all (56.9 per cent vs. 91.9 per cent; $\chi^2 = 5.3$, 1 d.f., $p < .05$) and offenders with a history of statutory social work supervision were less likely to be reconvicted the more rewarding they had found community service to be (66.7 per cent vs. 91.9 per cent; $\chi^2 = 5.8$, 1 d.f., $p < .01$). Offenders who were married, co-habiting, separated or divorced were, similarly, less likely to have been reconvicted if they had viewed their experiences of community service as being very worthwhile (56.9 per cent vs. 81.0 per cent; $\chi^2 = 5.3$, 1 d.f., $p < .05$).

169

In addition to there being an association between offenders' experiences of community service and their subsequent levels of reconviction, the types of offences committed by the sample in the three years after being sentenced also differed according to how worthwhile they had believed community service to have been. Offenders who had found their experience of community service to be very worthwhile were substantially less likely than other offenders to be reconvicted of offences involving dishonesty (39.0 per cent vs. 69.8 per cent; $\chi^2 = 6.8$, 1 d.f., p<.01) even though they were as likely as these other offenders to have received their community service orders for dishonesty offences (46.3 per cent vs. 53.5 per cent) or to have had convictions for such offences in the two years prior to being sentenced to community service (73.2 per cent vs. 74.4 per cent).

How well are offenders able to predict whether they will re-offend?

Offenders with higher numbers of previous convictions, those with a recent history of statutory social work supervision and those who were known to have alcohol-related problems when sentenced to community service were more likely on completing their community service orders to have predicted that they would re-offend. Each of these factors was subsequently found to be associated, though not always strongly, with the likelihood or frequency of reconviction. How well, then, were offenders able to predict whether they would re-offend?

Table 8.9 shows a clear relationship between offenders' earlier predictions and their subsequent rate and frequency of reconviction. Each of the eight offenders who believed that they were very likely to re-offend were reconvicted, and they were convicted on a significantly higher number of occasions than the other offenders in the sample. The majority of the 23 offenders who considered it fairly likely that they would re-offend were reconvicted on at least one occasion and, while they were reconvicted less frequently than those who believed themselves very likely to re-offend they had, on average, more new convictions than those who had suggested that further offending was unlikely.

The group who appear to have been least accurate in their predictions were those who indicated that it was unlikely that they would re-offend. Some of these offenders may have been overly optimistic in their original predictions while others may simply have been unwilling to admit in the earlier study that they were likely to re-offend.

Table 8.9
Actual reconviction and predicted likelihood of re-offending

	Likelihood of re-offending		
	Very	Fairly	Not at all
% reconvicted[1]	100.0	82.6	56.1
Average number of reconvictions[2]	7.1	4.4	3.0

[1] $p < .01$
[2] $p < .02$

In any case, it does appear that offenders' self-predictions can usefully serve as broad indicators of the likelihood and frequency of later offending behaviour as evidenced by official reconviction data. The implications of this finding will be considered in the concluding chapter.

Some methodological issues

There are certain inherent limitations associated with the use of official conviction data which are common to all reconviction studies. Mair and Nee (forthcoming) provide a useful rehearsal of some of these problems. An issue more specific to the present study concerns the generalisability of the findings in view of the relatively small sample size and the lack of complete comparability of the sample with the larger group of offenders from which it was drawn. Although the two groups were comparable across a range of personal characteristics and were indistinguishable in terms of a range of criminal justice variables (for further details see McIvor, 1992a), offenders who were breached were under-represented in the present sample. This is of particular significance in light of the Home Office's (1983) finding that offenders whose community service orders were breached were more likely to be reconvicted than those whose orders were successfully completed.

Owing to the small numbers of offenders who had been breached for failure to comply, it did not prove possible in the present study to examine the relationship between reconviction and the final outcomes of orders. There was, however, found to be an association between offenders' compliance with the requirements of their community service orders and both the likelihood and frequency of reconviction. Offenders who were reconvicted had sustained more unacceptable and acceptable absences while completing their community service orders than those with no new convictions in the follow-up period (1.9 vs. 0.7 unacceptable absences; $t=5.3$, $p<.05$: 3.7 vs. 2.1 acceptable absences; $t=4.9$, $p<.05$). Likewise, offenders who had one or more unacceptable absences from placement were more likely to have been reconvicted on at least one occasion (78.2 per cent vs. 53.2 per cent; $\chi^2= 7.7$, 1 d.f., $p<.01$) and were, on average, reconvicted more often (4.7 vs. 2.8; $t=5.6$, $p<.05$) than offenders who had none. It seems likely, then, that had the sample contained a more typical proportion of offenders who had been breached for failure to comply with the requirements of their community service orders, a slightly high rate of reconviction would have been achieved.

Summary

Although most offenders thought it unlikely that they would re-offend, just over three-fifths were reconvicted and around a quarter were imprisoned in the three years after being sentenced to community service. Slightly fewer than a third were reconvicted while completing their community service orders.

Offenders tended to be reconvicted for the first time of offences similar to those for which they had been convicted in the two years prior to receiving their community service sentence. Most of those who were reconvicted were reconvicted at most on two occasions: a small number of persistent offenders accounted for the majority of new convictions. Offenders tended to be reconvicted of less serious offences, though they were more likely to be imprisoned following community service.

As in other studies, the risk of reconviction decreased with age and increased linearly with the number of convictions in the two years prior to sentence. Offenders were more likely to be reconvicted the shorter the gap between their community service sentence and their most recent previous court appearance.

The rate and frequency of reconviction were highest among offenders who were already subject to some other statutory order when sentenced or who had been subject to statutory supervision by the social work department in the previous two years. Single offenders were more likely to be reconvicted and offenders who had no prior work experience were more often reconvicted in the three year follow-up period.

Offenders who had previous convictions for criminal justice offences (mainly breaches of bail) were more likely to have been reconvicted. This was also true of offenders who had been sentenced to community service or who had received a custodial sentence in the recent past.

The small number of offenders who were repeatedly reconvicted in the three years after being sentenced to community service were distinguishable in a number of ways from those who were not reconvicted or who were reconvicted less often.

Offenders whose experiences of community service had been particularly rewarding were less often reconvicted and fewer were reconvicted of offences involving dishonesty, such as burglaries and thefts. The quality of community service appears to have been most significant for certain offenders who had perhaps had less opportunity than others to make a valued contribution to their communities in the past.

Offenders, it appeared, had been reasonably well able to judge how likely they were to re-offend. Those who had earlier believed they would probably re-offend were most likely to have been reconvicted and were reconvicted more often than other offenders in the sample.

9 Progress and prospects

Community service: what has been achieved?

Reflecting on the first five years of community service in England and Wales, Baroness Wootton acknowledged that the new penal option had 'caught on much better' than she had dared hope (Wootton, 1977, p.110). She was, nonetheless, reluctant to assume that the apparent popularity of the community service order would, in the longer term, inevitably be sustained:

> Fashions in sentencing come and go; and it will largely be the recommendations of probation officers which determine whether the rising popularity of community service is just a flash in the pan, or whether this new sentence becomes a powerful and lasting addition to our armoury.
>
> (Wootton, 1977, p.112)

Similar concerns were expressed by Hood (1974), who questioned whether community service could 'have in the long run - after the initial impetus generated by the new scheme - more than a symbolic appeal' (p. 417). It is clear, almost twenty years on, that community service has been more than a 'flash in the pan' with exclusively symbolic appeal, but has become firmly established among the repertoire of sentences available to

British courts. Community service orders were imposed for 7 per cent of indictable offences in England and Wales in 1989, compared with only 3 per cent ten years earlier (Home Office, 1990a). Although the use of community service had dipped in 1989 (to just over 34,000 orders), there was a substantial increase in the number of orders imposed the following year (37,490), this rise being attributed, at least in part, to the introduction of national standards in April 1989 (Lloyd, 1991). While the use of community service relative to other disposals has been lower in Scotland than in England and Wales, the numbers of orders made by the Scottish courts has increased steadily since this sentencing option was introduced, from 220 orders in 1979 to 4,190 orders in 1989, in which year community service orders were imposed upon 2.3 per cent of persons against whom a charge was proved (Social Work Services Group, 1990). This increase can be partly accounted for by the incremental development of community service in Scotland, with additional schemes being developed each year. The more dramatic increases in recent years, however, (from 3,351 orders in 1988 to 4,520 in 1990) reflect the increased availability of orders in existing schemes following the introduction of 100 per cent funding for community service by the Scottish Office.

In 1986, community service was described by the Council of Europe as 'probably the most progressive alternative measure introduced in European criminal law in the last ten years, the one which seems to offer the most possibilities and the one which raises the most hopes among experts'. The widespread appeal of the community service order with the courts has been attributed to its supposed ability to encompass a variety of penal philosophies (Advisory Council on the Penal System, 1970; Carnie, 1990; Carnie and McIvor, 1991; Prison Reform Trust, 1988) even though, as Wootton (1978) notes, the Council's 'undisguised attempt to curry favour with everyone' (p. 128), of which she confesses to being somewhat ashamed, has also been widely criticised (e.g. Hood, 1974; Pease, 1985).

Notwithstanding such confusion about its underlying penal philosophy, it is clear from the research described in this book that various policy objectives associated with the community service order in Scotland have, in large measure, been achieved.

Benefit to the community

In his call for increased clarity about the purpose that the community service order is intended to fulfil, Pease (1985) has argued that the sentencing objectives should be defined in strictly retributive terms. As such, he suggests that 'the touchstone of success of the community service order would be the recognition by all concerned of the usefulness of the work being done and feelings of reconciliation resulting from the work' (p. 60).

The survey of beneficiaries, reported in Chapter 6, amply demonstrated that in most instances the work performed by offenders on community service orders was highly valued by the beneficiaries, whether they were individual members of the public or agencies that provided a range of services to their local communities. Most recipients were happy with the standard of work, believed it to have been of considerable benefit to them, and were willing to make further use of their local community service schemes. The quality of supervision of team placements was reported to be high and agency staff were generally happy with the support they received from their local scheme when supervising offenders on community service placements. Agencies often benefited in the longer term when offenders continued to attend their placements as paid workers or, more usually, as volunteers after completing their community service orders. There is no doubt too that, in many instances, beneficiaries' preconceived or stereotyped views of offenders will have been altered, in a positive direction, by their experiences.

Other studies that have examined agencies' experiences of offering placements to community service offenders have produced comparable findings (Godson, 1980; Leibrich et al., 1984b; Allen and Treger, 1990; Berk and Feeley, 1990). In Berk and Feeley's (1990) study, for example, only ten per cent of agencies were found to be unsatisfied with work that had been carried out. Similarly, Allen and Treger (1990) found that agencies were satisfied with the performance of offenders in 87 per cent of cases. In 27 per cent of cases the response of offenders on community service was described as better than that of volunteers; in a further 57 per cent of cases the offenders' performance was said to equal that of other volunteers. Eighty-eight per cent of the community service sponsors in Leibrich et al.'s (1984b) study indicated that their organisation had benefited directly from the work that had been carried out. Just under two-thirds of the offenders in Allen and Treger's (1990) study had continued to be associated with their placement agency by performing some type of voluntary work while this was true of 22 per cent of offenders in the research conducted by Leibrich et al. in New Zealand.

Because the costing of unpaid work by offenders creates technical difficulties (the tasks undertaken are intended to be those which would not otherwise be done, raising questions about their market value) no attempt was made to attach a financial value to the work that had been carried out. Nevertheless, the economic benefits are clearly large. McDonald (1986), for instance, estimated that in 1982 the Vera Institute community service project in New York provided services to the community worth

176

between $119,000 to $160,000. The same project was estimated in 1990 to have contributed services to the value of $350,000 (Center for Alternative Sentencing and Employment Services, 1991).

Although the benefits are evident, there are associated costs. Some agencies, for example, referred to the extra burden placed upon staff when required to oversee the activities of offenders on community service orders. As other studies (Godson, 1980; Leibrich et al., 1984b) have similarly found, absenteeism was highlighted as a problem by several agencies: it could be a source of frustration for staff and required liaison with the local community service scheme which could divert staff time from other important activities. The negotiation and arrangement of placements placed further demands upon agency resources but was recognised by many agencies as essential for a successful placement to be achieved.

The possibility of offending against the beneficiaries is an ever-present risk, and was the explanation most often offered by agencies for excluding offenders who had been convicted of particular types of crimes. Fortunately, though, the actual incidence of offending in placements was low, especially in work teams where, as a rule, closer supervision could be provided.

In general, then, it appears that the benefits to the recipients of unpaid work by offenders on community service outweighed the costs. Individual beneficiaries and agencies also recognised the potential value of community service to the offenders. Community service was thought by some to enhance offenders' self-esteem, improve their social skills and increase their self-reliance and responsibility. Several suggested that a community service order was more likely than a prison sentence to effect a positive change in offenders' attitudes and behaviour.

Benefit to the offenders

As in other studies (e.g. Polonoski, 1980; Thorvaldson, 1978; Varah, 1981) most offenders sentenced to community service found their orders to be a constructive and rewarding experience. Most considered the work interesting and enjoyable and believed that it would be of benefit to the recipients. Many offenders acquired new practical or interpersonal skills or improved upon those they already possessed and most felt that they had gained something from being on community service and that their experience had been worthwhile. Half of those interviewed expressed a willingness in principle to continue their work on a voluntary basis after completing their orders, though in some instances to do so was impractical.

At the same time, it is clear that for most offenders community service was no soft option. Even though their experiences of performing unpaid work had been generally positive, offenders still acknowledged community service to have been an intrusive and demanding sentence. References were made to the length of time over which a commitment had to be sustained and to the limitations that an order placed upon their leisure time.

No clear preferences emerged with regard to the types of settings in which offenders performed their community service work or the broad characteristics (practical or personal) of the tasks carried out. However, offenders most valued placements which maximised their contact with the beneficiaries, which enabled them to gain new skills and which allowed them to engage in work that they could recognise as being of benefit to the recipients. The importance of the offenders' relationships with their placement supervisors was also stressed.

Group and agency placements offered different, but equally valued, experiences to offenders. Team placements were more often regarded as offering work which was skilful and which was of direct benefit to the recipients. Agency placements, on the other hand, were more likely to bring offenders into contact with the beneficiaries of their work. If anything, practical placements in voluntary or statutory agencies were viewed by offenders as least rewarding. Practical agency placements were more likely than personal ones to involve offenders in relatively unskilled and unchallenging tasks. Offenders who completed their community service orders in placements of this type were less well integrated with agency staff and were less likely to have been brought into contact with those individuals or groups for whom the agency's services were provided.

There appeared to be a relationship between the quality of offenders' experiences on community service and the frequency and nature of reconviction in the three years after their orders were imposed. Offenders were less often reconvicted if they had found community service to be particularly worthwhile and this group were less likely to have been reconvicted of offences involving dishonesty, such as burglaries and thefts. The findings from the reconviction study contrasted with Phillpotts and Lancucki's (1979) observation that 'offenders are likely to 'turn to' theft if they continue their criminal career' (p. 35).

While necessarily speculative, some tentative explanations for these findings can be offered. Perhaps, as the Wootton Committee (Advisory Council on the Penal System, 1970) implied, contact with those who are more disadvantaged than themselves may put into perspective the offenders' own problems and circumstances and provide them with increased insight into the practical and emotional consequences of their offending upon other people. If this is true, a greater impact would be expected upon premeditated crimes which result in injury or loss to the victim (and certain offences involving dishonesty fall most readily into this category) and less upon offences which are committed upon impulse or which have no readily identifiable victim.

Community service might have had an influence upon reconviction in other ways. Offenders' self-confidence and self-esteem may have been enhanced through the development of practical and interpersonal skills and through the knowledge that they had made a valued contribution to their local communities, and especially to those in need. A similar explanation was offered by Ervin and Schneider (1990) to account for lower levels of recidivism among juveniles who participated in restitution programmes. Personal development and the experience of being valued will be particularly significant for those offenders who are lacking in confidence at the outset and who have had little or no opportunity to contribute in a positive way to their communities in the past. In addition, the opportunity to continue their work on a voluntary basis, and in so doing develop an additional interest, may have made crime a less attractive option for some offenders and encouraged them to lead a more law-abiding life.

The practical implications of these findings are three-fold. First, the data reinforce the importance of community service schemes making available work placements which will be construed by offenders as being rewarding and worthwhile. Such placements are characterised by high levels of contact with the beneficiaries, by work which is skilful and by tasks which offenders can readily identify as being of benefit to those in need. They are associated with lower levels of absenteeism and are more likely to lead, in the longer-term, to reductions in the frequency of reconviction and to changes in the types of offences for which offenders are subsequently reconvicted. Brief questionnaires, completed by offenders at the end of their orders, would enable schemes to monitor the quality of placement provision and ensure that the value of community service, both to the beneficiaries and to the offenders, is maintained. Schemes should think seriously about whether they wish to make continued use of placements which may be of benefit to the recipients of the work, but which are experienced by offenders as unrewarding, isolating and lacking in interest.

Second, there was some evidence, albeit from a small sample, that offenders who experienced personal or social problems while completing their orders had more absences from placement and were more often reconvicted in the three years after sentence. This is consistent with a growing body of research (e.g. Byrne, 1990; Erwin, 1990; McIvor, 1992b; Raynor, 1988) which suggests that offenders are more likely to re-offend if problems which are associated directly or indirectly with their offending

179

behaviour are not adequately resolved. The importance of offenders on community service having access, as necessary, to assistance with a range of practical and personal difficulties has been stressed by McIvor (1991b) and by McWilliams (1989).

This is not, however, a plea for the increased 'probationisation' of community service for this would, as McWilliams and Pease (1980) predicted, almost certainly reduce its credibility with the courts and lead to even greater inconsistency in its use. Equity is more likely to be achieved if community service is clearly recognised as a tariff measure where the number of hours ordered is commensurate with the seriousness of the offence, rather than as a sentence in its own right whose use is influenced by perceptions of need. But the social work values which underpin work with offenders (Bottoms, 1989; Harris, 1989) should be articulated in the day-to-day operation of community service schemes. Offenders should be given the opportunity to maximise their potential in ways which preserve, or better still, enhance their dignity and self-respect.

Third, the reconviction study revealed that offenders' predictions of future offending could serve as broad indicators of their rate and frequency of reconviction. The application of this method both to practice and to research merits further exploration. In a research context it might, at the very least, enable the relationship between predicted re-offending and other outcome measures, such as a reduction in the incidence and severity of personal and other problems, to be examined. Were the method found to be sufficiently reliable, it could be adopted by practitioners at the outset and conclusion of intervention to obtain useful feedback about the effectiveness of the services they have provided.

The absence of a comparison group prevented the examination of reconviction following community service with that following other sentences though some limited comparison with other studies is possible. Pease et al. (1977) concluded that community service was no less effective than other sentences (custodial and otherwise) with respect to reconviction. A similar conclusion was reached by the Home Office (1983) whose reconviction rates for standard list offences were only slightly lower than the more broadly based reconviction figures reported here.

Phillpotts and Lancucki (1979) found that approximately 63 per cent of offenders who received an immediate custodial sentence (including detention centre and borstal) in 1971 had been reconvicted of standard list offences within four years. Sixty-eight per cent of the offenders who attended the Hereford and Worcester Probation Service Young Offender Project were reconvicted within two years (Roberts, 1989) and, on average, 63 per cent of offenders attending day centres in England and Wales had at least one new conviction in the two years following sentence (Mair and

Nee, forthcoming).

The reconviction rates reported in Chapter 8 appear to compare favourably with those obtained in these other recent studies. However, the offenders in the present sample had, on the basis of their previous sentencing histories, a lower risk of reconviction than the offenders whose reconviction data were examined in the research by Roberts (1989) and by Mair and Nee (forthcoming). It might tentatively be concluded that reconviction is, overall, at least no worse following community service than following other sentences. But before any definitive conclusions can be reached about the relative effectiveness in this respect of community service and other sentences, carefully conducted analyses of reconviction among comparable groups of offenders will be required.

It is easy to fall prey to the allure of reconviction statistics and to over-estimate their significance. Community service is not an expressly rehabilitative sanction and to judge its success solely or substantially on this basis can be misleading and unfair. Such analyses are particularly dangerous when attempted on a global scale. Witness the widespread abandonment of rehabilitative aspirations following the over-simplistic conclusions of Martinson (1974) and others in the 1970s. Fortunately, researchers are now becoming increasingly sensitised to the need to ask not simply whether a particular sentencing option 'works' but to define effectiveness more broadly and explore, as this book has done, under which circumstances and for which offenders it works best.

Diversion from custody

The limited diversionary impact of the community service order has, perhaps, proved the greatest source of disappointment. As in previous studies (e.g. Pease et al., 1977) fewer than half the community service orders imposed were estimated to have replaced sentences of detention or imprisonment. The differing views among probation staff and among sentencers about whether community service should be reserved as an alternative to a custodial sentence have been well documented. Such divergence of opinion is understandable in view of the discrepancy between the government's apparent intentions and the legislation which was subsequently introduced.

Neither is this confusion in purpose and in practice limited to community service. The suspended sentence in England and Wales functions as an alternative to imprisonment in around the same percentage of cases as does the community service order (Bottoms, 1981, 1987; Sparks, 1971). The limited diversionary impact of so-called alternatives to custody has been attributed, at least in part, to the rather tortured logic that the imposition of such sentences requires (e.g. Pease, 1985). First the court must decide that a custodial sentence is the only realistic option in a particular case. Then the sentencer must consider whether, having decided that imprisonment is necessary, an alternative non-custodial sanction can be imposed.

It also appears that sentencers are keen to impose community service orders across a broader spectrum of cases because of the limited range of non-custodial disposals available and because community service, through its ability to combine a number of sentencing objectives, has a certain intuitive appeal (Carnie, 1990). Nevertheless, it appears that lack of consistency in the use of community service by the courts can, in some instances, disadvantage offenders by placing them at risk of a custodial sentence earlier in their offending careers.

Several options have been identified which, it has been argued, might lead to greater consistency in the way in which the community service order is used. Pease (1978), for instance, proposed the introduction of a split tariff in which orders with smaller numbers of hours could serve as alternatives to fines and longer orders could replace prison sentences of differing lengths. Alternatively, sentencers might be required, as in the Republic of Ireland, to indicate at the point of sentence, what community service had replaced so that this information could be available to sentencers if the offender was breached or subsequently re-appeared in court on a further occasion. Both approaches would enable offenders to consent to the making of a community service order in the knowledge of what the alternative would be. They also might encourage the courts to make increasing use of shorter community service orders, thereby undermining the potential impact of the sentence on the use of custodial sentences and creating practical difficulties, in terms of appropriate placement provision, for schemes.

In Scotland, there was a clear risk that community service might slip yet further down the sentencing tariff as the courts became increasingly frustrated by the ineffectiveness and inappropriateness, for many offenders, of fines. The reluctance of the government to extend the availability of community service to the District Courts, the introduction of national objectives and standards for community service schemes and the amendment of the original legislation reflected the concern of the Scottish Office to ensure that community service orders were imposed to a greater degree than had hitherto been the case as an alternative to custody.

If the government's objective is achieved to any significant extent by these recent legislative and policy developments, a number of practical consequences may arise. If community service schemes are required to deal with increasing proportions of more persistent offenders, then higher levels of non-compliance are likely to result. As in previous studies (e.g. Pease et al., 1975) offenders with more extensive criminal histories were found to have higher levels of absenteeism and breach. Community service staff would, therefore, find themselves having to devote more time to following up absences and submitting breach applications. The courts would need to be re-assured that an increased breach rate reflected the change in sentencing practices in order for their confidence in community service to be maintained.

Higher levels of reconviction might also be expected if there was a substantial shift in the tariff position of community service. In common with earlier studies (e.g. Pease at al., 1977; Phillpotts and Lancucki, 1979) the likelihood of reconviction increased linearly with the number of convictions in the previous two years. Since the majority of first reconvictions occurred relatively soon after the community service order was imposed, the ability of community service to offer adequate public protection from more persistent offenders might increasingly be called into question.

There may, finally, be direct implications for placement provision. Although many agencies indicated that they would be happy to offer a placement to any offender who was deemed suitable by the community service scheme, most expressed reservations about accepting offenders who might pose a risk to their clients or staff. To minimise the risk of offending against the beneficiaries, a greater reliance might have to be placed upon the use of team placements in which direct supervision and oversight can be more effectively provided. This would have the effect of limiting the ability of schemes to match offenders to placements with regard to a wider range of criteria.

It is possible, on the other hand, that the new legislation will serve instead to limit the pool of offenders upon whom the courts consider that community service orders can reasonably be imposed. Reluctant to extend the use of community service to embrace more serious offenders or offences, and restricted in their ability to impose community service orders where a custodial sentence is unwarranted, sentencers may make less use of community service orders (especially as a stand alone option) over coming years. In view of the success that community service has, in many ways, been, this would be a disappointing turn of events, but one which would be preferable to the inequities that would be perpetuated if the new legislative requirements were on occasion side-stepped or ignored.

The future of community service revisited

In 1980, McWilliams and Pease speculated upon the future directions that the development of community service might take. The standardisation of practice on a national basis, which was their most optimistic scenario, has now been introduced in Scotland and in England and Wales.

In principal, the desirability of national standards which strive to achieve equity and consistency and which seek to eliminate unnecessary (and even damaging) discretion cannot be disputed. However, the guidelines that were developed in Scotland, and which placed a greater emphasis on maximising the value of community service for the offender, received a more enthusiastic reception than did their counterparts in England and Wales in which elements of McWilliams and Pease's (1980) penalisation cameo could be discerned. In an attempt to promote community service as a tough and credible alternative to prison (and to counteract any 'probationisation' of the measure which might have contributed to its decreased use by the courts), the Home Office (1988b) introduced a requirement that most offenders sentenced to orders of 60 hours or more should be required to complete the first 21 hours of their orders engaged in demanding physical tasks which improve the appearance or amenities of a neighbourhood. The types of work envisaged by the government are unlikely to expose offenders to the kinds of experiences that they find rewarding and worthwhile and which serve to maintain the necessary commitment and motivation that they require to complete their community service orders. This requirement, combined with a tighter and less flexible enforcement policy has led some (e.g. Allen, 1988; McIvor, 1991a; McWilliams, 1989) to predict a sharp increase in the proportions of offenders breached, which might, as a consequence, decrease rather than increase the credibility of community service with sentencers.

The increased use of community service in England and Wales since the implementation of the national standards has been accompanied by an increase in the proportions of offenders who are returned to court for failure to comply with the requirements of their community service orders. Lloyd (1991) has suggested that the national standards are at least in part responsible for the higher levels of breach and has warned that the government's attempts to increase the diversionary potential of community service and its credibility could backfire if higher proportions of offenders end up in custody through their orders being revoked and if sentencers become irritated by the larger numbers of breached offenders appearing before the courts.

Scotland has also witnessed an increase in the numbers of offenders breached since the implementation of national standards. A further

184

increase in the breach rate seems likely following the further revision of the enforcement policy in April 1991 to bring it into line with the national standards for probation (Social Work Services Group, 1991b). Community service schemes are now required to initiate breach proceedings following the third (rather than fourth) failure to comply.

It is possible, though, that higher completion rates will, in due course, again be achieved. It was shown in Chapter 4 that the more stringent enforcement of orders produced increased compliance and did not necessitate greater numbers of offenders being returned to court. It appeared that offenders were well aware of the extent to which staff would tolerate absenteeism and that while many took full advantage of the leeway that existed, few were prepared to overstep the mark and risk being breached. Assuming that community service staff clearly communicate their expectations to offenders and make them fully aware of the implications if they fail to comply, then breach rates may revert to a more typical level as offenders adjust to the more rigorous expectations placed upon them by staff.

This also assumes, though, that unacceptable absences are defined as such only if they constitute 'a wilful refusal to work' (McWilliams, 1989). The introduction of standardised criteria can prevent the worst excesses of unfettered discretion. There is a risk, however, that inappropriately rigid adherence to a pre-determined checklist may result in some offenders being breached as a result of their inability rather than their unwillingness to complete their community service work.

How in other respects are recent policy developments likely to influence the future of community service by offenders? In Scotland, the introduction of full central funding and the implementation of national standards for court services, through care and probation is intended to encourage increased use of community-based social work disposals for offenders who would otherwise be deprived of their liberty. If the national standards have their desired effect, then we will witness an overall growth in the use of probation in Scotland over the next few years and an increase, more especially, in the numbers of offenders made subject to probation orders who would otherwise face sentences of imprisonment. In the interests of public protection or to mark the gravity of offences, the courts may make increasing use of a range of additional requirements, such as community service or attendance at specialised projects, when placing more serious or persistent offenders on probation. Sheriffs clearly value the ability to combine community service and probation (Carnie, 1990) not least because it enables a greater degree of control to be exercised over offenders who are allowed to retain their liberty by performing unpaid work. The risk is that the use of community service as a stand alone measure will decrease as greater use is made of Section 7 (combined) orders by Scottish courts.

A similar situation may arise in England and Wales with the implementation of the 1991 Criminal Justice Act, which will enable for the first time the combined use of probation and community service in these countries. The 1991 Act will also permit the courts to attach an array of requirements (such as residence requirements, treatment for drug or alcohol dependency and attendance at probation centres) to probation and combination orders and to impose them alongside other community sentences such as curfew orders (possibly enforced by electronic monitoring) and compensation orders. In effect, the new community sentences may come to resemble the intensive supervision programmes that were developed during the 1980s in the United States in response to record levels of imprisonment and prison overcrowding. Such programmes place a considerable emphasis upon surveillance and control but, as McIvor (1990c, 1992b) has argued, their effectiveness is increasingly being called into question.

Intensive supervision programmes have been criticised for their apparent lack of impact upon recidivism (Petersilia and Turner, 1990) which in some instances has been attributed to their lack of attention to offenders' underlying problems and needs (Byrne, 1990; Erwin, 1990). On the other hand, the rate of revocation has been high and has usually resulted in offenders being imprisoned for the original offence, even though most revocations have been prompted by technical violations rather than by continued offending by the probationer (e.g. Pearson, 1988; Pearson and Harper, 1990). These findings would be slightly less worrying were it certain that the intensive supervision cases had, at the outset, been genuinely prison-bound. However the diversionary impact of these programmes has been questioned (Morris and Tonry, 1990; Tonry, 1990), rasing doubts about their cost-effectiveness (United States General Accounting Office, 1990) and concerns on ethical grounds about imposing such restrictive sanctions upon offenders who would otherwise be dealt with by means of some other less intrusive penalty (von Hirsch, 1990).

The most pertinent lesson to be learned from these recent experiences in North America is that the more restrictions and requirements that are placed upon offenders, the greater the likelihood that they will fail. Probation officers may be tempted to advocate the use of combined orders with associated conditions to enhance the credibility of probation recommendations with the courts and sentencers may seize upon the new opportunities presented to them to satisfy themselves that increased public protection can be achieved. But Clear and Hardyman (1990) have warned that when controls are imposed upon offenders who would otherwise adjust well in the community, the potential of the controls to backfire must be assessed. The risk, in other words, is that some offenders who could have successfully completed a period of standard probation may be breached for failing to comply with unnecessary additional requirements or sentences and imprisoned as a result.

If the new combination orders prove popular with the courts, and especially if they are used frequently in conjunction with other restrictive community sentences, then it appears almost inevitable that increasing proportions of offenders will fail to complete their community service orders, not necessarily through failure to comply with the requirements specific to the community service sentence, but through being returned to court and re-sentenced, either because they have committed new offences or, more probably, because they have failed to comply with the other requirements placed upon them.

Should this occur, there would be major practical repercussions for community service schemes. Placement-providing agencies, who often comment on the need for offenders to go through a period of adjustment and familiarisation before they are able to contribute most effectively to the agency's work, would become increasingly irritated by the unreliability and high turnover of offenders on community service orders. Faced with the prospect of losing agency placements, schemes would find themselves reserving such placements for offenders sentenced to community service alone, while offenders given combined community sentences would be allocated automatically to workshops and teams. The policy of carefully matching offenders to appropriate work placements would need to be abandoned, the proportionate use of team placements would increase and, finding themselves with a lack of suitable alternative tasks to occupy the teams, increasing emphasis would be placed by community service schemes upon environmental tasks such as cleaning beaches and canals, picking up litter and clearing waste ground.

This gloomy scenario, which is not entirely fanciful, could logically be extended to embrace the decline of staff morale, lowered motivation among offenders, heightened levels of absenteeism and breach and so on. It highlights the importance of community service being retained as a distinctive and, as far as possible, discrete penal option. Just as probation officers were of central importance in establishing community service as a much-valued addition to the repertoire of sentences available to British courts, so will they have a crucial role to play in ensuring, through their recommendations to sentencers, that the credibility and distinctiveness of the community service order is preserved.

The fate of community service may be uncertain, but its achievements as well as its shortcomings are clear. The community service order may not have lived up to initial hopes that it would make a significant contribution to reducing the reliance of courts upon the use of custodial sentences. It is, however, a less costly option than imprisonment, one which many offenders find to be rewarding and worthwhile and one which appears to be no less effective than other court disposals in reducing recidivism. In most instances, the unpaid work performed by offenders sentenced to community service is highly valued both by placement-providing agencies and by disadvantaged members of the public who have been the recipients of unpaid work.

Although some worrying inconsistencies, which have plagued community service from the outset, will probably remain (it is questionable, for example, whether parity across courts in the use of community service will ever be achieved) community service schemes should be encouraged to build upon their successes, publicise their achievements and strive to ensure that the future of community service as a constructive and distinctive sentencing option is assured.

Bibliography

Advisory Council on the Penal System (1970) *Non-Custodial and Semi-Custodial Penalties,* London: HMSO.

Albrecht, H. & Schädler, W. (1986) *Community Service: A New Option in Punishing Offenders in Europe,* Freiburg: Max Planck Institute for Foreign and International Penal Law.

Allen, G.F. & Treger, H. (1990) Community service orders in federal probation: Perceptions of probationers and host agencies, *Federal Probation, 54, 3,* 8-14.

Allen, R. (1988) Punishment in the community, *Social Work Today, 11 August,* 25.

Association of Directors of Social Work (1987) *Report of a Working Party on Fines and Fine Default,* Glasgow: ADSW.

Australian Institute of Criminology (1983) *Community Service Orders in Australia and New Zealand,* Canberra: Australian Institute of Criminology.

Bailey, W.C. (1966) Correctional outcome: An evaluation of 100 reports, *Journal of Criminal Law, Criminology and Police Science, 57,* 153-60.

Berk, R. & Feeley, M.M. (1990) *An Evaluation of the Community Service Order Scheme in the US District Court for the Northern District of California,* Center for the Study of Law and Society, University of California at Berkeley.

Bishop, N. (1988) *Non-Custodial Alternatives in Europe,* Helsinki: Government Printing Office.

Borders Social Work Department (1987) *Community Service by Offenders Scheme,* Unpublished research report.

Bottoms, A.E. (1981) The suspended sentence in England 1967-78, *British Journal of Criminology, 21,* 1-26.

Bottoms, A.E. (1987) Limiting prison use: Evidence in England and Wales, *The Howard Journal, 26,* 177-202.

Bottoms, A.E. (1989) The place of the probation service in the criminal justice system, in *Central Council of Probation Committees: The Madingley Papers ll,* Cambridge: University of Cambridge Institute of Criminology.

Bryant, M.J. (1983) Community service as an alternative to custody, *Justice of the Peace, 147,* 62.

Bucknell, P. (1980) Community service, *Justice of the Peace, 144,* 251.

Byrne, J.M. (1990) The future of intensive probation supervision and the new intermediate sanctions, *Crime and Delinquency, 36,* 6-41.

Carnie, J. (1990) *Sentencers' Perceptions of Community Service by Offenders,* Edinburgh: Scottish Office Central Research Unit.

Carnie, J. & McIvor, G. (1991) Sentencing offenders to community service in Scotland, in M. Adler and A.R. Millar (Eds.) *Socio-Legal Research in the Scottish Courts: Volume 2,* Edinburgh: Scottish Office Central Research Unit.

Center for Alternative Sentencing and Employment Services (CASES) (1991) *Annual Report 1990,* New York: CASES.

Clear, T.G. & Hardyman, P.L. (1990) The new intensive supervision movement, *Crime and Delinquency, 36,* 42-60.

Curran, J.H. & Chambers, G.A. (1982) *Social Enquiry Reports in Scotland,* Edinburgh: HMSO.

Duguid, G. (1982) *Community Service in Scotland: The First Two Years,* Edinburgh: Scottish Office Central Research Unit.

Ervin, L. & Schneider, A.L. (1990) Explaining the effects of restitution on offenders: Results from a national experiment in juvenile courts, in B. Galaway and J. Hudson (Eds.) *Criminal Justice, Restitution, and Reconciliation,* Monsey: Criminal Justice Press.

Erwin, B.S. (1990) Old and new tools for the modern probation officer, *Crime and Delinquency, 36,* 61-74.

Flegg, D. (1976) *Community Service: Consumer Survey 1973-76,* Nottingham: Nottingham Probation Service.

Fletcher, A.E. (1983) *Organisational Diversity in Community Service,* Department of Social Administration, University of Manchester.

Godson, D. (1980) *Community Service by Offenders: The Agencies' Experiences in Hampshire,* Department of Sociology and Social Administration, University of Southampton.

Godson, D. (1981) Community service as a tariff measure, *Probation Journal, 28,* 124-9.

Harland, A.T. (1980) Court-ordered community service in criminal law: The continuing tyranny of benevolence?, *Buffalo Law Review, 29,* 425-86.

Harris, R. (1989) Social work in society or punishment in the community?, in R. Shaw and K. Haines (Eds.)*The Criminal Justice System: A Central Role for the Probation Service,* Cambridge: University of Cambridge Institute of Criminology.

Hillsman, S.T. (1990) Fines and day fines, in M. Tonry and N. Morris (Eds.) *Crime and Justice: A Review of Research Volume 12,* Chicago: University of Chicago Press.

Hoggarth, E.A. (1991) *Selection for Community Service Orders,* Aldershot: Avebury.

Home Office (1965) *The Adult Offender, Cm 2852,* London: HMSO.

Home Office (1969) *People in Prison (England and Wales), Cm 4212,* London: HMSO.

Home Office (1983) Reconvictions of those given community service orders, *Home Office Statistical Bulletin,* London: HMSO.

Home Office (1988a) *Punishment, Custody and the Community, Cm 424,* London: HMSO.

Home Office (1988b) *National Standards for Community Service Orders,* Home Office.

Home Office (1989) *National Standards for Community Service Orders,* Home Office Circular 18/89.

Home Office (1990a) *Criminal Statistics England and Wales 1989, Cm 1322,* London: HMSO.

Home Office (1990b) *Crime, Justice and Protecting the Public, Cm 965,* London: HMSO.

Hood, R. (1974) Criminology and penal change: A case study of the nature and impact of some recent advice to governments, in R. Hood (Ed.) *Crime, Criminology and Public Policy: Essays in Honour of Sir Leon Radzinowicz,* London: Heinemann.

Jardine, E., Moore, G. & Pease, K. (1983) Community service orders, employment and the tariff, *Criminal Law Review,* 17-20.

Kilbrandon Committee (1964) *Report of the Committee on Children and Young Persons, Cmnd. 2306,* Edinburgh: HMSO.

Knapp, M., Robertson, E. & McIvor, G. (1989) *Community Service Orders as Alternatives to Custody: Evidence on Comparative Costs,* Discussion Paper 644, Personal Social Services Research Unit, University of Kent at Canterbury.

Knapp, M., Robertson, E. & McIvor, G. (1992) The comparative costs of community service and custody in Scotland, *The Howard Journal, 31,* 8-30.

Leibrich, J. (1984) Criminal history and reconvictions of two sentence groups: Community service and non-residential periodic detention, in J. Leibrich, B. Galaway and Y. Underhill (Eds.) *Community Service Orders in New Zealand: Three Research Reports,* Wellington, New Zealand: Department of Justice.

Leibrich, J. (1985) Use of community service in New Zealand, *Australia and New Zealand Journal of Criminology, 18,* 85-94.

Leibrich, J., Galaway, B. & Underhill, Y. (Eds.) (1984a) *Community Service Orders in New Zealand: Three Research Reports,* Wellington, New Zealand: Department of Justice.

Leibrich, J. Galaway, B. & Underhill, Y. (1984b) Survey of people connected with the community service sentence, in J. Leibrich, B. Galaway and Y. Underhill (Eds.) *Community Service Orders in New Zealand: Three Research Reports,* Wellington, New Zealand: Department of Justice.

Lewis, P. (1981) Spider's stratagem, *Social Work Today, 13, 5,* 12.

Lipton, D., Martinson, R. & Wilks, J. (1975) *Effectiveness of Correctional Treatment: A Survey of Treatment Evaluation Studies,* Springfield: Praeger.

Lloyd, C. (1991) National standards for community service orders: The first two years of operation, in *Home Office Research and Statistics Department Research Bulletin No. 31,* London: Home Office Research and Planning Unit.

Lothian, A. (1991) A prescription for the sick man of the system, *Glasgow Herald,* 9 January.

Mair, G. & Nee, C. (forthcoming, 1992) Day centre reconviction rates, *British Journal of Criminology.*

Martinson, R. (1974) What works?: Questions and answers about prison reform, *The Public Interest, 23,* 22-54.

McDonald, D.C. (1986) *Punishment Without Walls: Community Service Sentences in New York City,* New Brunswick: Rutgers University Press.

McIvor, G. (1989) *An Evaluative Study of Community Service by Offenders in Scotland,* Social Work Research Centre, University of Stirling.

McIvor, G. (1990a) *Community Service by Offenders: Assessing the Benefit to the Community,* Social Work Research Centre, University of Stirling.

McIvor, G (1990b) Community service and custody in Scotland, *The Howard Journal*, 29, 101-13.

McIvor, G. (1990c) *Sanctions for Serious or Persistent Offenders: A Review of the Literature*, Social Work Research Centre, University of Stirling.

McIvor, G. (1991a) Community service work placements, *The Howard Journal*, 30, 19-29.

McIvor, G. (1991b) Social work intervention in community service, *British Journal of Social Work*, 21, 591-609.

McIvor, G. (1992a) *Reconviction Among Offenders Sentenced to Community Service*, Social Work Research Centre, University of Stirling.

McIvor, G. (1992b) Intensive probation supervision: Does more mean better?, *Probation Journal*, 39, 2-6.

McWilliams, B. (1980) *Community Service Orders: Discretion and the Prosecution of Breach Proceedings*, Department of Social Administration, University of Manchester (mimeo).

McWilliams, B. & Murphy, Y.N. (1980) Breach of community service, in K. Pease and W. McWilliams (Eds.) *Community Service by Order*, Edinburgh: Scottish Academic Press.

McWilliams, W. (1980) Selection policies for community service: Practice and theory, in K. Pease and W. Mcwilliams (Eds.) *Community Service by Order*, Edinburgh:Scottish Academic Press.

McWilliams, W. (1989) Community service national standards: Practice and sentencing, *Probation Journal*, 36, 121-6.

McWilliams, W. & Pease, K. (1980) The future of community service, in K. Pease and W. McWilliams (Eds.) *Community Service by Order*, Edinburgh: Scottish Academic Press.

Menzies, K. (1996) The rapid spread of community service orders in Ontario, *Canadian Journal of Criminology*, 28, 157-69.

Menzies, K. & Vass, A.A. (1989) The impact of historical, legal and administrative differences on a sanction: Community service orders in England and Ontario, *The Howard Journal*, 28, 204-17.

Morgan, C. & Ruffles, M. (1980) Community service and community agencies, in K. Pease and W. McWilliams (Eds.) *Community Service by Order*, Edinburgh: Scottish Academic Press.

Morris, N. & Tonry, M. (1990) *Between Prison and Probation: Intermediate Punishments in a Rational Sentencing System*, New York: Oxford University Press.

National Association of Probation Officers (1977) *Community Service Orders: Practice and Philosophy*, Thornton Heath: Ambassador House.

Nicholson, L. (1990) *A Survey of Fine Defaulters in Scottish Courts*, Edinburgh: Scottish Office Central Research Unit.

Nicholson, L. & Millar, A.R. (1989) *An Evaluation of the Fines Officers Scheme,* Edinburgh: Scottish Office Central Research Unit.

O'Boyle, F. & Parsloe, P. (1980) *Community Service by Offenders: Report of a Research Project in the Grampian Region,* Department of Social Work, University of Aberdeen.

Pearson, F.S. (1988) Evaluation of New Jersey's intensive supervision program, *Crime and Delinquency, 34,* 437-48.

Pearson, F.S. & Harper, A.G. (1990) Contingent intermediate sentences: New Jersey's intensive supervision program, *Crime and Delinquency, 36,* 75-86.

Pease, K. (1978) Community service and the tariff, *Criminal Law Review,* 546-8.

Pease, K. (1980a) A brief history of community service, in K. Pease and W. McWilliams (Eds.) *Community Service by Order,* Edinburgh: Scottish Academic Press.

Pease, K. (1980b) Community service and prison: Are they alternatives,? in K. Pease and W. McWilliams (Eds.) *Community Service by Order,* Edinburgh: Scottish Academic Press.

Pease, K. (1983) Penal innovations, in J. Lishman (Ed.) *Research Highlights No. 5: Social Work with Adult Offenders,* Aberdeen: Department of Social Work, University of Aberdeen.

Pease, K. (1985) Community service orders, in M. Tonry and N. Morris (Eds.) *Crime and Justice: An Annual Review of Research Volume 6,* Chicago: University of Chicago Press.

Pease, K. Billingham, S. & Earnshaw, I. (1977) Community service assessed in 1976, *Home Office Research Study No. 39,* London: HMSO

Pease, K., Durkin, P., Earnshaw, I., Payne, D. & Thorpe, J. (1975) Community service orders, *Home Office Research Study No. 29,* London: HMSO.

Pease, K. & McWilliams, W. (1980) *Community Service by Order,* Edinburgh: Scottish Academic Press.

Petersilia, J. & Turner, S. (1990) Comparing intensive and regular supervision for high-risk probationers: Early results from an experiment in California, *Crime and Delinquency, 36,* 87-111.

Phillpotts, G.J.O. & Lancucki, L.B. (1979) Previous convictions, sentence and reconviction: A statistical study of a sample of 5000 offenders convicted in January 1971, *Home Office Research Study No. 53,* London: HMSO.

Polonoski, M. (1980) *The Community Service Order Programme in Ontario (2): Participants and their Perceptions,* Scarborough, Ontario: Ontario Ministry of Correctional Services.

Polonoski, M. (1981) *The Community Service Order Programme in Ontario (4): Summary,* Scarborough, Ontario: Ontario Ministry of Correctional Services.

Prison Reform Trust (1988) *'The Most Progressive Alternative': Community Service by Offenders,* London: Prison Reform Trust.

Ralphs, P. (1980) Community service: A growing concern but where to?, *International Journal of Offender Therapy and Comparative Criminology, 24,* 234-40.

Raynor, P. (1988) *Probation as an Alternative to Custody,* Aldershot: Avebury.

Read, G. (1980) Area differences in community service operation, in K. Pease and W. McWilliams (Eds.) *Community Service by Order,* Edinburgh: Scottish Academic Press.

Rifkind, M. (1989) Penal policy: The way ahead, *The Howard Journal, 28,* 81-90.

Roberts, C.H. (1989) *First Evaluation Report: Young Offender Project,* Hereford and Worcester Probation Service.

Roberts, J. & Roberts, C. (1982) Social enquiry reports and sentencing, *The Howard Journal, 21,* 76-93.

Robison, J. & Smith, S. (1971) The effectiveness of correctional programs, *Crime and Delinquency, 17,* 67-80.

Rook, M.K. (1978) Tasmania's work order scheme: A reply to Varne, *Australia and New Zealand Journal of Criminology, 11,* 81-8.

Schneider, A.L. (1986) Restitution and recidivism rates of young offenders: Results from four experimental studies, *Criminology, 24,* 633-52.

Schneider, A.L. & Schneider, P.R. (1985) The impact of restitution on recidivism of juvenile offenders: An experiment in Clayton County, Georgia, *Criminal Justice Review, 10,* 1-10.

Scottish Community Service Group (1986) *Policy Sub-group Final Report,* Scottish Community Service Group.

Scottish Home and Health Department (1990) *Prison Statistics Scotland,* Edinburgh: Government Statistical Service.

Scottish Office (1966) *Social Work and the Community, Cmnd. 3065,* Edinburgh: HMSO.

Scottish Office (1987) *Government to Provide Total Funding for Community Service Schemes,* Edinburgh: Scottish Information Office.

Shaw, S. (1980) *Paying the Penalty: An Analysis of the Costs of Penal Sanctions,* London: NACRO.

Social Work Services Group (1980) *Guidelines for Local Authority Social Work Departments on Introduction and Operation of Schemes for Community Service by Offenders,* Edinburgh: Scottish Office.

Social Work Services Group (1988) *Statistical Bulletin: Community Service by Offenders in 1986,* Edinburgh: Government Statistical Service.

Social Work Services Group (1989) *National Standards and Objectives for the Operation of Community Service by Offenders Schemes in Scotland,* Edinburgh: Scottish Office.

Social Work Services Group (1990) *Statistical Bulletin: Community Service by Offenders in 1987, 1988 and 1989,* Edinburgh: Government Statistical Service.

Social Work Services Group (1991a) *Social Work Services in the Criminal Justice System: Summary of National Objectives and Standards,* Edinburgh: Scottish Office.

Social Work Services Group (1991b) *National Standards and Objectives for Social Work Services in the Criminal Justice System,* Edinburgh: Scottish Office.

Sparks, R.F. (1971) The use of suspended sentences, *Criminal Law Review,* 384-401.

Tak, P.J.P. (1986) Community service orders in Western Europe: A comparative survey, in H. Albrecht and W. Schädler (Eds.) *Community Service: A New Option in Punishing Offenders in Europe,* Freiburg, Germany: Max Planck Institute for Foreign and International Penal Law.

Thorvaldson, S.A. (1978) *The Effects of Community Service on the Attitudes of Offenders,* Unpublished PhD thesis, University of Cambridge.

Tonry, M. (1990) Stated and latent features of ISP, *Crime and Delinquency,* 36, 174-91.

United States General Accounting Office (1990) *Intermediate Sanctions: Their Impacts on Prison Crowding, Costs, and Recidivism are Still Unclear,* Report to the Chairman, Select Committee on Narcotics Abuse and Control, House of Representatives, Washington, D.C.

van Kalmthout, A.M. & Tak, P.J.P. (1988) *Sanction-Systems in the Member-States of the Council of Europe: Part 1,* London: Kluwer/Gouda Quint.

Varah, M. (1981) What about the workers?: Offenders on community service orders express their opinions, *Probation Journal,* 28, 121-3.

Vass, A.A. (1984) *Sentenced to Labour: Close Encounters with a Prison Substitute,* St. Ives: Venus Academica.

Vass, A.A. and Menzies, K. (1989) The community service order as a public and private enterprise: A comparative account of practices in England and Ontario, Canada, *British Journal of Criminology,* 29, 255-72.

von Hirsch, A. (1990) The ethics of community-based sanctions, *Crime and Delinquency,* 36, 162-73.

Wasik, M. & Taylor, D. (1991) *Blackstone's Guide to the Criminal Justice Act 1991,* London: Blackstone Press Limited.

West, J.S.M. (1976) Community service orders, in J.F.S. King and W. Young (Eds.) *Control Without Custody,* Cambridge: Cambridge Institute of Criminology.

West, J.S.M. (1977) Community service orders: How different?, *Probation Journal, 24,* 112-20.

West, J.S.M. (1978) Community service for fine defaulters, *Justice of the Peace, 142,* 425-8.

Williams, B., Creamer, A. & Hartley, L. (1991) Probation as an alternative to custody, in M. Adler and A.R. Millar (Eds.) *Socio-Legal Research in the Scottish Courts: Volume 2,* Edinburgh: Scottish Office Central Research Unit.

Willis, A. (1977) Community service as an alternative to imprisonment: A cautionary view, *Probation Journal, 24,* 120-6.

Willis, A. (1978) Community service and the tariff: A critical comment, *Criminal Law Review,* 540-4.

Wootton, B. (1977) Some reflections on the first five years of community service, *Probation Journal, 24,* 110-2.

Wootton, B. (1978) *Crime and Penal Policy,* London: George Allen and Unwin.

Wright, M. (1984) *In the Interests of the Community: A Review of the Literature on Community Service Orders,* Department of Social Administration, University of Birmingham.

Young, W.A. (1979) *Community Service Orders: The Development and Use of a New Penal Measure,* London: Heinemann.

Index

absences
  acceptability of 48-52, 56, 185
  agencies' concern about 105,
    120, 177, 187
  incidence of 83; and
    enforcement practices 60,
    68-72, 80, 185; and
    offenders' perception of
    work placement 74, 80; as
    outcome measure 22;
    placement allocation
    procedures unrelated to
    63; pre-sentence
    interviews unrelated to 60;
    problems contributing to
    75; and reconviction 172;
    variation in 68; and work
    placement setting 73-4, 80
  notification of 74
  orders breached due to 47,
    48, 56
  prior notification of 49, 50,

51, 56
  and time to complete
    community service 67, 80
  unacceptable: definition of
    48-52, 56, 185; from
    practical work
    placements 74; and
    offenders' perception of
    work placements 74, 80;
    and reconviction 172;
    tolerance of 69-70, 71, 80
accommodation 36
accommodation problems
  and reconviction 167
  and risk of breaching 54
  and social work history 37
Advisory Council on the
    Penal System
  see Wootton Committee
age 35
  and breaching 52
  and criminal history 37

and likelihood of re-offending
153
minimum for community
service 4, 9
and offence type 38
and perception of work
placements 89
and placement allocation 46
and pre-sentence custody 37
and reconviction 151, 152,
163, 166-7, 168, 169, 172
and risk of custodial
sentence 134
see also young offenders
agencies
attitude to local offenders 125
client groups served by 114
offenders' integration within
118, 119, 178
offenders' voluntary
continuance at 98-100, 102,
118-19, 176, 179
satisfaction with support from
community service staff
121-3, 127-8
suggestions for improvements
to community service
122-3, 125
willingness to continue
offering placements 123-5
agency placements
absences from 73-4, 80, 105,
120, 177, 187
allocation to 46, 55-6, 63
benefits of: to agencies 30-1,
105, 118, 119-20, 123-4,
126-7, 176-7; to offenders
123, 124, 125, 126-7, 150,
177
costs to agencies 177
low likelihood of breach 72-3
offenders' perceptions of

90-1, 92, 94, 178
problems with 119-21, 125-6,
127, 177, 187
proportion of offenders
allocated to 44, 45
restrictions on offenders
accepted for 115-16, 127
team (group) placements
regarded as inferior to 89
type of work carried out in
43, 44, 117-18, 127
Albrecht, H. 2
alcohol-related problems 36
and criminal history 37
and likelihood of re-offending
153
and reconviction 164
and social work history 37
Allen, G.F. 83, 105, 176
Allen, R. 7, 184
Association of Directors of
Social Work (ADSW)
recommendations on fines
and fine default 15
Australian Institute of
Criminology 2

Bailey, W.C. 3
beneficiaries
benefit of community service
to 30-2, 118, 123-4, 125,
126, 127, 176-7; offenders'
perception of 85, 88, 90,
92, 102, 104-5, 177;
previous research on 105
offenders' contact with 85,
86-7, 102; in agencies 118;
value of 89, 178
offenders' good relationship
with 107-8, 111-12, 113,
127
problems experienced by 109,

119-21, 125-6, 127, 177, 187

questionnaires completed by 31-2, 106

referral to community service 106

satisfaction 105, 108-13, 127, 176-7

suggestions for improvements to community service 112-13, 122-3, 135

type of work done for 106-7, 127

willingness to use community service again 109-12, 127

see also agencies; individual beneficiaries

Berk, R. 105, 151, 176

Bishop, N. 2, 151

Borders Community Service Scheme 31, 105

Bottoms, A.E. 180, 181

breach

  costs 28

  incidence of: and accommodation problems 54, 56; and age 52; contribution of comprehensive social work service to reduction in 76-7, 80; contribution of national standards to 184-5; and criminal history 53, 56; and delay in starting work 67; and employment status 54; and enforcement strictness 71-2, 80; and offence type 53; pre-sentence interviews unrelated to 60; and sentencing practice 183; and social work history 53,

54, 56; and type of work placement 72-3, 80; work placement allocation procedures unrelated to 63-5

  reasons for 47-8, 56

  and reconviction 171-2

  sentences imposed following 131, 134-7, 142-3, 148

  under-representation among questionnaire respondents 83

breach proceedings

  inconsistent initiation of 6, 10, 69-72, 80, 185; *see also* absences

  Scottish Community Service Group recommendations 11

Bryant, M.J. 130

Bucknell, P. 151

Byrne, J.M. 179, 186

Carnie, J. 14, 29, 30, 32, 38, 43, 59, 65, 72, 136, 138, 139, 140, 141, 143, 147-8, 150-1, 175, 182, 185

Chambers, G.A. 17

Clear, T.G. 186

combined orders 7, 8-9, 42, 185-7

community

  benefit of community service to 30-2, 104-28, 175-7

community service

  aims and objectives 100-1, 103, 104, 142, 150-1; achievement of 82, 174-83, 187-8; ambiguity 5, 130-1, 175; Home Office circular on 6; Scottish Office on 9; *see also* punishment;

rehabilitation; reparation
beneficiaries *see* beneficiaries
benefit to community 30-2,
104-28, 175-7
benefit to offenders 93-4,
102-3, 177-81, 188;
agencies' perception of
123, 124, 125, 126-7, 150;
individual beneficiaries'
perception of 112, 113,
127, 150
costs *see* cost-effectiveness;
costs
credibility: implications of
national standards for 6,
14, 18, 184; undermined by
inadequate funding 12, 65
development: England and
Wales 3-8, 174-5, 186;
Scotland 8-18, 20-1, 131-2,
175, 185-6
distinctiveness: importance of
preserving 187
diversionary impact on
imprisonment *see*
imprisonment
effectiveness: aims of
research into 19-24, 26-7,
28-9, 30-1, 32-3;
methodology of research
into 24-5, 27-8, 29-30, 31-2,
33-4, 83, 171-2; need for
research into xii-xiii
excess demand for 65, 79
experimental schemes *see*
experimental schemes
funding *see* funding
integration within social work
services to criminal justice
system 17-18, 81
operational diversity 5-6,
10-11, 57; aims of research

into 19-24; methodology of
research into 24-5;
reduction in 80-1
perceptions of *see*
beneficiaries; sentencers;
work placements
popularity 3, 29, 174-5
previous research into xii, 20,
26, 30-1, 33, 82-3, 105
probationisation: dangers of
130, 180
punitive element *see*
punishment
reconviction before and after
see reconviction
success, measurement of 82
suggestions for improvements
to: from agencies 122-3,
125; from beneficiaries
112-3; from offenders 97-8
suitability for *see* community
service assessment
temporary closure and delays
65
worldwide use 1-3
see also community service
orders; work placements
community service assessment
criteria for 25, 38-41
procedures 57-61, 79
referral for 37, 40
Community Service by
Offenders (Scotland) Act
1978 8, 41-2
community service orders
community service staff views
on use of 141-2
delays in starting 65-7, 79-80,
81
enforcement *see* enforcement
future use 183
inconsistent use of 11, 29,

130-1, 148, 180, 182, 188;
economic implications 146;
impact of national
standards on 139-40, 142,
147-8, 149
increasing use of 6, 10, 175
informed consent to 146, 182
length 4, 7, 41-3; breaching
unrelated to 52-3; and type
of work 6, 184
non-compliance with *see*
breach
outcomes 22-3, 47-52, 56;
impact of national
standards on 184-5; and
reconviction 171-2; *see also*
breach
revocation 47, 48
as sentence in its own right 6,
139, 140-1, 142, 180;
uncertainty about 5, 23-4,
130
sentences replaced by:
community service staff
views on 141-2; offenders'
perception of 144-6;
sentencers' views on 29-30,
138-41, 148, 149, 181-2,
183; *see also* fines;
imprisonment;
non-custodial sentences
successful completion 22, 47,
48, 56, 82; *see also* breach
tariff position 5, 11, 130, 140,
180, 182, 183
time to complete 65-7, 80
Community Service Orders
Rules 1989 6
community service staff
agencies' satisfaction with
121-3, 127-8
assessment of offenders'

suitability for community
service 39-41
interviews and questionnaires
25
offenders' suggestions about
98
perception of sentencing
practice 141-2
pre-sentence interviews with
offenders 58-61, 79
and social enquiry report
preparation 58-61
social work service to
offenders 75-9, 80
cost-effectiveness
community service assessment
procedures 61, 79
and enforcement procedures
72
intensive supervision
programmes 186
work placement allocation
procedures 64
costs
community service 26, 27, 28,
146, 149
imprisonment 26, 27-8, 146,
149
supervision 72
work placement allocation 64
Council of Europe, community
service praised by 175
courts *see* District Court;
Sheriff Court
criminal history 37
and likelihood of re-offending
153
and reconviction 164-6, 167-8,
172, 173
and risk of breaching 53
and risk of custodial sentence
134

and suitability for community
service 39, 55
Criminal Justice Act 1972 3
Criminal Justice Act 1982 4
Criminal Justice Act 1991 7-8,
186
criminal justice, offences against
38, 155, 156, 166, 167, 168,
173
Curran, J.H. 17
custody *see* imprisonment

dishonesty, offences
involving 38
and agency placements 116
reconviction for 155, 156, 158,
159, 160, 167, 170, 173, 178
and risk of breaching 53
District Courts
attitude to community service
30, 140-1
reluctance to extend
community service to 11,
182
drug-related problems 36
Duguid, G. 9, 21, 23, 35, 131-2

employment, contribution of
community service to
chances of 85
employment status 35, 37
and length of community
service orders 42-3
and likelihood of
non-custodial sentence 43
and perception of work
placements 169
and reconviction 164, 168,
169
and risk of breaching 54
and risk of custodial sentence
134

and suitability for community
service 40
see also unemployment
enforcement
inconsistencies in 10, 80
standards for 11, 72, 81, 185
strictness: and incidence of
absence 60, 68-72, 80, 185;
offenders' perception of
70-1
England and Wales,
development of community
service in 3-8
see also experimental schemes
Ervin, L. 151, 179
Erwin, B.S. 179, 186
Europe, community service in 2
experimental schemes 3, 8
evaluation xii, 4-5, 9, 82,
131-2, 151-2

family commitments
acceptability of absences due
to 49, 50, 51, 52, 56
and allocation to work
placements 45
family problems, community
service staff help with 75-6
family relationships 36, 37
Feeley, M.M. 105, 151, 176
fine defaulters, supervised
attendance order for 15-16
fines, community service orders
imposed in place of 139,
140-1, 182
Flegg, D. 85
Fletcher, A.E. 5
Forsyth, M. 12
funding
from Scottish
11-12, 16, ?
inadequate: c

203

service credibility
undermined by 12, 65
in United States 1-2

gardening 44, 106, 107
beneficiaries' satisfaction with
108-9, 111, 127
gender 35
and allocation to work
placements 46
and criminal history 37
and reconviction 164
Godson, D. 30, 105, 115, 131,
176, 177

Hampshire, satisfaction with
community service in 105
Hardyman, P.L. 186
Harland, A.T. 151
Harper, A.G. 186
Harris, R. 180
Hillsman, S.T. 15
Hoggarth, E.A. 1, 39
Home Office
national standards introduced
by 6-7
reconviction studies 151-2,
171
Home Office Research Unit
evaluation of experimental
schemes *see* Pease
Hood, R. 174, 175
hours worked *see* community
service order, length

illness, acceptability of absences
due to 48, 49, 50, 51, 52,
56
imprisonment
community service as
alternative to 2, 3, 4,
13-14; community service

staff view on 141-2; cost
implications 146, 149;
decline in 29, 130, 131-2;
divergent views on 5, 23-4,
129-31, 181-3;
encouragement of 14-15,
28-9, 139-40, 182;
estimation of extent 31-2,
133-8, 148, 181; legislation
on 14-15, 148; offenders'
perception of 144-6;
sentencers' views on
138-42, 181-2, 183
community service orders
revoked due to 48
costs 26, 27-8, 146, 149
fine defaulters 15
following breaching 131,
134-6, 142-3, 148
government aim to reduce
use of 13-14, 28-9, 139
high level of 13
ineffectiveness 3
previous experience of 37;
and risk of breaching 53,
54, 56; and suitability for
community service 39, 40,
55
prior to sentencing 37; and
risk of custodial sentence
134; and suitability for
community service 40, 55
reconviction following 151
risk of: and custodial
sentencing 137-8; following
reconviction 156, 161-2,
172; and likelihood of
breach 143-4; offenders'
perception of 144-6, 148-9
unsuccessful referrals 39,
131-2, 133-4, 137-8
see also non-custodial

sentences
individual beneficiaries
  characteristics 106
  offenders' perception of value
    of community service to
    90, 92
  problems experienced by 109
  satisfaction 105, 108-13, 176,
    177
  suggestions for improvements
    to community service
    112-13
  type of work done for 106-7
  willingness to use community
    service again 109-12
interviews
  with community service staff
    25
  with offenders 23, 25, 83
  with sentencers 29-30

Jardine, E. 42

Kilbrandon Committee 8
Knapp, M. 26, 27, 57, 72, 146

Lancucki, L.B. 152, 162, 178,
  180, 183
Law Reform (Miscellaneous
  Provisions) (Scotland) Act
  1990 15-16, 148
legislation 3, 4, 5, 7, 8-9, 16, 186
  aim to promote consistent use
    of community service
    14-15, 148
  see also specific acts
Leibrich, J. 2, 30, 83, 105, 151,
  176, 177
Lewis, P. 130
Lipton, D. 3
Lloyd, C. 175, 184
Lothian, A. 17

McDonald, D.C. 2, 101, 105,
  151, 176
McIvor, G. 27, 29, 32, 33, 39, 48,
  75, 76, 137, 171, 175, 179,
  180, 184, 186
McWilliams, B. 5, 6, 22, 44, 52,
  72, 74
McWilliams, W. 7, 39, 130, 180,
  184, 185
magistrates
  attitudes to community
    service 139
Mair, G. 171, 180, 181
marital status 35
  and perception of work
    placements 169
  and reconviction 164, 166,
    169
  and suitability for community
    service 39, 40
Martinson, R. 3, 181
Menzies, K. 2
Millar, A.R. 15
Morgan, C. 98
Morris, N. 2, 186
motivation
  maintained by good
    supervisor/worker
    relationship 85
  unsuccessful referrals' lack of
    40, 41, 55
Murphy, Y.N. 72

Nee, C. 171, 181
New Zealand, community
  service in 83
Nicholson, L. 15
non-custodial sentences
  community service as
    alternative to 5, 6, 15-16,
    23-4, 182; community

service staff view on 141-2;
cost implications 146, 149;
increasing use of 29, 131-2;
sentencers' views on 138-9,
140-1; and tariff esclation
142-3, 148
employment status in relation
to 43
Northern Ireland, length of
community service orders
in 42-3

O'Boyle, F. 9
offences, types of 38
and allocation to work
placements 45, 46
and exclusion from agency
placements 115-16, 127
and reconviction 155-6,
158-62, 166, 167, 170, 172,
173, 178
and risk of breaching 53
and suitability for community
service 38-9, 55
offenders
allocation to work placements
see work placements
beneficiaries' contact with see
under beneficiaries
benefit of community service
to 93-4, 177-81, 188;
agencies' perception of
123, 124, 125, 126-7, 150;
individual beneficiaries'
perception of 112, 113,
127, 150
categories excluded from
agency placements 115-16,
127
criminal history see criminal
history
informed consent to

community service order
146, 182
interests and skills see skill
acquisition; skills
interviews with 23, 25, 83
involvement in work
placement allocation 62-3,
81; compliance unrelated
to 63-5, 79
offences committed by see
offences
perception of enforcement
strictness 71
perception of risk of
imprisonment 144-6, 148-9
perception of work
placements see under work
placements
persistent: characteristics
162-8, 173; non-compliance
with community service
order 182-3
personal development:
contribution of community
service to 93-4, 126-7,
178-9
pre-sentence interviews with
community service staff
58-61, 79
questionnaires completed by
23, 25, 83
re-offending by, self-predicted
likelihood of 153-4, 168-9,
170-1, 173, 180
reconviction see reconviction
rehabilitation see
rehabilitation
risk of imprisonment see
under imprisonment
social work history see
statutory social work
supervision

social work service for 16-18,
74-9, 80, 81, 180
socioeconomic characteristics
21-2, 25, 35-7; and
reconviction 162-4, 166-8;
and suitability for
community service 39-41,
55; in United States 2; *see
also particular
characteristics, e.g.* age;
unemployment
suitability for community
service *see* community
service assessment
supervisors' relationships with
85, 89
unreliability of self-report
data on reconviction 157

painting and decorating 44, 106,
107
beneficiaries' satisfaction with
108-9, 110, 113, 127
Parsloe, P. 9
Pearson, F.S. 186
Pease, K. 3, 4, 5, 21, 29, 33, 35,
82, 130, 131, 144, 151, 162,
175, 180, 181, 182, 183, 184
personal development,
contribution of community
service to 93-4, 126-7,
178-9
personal services, work
placements involving 117,
118, 119
allocation to 46
low level of absenteeism from
74, 80
offenders' perception of 91-2,
94
Personal Social Services
Research Unit

research into cost of
community service 26-8, 57
Petersilia, J. 186
Phillpotts, G.J.O. 152, 162, 178,
180, 183
Polonoski, M. 2, 177.
practical work 44
in agencies 117, 118-19, 127
allocation to 46
appropriateness for certain
offenders 89-90
Home Office rules on 6, 184
incidence of absences from
74, 80
likely increase in 187
offenders' perception of 90-2,
178
see also gardening; painting
and decorating
pre-sentence allocation to work
placements 62
pre-sentence interviews 57-60
effectiveness not evident 60-1,
79
Prison Reform Trust 175
prisons
disturbances in 13
overcrowding 3
see also imprisonment
probation
community service as
requirement of 7, 8-9, 42,
185-6
increasing use of 185
need to maintain distinction
between community
service and 78
previous experience of 36;
and suitability for
community service 40
reluctance to use 16-17
social work departments'

responsibility for 8, 16-17
suitability for offenders with
    personal problems 74-5
probation services
    divergent views on
        community service aims 5,
        130, 181
    responsibility for community
        service 3-4, 187
probationisation, dangers of 130,
    180
public order offences 38
    reconviction for 155, 156, 158,
    159, 160, 167
punishment, community service
    as 9
    offenders' perception of
    100-1, 102, 178

questionnaires
    beneficiaries 31-2, 106
    community service staff 25
    offenders 23, 25, 83

Ralphs, P. 23, 89
Raynor, P. 179
re-offending, self-predicted
    likelihood of 153-4, 168-9,
    170-1, 173, 180
Read, G. 5
recidivism *see* reconviction
reconviction
    accuracy of offenders'
        prediction of 170-1, 173,
        180
    before and after community
        service 157-62
    and breaching 171-2
    community service experience
        and 32-3, 150, 178-9, 180-1
    data on 33-4, 154; limitations
        of 171-2

factors associated with 151,
    152, 162-70, 183
following imprisonment 151
impact of intensive
    supervision programmes
    on 186
imprisonment following 156,
    161-2
offences associated with
    155-6, 158-60, 166, 170,
    172, 173, 178
previous research into 33,
    151-2
rate of 154-5, 157, 158, 172,
    180-1
while completing community
    service 156-7
and work placement
    characteristics 32-3, 150-1,
    152, 153-4, 168-70, 173
see also re-offending
rehabilitation
    imprisonment ineffective 3
    through community service 9,
    14, 32, 150-1, 178-9, 181;
    estimation of *see* reconviction
remand status 37
    and risk of custodial sentence
    134
    and suitability for community
        service 40, 55
reparation
    through community service 9,
    30, 104, 175-7
research methodology 24-5, 27-8,
    29-30, 31-2, 33-4, 83, 171-2
    see also interviews;
    questionnaires
revocation, sentences following
    134-7, 142-3
Rifkind, M. 13
Roberts, C.H. 180, 181

Roberts, J. 17
Robertson, E. 26
Robison, J. 3
Rook, M.K. 2
Ruffles, M 98

sampling strategy 24, 171
Schädler, W. 2
Schneider, A.L. 151, 179
Scottish Community Service
    Group
    survey and recommendations
    10-11, 20
Scottish Office
    on community service aims 9
    evaluation of experimental
        schemes 9
    funding from 10, 11-12, 16,
        26-7, 65, 175
    national guidelines 57, 65-6,
        78-9, 80-1
    proposals for restructuring
        social services 8
    supervised attendance order
        introduced by 16
Section 7 orders 7, 42
sentencers
    attitudes to sentencing
        following breach 136, 143,
        148
    attitudes to use of community
        service 28-30, 138-41, 148,
        149
    combined orders valued by
        186
    recognition of sentencing
        inconsistencies 147, 148
    use of community service as
        alternative to non-custodial
        sentence 23-4, 29, 131,
        138-9, 140-1, 142
    views on rehabilitative impact

of community service 150-1
sentencing
    following breaching 131,
        134-7, 142-3, 148
    following reconviction 156,
        160-2
    inconsistencies in 7-8,
        130-1, 141-2, 182; cost
        implications 146, 149;
        impact of national
        standards on 14, 139-40,
        147-8, 149
    interviews with community
        service staff prior to 58-61,
        79
    policy debate 23-4
    risk of imprisonment in
        relation to 137-8
    of unsuccessful referrals
        131-2, 133-4
sexual offenders, agency
    placements not offered to
    116
Shaw, S. 26
Sheriff Court
    length of community service
        orders imposed by 42
    referrals for community
        service assessment by 37
sheriffs
    assessment of offenders'
        suitability for community
        service 38-9
    attitudes to use of community
        service 30, 138-40, 148, 149
    combined orders valued by
        186
    perception of rehabilitative
        effect of community
        service 151
    pre-sentence interviews by
        community service staff

supported by 59
recognition of sentencing
  inconsistencies 147, 148
sentences imposed by:
  following breach 136, 143,
  148; influence of offenders'
  employment status on 43
use of community service as
  alternative to non-custodial
  sentences 23-4, 29, 138-9,
  142
skill acquisition
  on work placements 84-93
  passim, 102, 178, 179
skills
  use on work placements 84,
  86, 88, 90, 91, 92
  and work placement
  allocation 45, 46, 55, 62, 63
Smith, S. 3
social enquiry reports 37, 40,
  58-61
social work departments
  creation 8; declining use of
  probation following 16-17
  responsibility for community
  service 12-13
  services for offenders 16-18,
  77, 81, 180
Social Work Research Centre
  research into community
  service xii-xiii 19-34
social work supervision *see*
  statutory social work
  supervision
social workers
  referrals for community
  service assessment by 37,
  40
solvent abuse 36
Spain, community service
  rejected in 2

Sparks, R.F. 181
standards, national 6-7, 11,
  12-13, 20
  on community service
  assessment procedures 58,
  59, 81
  and community service
  objectives 142
  enthusiasm for 184
  impact on breach rate 184-5
  impact on sentencing practice
  14, 139-40, 147-8
  on offenders' access to social
  work service 78-9, 81
  operational diversity reduced
  by 18, 80-1
  on punitive element in
  community service 101,
  184
  relevance of SWRC research
  to 20-1, 57
  reparation emphasised in 104
  on work placement allocation
  63, 81
statutory social work
  supervision, experience of
  36-7
  and absenteeism from work
  placements 73
  and allocation to work
  placements 46, 55-6
  and criminal history 37
  and likelihood of re-offending
  153
  and perception of work
  placements 169
  and reconviction 164, 166-7,
  169, 172
  and risk of breaching 53, 54,
  56
  and suitability for community
  service 40, 41, 55

substance abuse 36
  and suitability for community
    service 41
supervised attendance order 15,
  16
supervision costs, contribution of
  lax enforcement to 72
supervision programmes,
  intensive 186
supervisors, offenders'
  relationships with 85, 89
suspended sentences 181-2
Sweden, community service
  rejected in 2

Tak, P.J.P. 1, 2
tariff escalation 130-1, 142-4,
  148
Taylor, D. 7-8
team placements 43-4, 45
  agency placements regarded
    as superior to 89
  allocation to 46, 55
  beneficiaries' complaints
    about 108-9
  Home Office rules on 6
  increased use of 183, 187
  likelihood of non-compliance
    on 72-3, 80
  offenders' perceptions of
    90-1, 92, 94, 178
  strict notification of
    absences 74
  work done by 106-7;
    beneficiaries' satisfaction
    with 107-13
Thorvaldson, S.A. 177
Tonry, M. 2, 186
transport
  to work placements:
    offenders' suggestions
    about 97-8

Treger, H. 83, 105, 176
Turner, S. 186

unemployment 35, 37
  and length of community
    service orders 42-3
  and perception of work
    placements 169
  and risk of breaching 54, 56
  and risk of custodial sentence
    134
  and suitability for community
    service 40
  see also employment status
United States
  community service 1-2, 83
  intensive supervision
    programmes 186
unreliability, beneficiaries'
  complaints about 109
unsuccessful referrals
  characteristics 25, 39-41, 55,
    134
  risk of imprisonment 137-8
  sentencing 131-2, 133-4

van Kalmthout, A.M. 1, 2
Varah, M. 83, 177
Vass, A.A. 2, 3, 5, 6, 52, 130,
  139
violent offences 38
  and placement allocation 116
  reconviction for 155, 156, 158,
    159, 160, 167
von Hirsch, A. 186

Wasik, M. 7-8
West, J.S.M. 15-16, 23, 89, 130,
  151
Williams, B. 17
Willis, A. 131, 146
women

criminal history 37
placement allocation 46, 56
as proportion of offenders 35
reconviction 164
Wootton, Baroness
on achievements of
community service 174
Wootton Committee
on aims of community
service 5, 104, 130
recommendations 3, 4, 129
on rehabilitation and
reconviction 150, 178-9
on value of offenders working
with volunteers 89
work commitments,
acceptability of absences
due to 49, 50, 51, 52, 56
work placements
in agencies see agency
placements
allocation to:
cost-effectiveness 64;
factors influencing 45-6,
55-6, 61-3; offenders'
involvement in 62-5, 79,
81, 84, 86
appropriateness for particular
offender 89-90
beneficiaries of see
beneficiaries
changes in 46-7
continued voluntary
attendance at 98-100, 102,
118-19, 176, 179
as enjoyable and interesting
experience 84, 86-7, 88, 92,
93, 94-5, 102, 103, 177; and
likelihood of re-offending
153
failure to attend see absences
need for commitment to

100-1, 102, 178
offenders' beliefs about gains
from 93-4, 102-3
offenders' likes and dislikes
about 94-6
offenders' perception of 23,
82-3, 84-9; age differences
in 89; and allocation to
desired work 86, 90; and
contact with beneficiaries
85, 86-7, 90, 91, 92, 102,
178; and incidence of
absenteeism 74, 80, 179;
influence of placement
type and work on 89-92,
102, 178; and involvement
in placement allocation 63,
64; and perceived
usefulness of work 88, 90,
92, 104-5, 179; and
reconviction 32-3, 150-1,
152, 153-4, 168-70, 173,
178, 179; and skill
acquisition 84, 86, 87, 88,
89, 93, 102, 178
offenders' suggestions for
improvements to 96-8
punitive element: offenders'
perception of 100-1, 102,
178
recommendations for 14
skill acquisition on 84, 86, 87,
88, 89, 90, 91, 92, 102
skills and experience used in
84, 86, 88, 90, 91, 92
supervisors 85, 89
type of work carried out on
187; in agencies 117-18,
127; for individual
beneficiaries 106-7, 127;
and integration into agency
118, 119; and likelihood of

re-offending 153, 169
types of 43-5; and likelihood
of non-compliance and
breach 72-4, 80; and
likelihood of re-offending
153, 169; and offenders'
perceptions of community
service 90-2
as worthwhile experience 84,
86-7, 88, 89, 92, 102, 169,
177, 188; and likelihood of
reconviction 153, 169-70,
173
see also types of work e.g.
practical work; specific
placements e.g. agency
placements
work teams see team placements

workshop placements 43, 44, 55
likelihood of breach on 72-3
offenders' perception of 90,
91
Wright, M. 3

young offenders
assessment of suitability for
community service 41
breach 52
criminal history 37
custody prior to sentence 37
likelihood of re-offending 153
placement allocation 46, 55-6
reconviction 151, 152
types of offences 38
Young, W.A. 1, 3, 5, 6, 130